UNSETTLED

Also by Ryan Hampton

American Fix

UNSETTLED

How the Purdue Pharma Bankruptcy
Failed the Victims of the American
Overdose Crisis

RYAN HAMPTON

with Claire Rudy Foster and Hillel Aron

ST. MARTIN'S PRESS
New York

First published in the United States by St. Martin's Press, an imprint of St. Martin's Publishing Group

www.stmartins.com

Design by Donna Sinisgalli Noetzel

Library of Congress Cataloging-in-Publication Data

Names: Hampton, Ryan, author. | Foster, Claire Rudy, author. | Aron, Hillel, author.
Title: Unsettled : how the Purdue Pharma bankruptcy failed the victims of the American overdose crisis / by Ryan Hampton, with Claire Rudy Foster and Hillel Aron.
Description: First edition. | New York : St. Martin's Press, [2021] | Includes bibliographical references and index.
Identifiers: LCCN 2021026643 | ISBN 9781250273161 (hardcover) | ISBN 9781250273178 (ebook)
Subjects: LCSH: Purdue Pharma L.P. | Pharmaceutical industry— Moral and ethical aspects—United States. | Opioid abuse— United States. | Bankruptcy—Moral and ethical aspects.
Classification: LCC HD9666.9.P87 H36 2021 | DDC 338.7/6161510973—dc23
LC record available at https://lccn.loc.gov/2021026643

First Edition: 2021

10 9 8 7 6 5 4 3 2 1

This book is for all those who were counted out.

Your stories and your voices matter. Never stop fighting.

And for Sean, my heart—I couldn't have done this without you.

CONTENTS

PREFACE

When I sat down to write *American Fix* in 2017, the world was a
very different place from what it is now. It feels silly to say that,
but at the time I had no idea what we were in for. I was early in
my recovery then. Idealistic. Untested. I was convinced that the
Sackler family had single-handedly engineered the crisis and that
they alone were responsible for the widespread, tragic carnage in
our homes and communities. I believed that exposing the Sacklers
and mobilizing people would be enough to right the scales of justice. That the karmic balance of the universe would correct itself if
enough people got involved. If I just *believed* enough.

I'm glad I felt that way at the time. The fire in my belly hasn't gone
out, but the things I've learned and experienced over the last few
years have seasoned me. I was on the front lines of the anti-Sackler
protests for years. If there was a rally, I was *there*. I stayed in the
homes of parents who'd lost kids to overdoses, mourned my dead
friends, and pushed for meaningful legislation to change the way
our nation treats substance use disorder. I was out-front, waving the
banner and yelling at anyone who would listen. I considered myself

an expert—and I was, but my expertise had limits, and the next few years showed me how narrow my perspective really was.

As a cis white man and a vocal advocate, I knew I could do a lot of good on the front lines. Loud voices get attention, and attention makes change. Yet, I knew I couldn't be the *only* voice. I couldn't speak for people from other groups, especially historically marginalized populations. I learned to be more mindful about how I talked about recovery as I learned more about other people's experiences. I knew addiction recovery was a transpolitical issue, but not until after the Black Lives Matter movement grabbed headlines and elevated the message of challenging old ideas about race, values, and identity did I really grasp the idea of intersectionality. *Your mileage may vary.* While we describe addiction as the "great equalizer," it was increasingly apparent to me that neither addiction nor recovery made people equal. Substance use disorder had inequitable effects on people. Addiction revealed privilege, security, and safety. If people were white, insured, middle-class or higher, and employed, they were more likely to survive. Take those qualities away, and the odds declined dramatically. A Black, trans, homeless woman on the South Side simply didn't have the same chance that a white cis woman with tenure at Berkeley did. Pretending otherwise was cruel and insincere.

I tried to bring the same sensitivity to other relationships within my community. For example, I finally started to understand the importance of protecting the rights of pain patients and people who use opioids for managing chronic conditions. I saw that a lot of the legislation and regulation that was designed to curb overdoses harmed pain patients, too; even well-intended regulatory "fixes" ignored patients and created massive upheaval in their lives. My long-held fantasy of destroying Purdue had more than one crack in it. Maybe abolishing opioid manufacturers wasn't the answer after all. If anything, I began to see how simplistic my view had been. I grew and listened and did the work and stayed willing. I am incredibly grateful for the people who took the time to educate me, answer my questions, and challenge my long-held beliefs. They prepared me for the journey I took in *Unsettled,* and I am a better person for it.

Learning how to use my voice was difficult, important work. Ironically, just as I felt I was making progress, I opted to silence myself to do something that was even more important to me—bearing witness to the bloodbath of the Purdue bankruptcy. I agreed to say nothing, but I couldn't shut off my feelings, and in the end, I couldn't betray my principles and let these secrets die in darkness. I wrote *Unsettled* in real time, as the case was unfolding. The book you're holding in your hands represents how I felt in the moment, as well as where I was in my life, where America was, and what happened during the excruciating Chapter 11 proceedings, Purdue's eventual restructuring, and the Sackler family's exit from any true accountability. This is real, it's raw, and large sections of it are recollected from my memory. I listened to hundreds of hours of testimony and lawyer talk. I sat in countless meetings. I read thousands of documents. At some point, I couldn't keep it to myself.

Throughout the bankruptcy, I struggled to keep quiet. It made my blood boil to see the Sacklers continue to perform for the media, offering a few reputation-polishing facts but never telling the whole truth. Other parties involved, who I thought had undertaken with me not to discuss the case during the proceedings, sang like canaries. Not me. This book was the outlet for my anger, and in retrospect I believe it made witnessing the process bearable. My only recourse was to take my rage and my frustration and, once again, funnel it onto paper.

In a perfect world, would Purdue even exist? I can't say. A friend asked me if we couldn't just pull OxyContin off the market. It was a sassy question, but I had to give a serious answer. No. We can't. Ironically, we *have* to keep selling it.

As I write this, Purdue is currently worth a little more than $1 billion on paper. The settlement they reach will be ten to twelve times that value. If they're going to pay their debts, they *have* to keep selling Oxy, as a restructured company. I had an idea to liquidate the company, take that billion dollars, give it to the victims, and call it a day. Walk away. My suggestion was practically laughed out of the room.

Progress is often less expensive than maintaining the status quo, and when it comes to implementing change, we're so often told there's "no money for that." There is money. Other people wanted to get paid more than they wanted to do something meaningful— something that could potentially save millions of lives. The paycheck won out, every time.

The goal of my work has never been to ban or outlaw opioids. Opioids aren't the problem. Greed is. Reckless capitalism is. Gross wealth inequality is. A so-called justice system that shields the ultrawealthy from the consequences of their actions is. A government that plays strictly within the lines, rarely advocating for the people they claim to represent, is. And a culture that misunderstands addiction as a moral failing is. We have ways of correcting and improving these systems, but reform is slow, and too often good ideas die by a thousand cuts. What we need in this country is universal health care, evidence-based prevention, recovery support on demand, housing for everyone, harm reduction in every community—and the list goes on and on. We need more than a hotline or a handful of Facebook pages. We need to build on the wildly effective foundation of existing mutual-aid networks and recovery community organizations—funding dreamers, outsiders, people with lived experience, and frontline providers who make a real difference.

Will we? A few years ago, I would have said yes. Now, I'm not so sure.

My experience with Purdue shook my faith to the core. Coming out of the fog, I am not sure what my next steps will be. I am a different person from who I was in 2017. I am older. I am tired. Writing *Unsettled* was a difficult, distressing undertaking in many ways. Yet, these things must be said. They must be shared. I have waited too long to say them.

INTRODUCTION

August 17, 2018. Thick thunderclouds darkened the horizon, turning the beautiful Stamford, Connecticut, sky from blue to nearly black. Within moments, my shirt was soaked with sweat as the August humidity crept down my collar. I heard the voices before I even got to the Purdue Pharma building. As I pulled into a parking spot, my ears started to ring. The shouting grew louder as I hustled toward the glittering monolith on Tresser Boulevard.

The police were already there, shielding the front of the building in a blockade formation. Hundreds of people crowded the plaza. The noise hit me like a wall, and I stumbled as I went into the press of bodies, working my way forward. The ground was covered in shreds of paper, "protest messages" that people were stuffing into orange plastic pill bottles and leaving on the steps. The officers didn't move. Locked in place, they were there to back Purdue.

Standing in the shadow of the building, my sweat turned to ice water. I looked up, craning my neck to take in the whole monstrosity. One Stamford Forum was the mother ship. Ten floors of glass windows and dark chrome reflecting the coming storm down at us. It felt nearly abandoned, even on a Friday afternoon, when people should have been coming and going to their jobs. The stillness was eerie, as though the building were listening to us, planning its next move. I felt as if I were looking up at the Death Star for the first time. *That's no moon.* One Stamford wasn't just a corporate office; it was a national monument to American greed.

The 505,000-square-foot building at 201 Tresser was stuffed with Purdue offices. This was ground zero. Inside these walls, the Sackler family–owned company had run the numbers, drawn up marketing plans, and executed their strategies. The company committed cold-blooded corporate genocide, rubber-stamped by the FDA and cosigned by the free market. More blood had been spilled in that building than I could comprehend. My stomach clenched with nausea. I felt as if I were standing at the gates of hell.

On the third floor, in one of the lacquered panes that overlooked the plaza, I could see figures standing at the window. Three or four people clustered together, holding their phones and pointing down at the crowd. I narrowed my eyes. They were taping us.

They were *laughing.*

I'd tear that place to pieces—with my own hands if necessary. My voice joined the chant that swelled around me. The protest was a furious hurricane, filling the plaza and battering the windows of the Purdue building.

I'll end them, I thought to myself. *If it's the last thing I do. I will take this place down—along with everything it ever stood for.*

I got the phone call a year later, on a beautiful, sunny Sunday afternoon in September 2019. It was the long Labor Day weekend, and I was at the Bronx Zoo with my two favorite people for a last-minute vacation. I let go of my fiancé's hand to answer my phone. Sean, who was used to work interrupting our dates and outings, smiled at me and turned away to talk to my mom. They pointed at the red pandas in the nearest enclosure while I pressed my phone to my ear.

"Purdue's filing for bankruptcy," the voice on the other end said.

"Yeah, whatever." I got lots of calls like this. Everyone had a theory about Purdue, and information spread like wildfire between advocates, reporters, and lobbyists. A lot of it was old news by the time it got to me. We all knew the same stuff because we'd worked tirelessly to take down Purdue and bring them to justice for encouraging and profiting off a national drug epidemic that had claimed hundreds of thousands of lives.

"No, it's really happening," she said.

What I learned in that phone call altered the course of almost two years of my life. (Though it felt like twenty.) I didn't know what it meant, but by the time I hung up and turned back to Sean and my mom, the gears of history were turning at lightning speed. Within two weeks, Purdue Pharma *did* file for bankruptcy. Before I knew it, I was in a room packed with every person I'd ever squared off with.

That day was the last calm moment I experienced for the next twenty-two months. Life before the Purdue case wasn't exactly smooth sailing, but I navigated the waves with some help from my partner and my friends. I wasn't new to being a disrupter, but I was about to be catapulted to a level of involvement I hadn't imagined was possible for people such as me.

Previously, I'd worked to support a range of policy issues and devoted countless hours to advance forward-thinking addiction recovery legislation. I knew what the numbers were in the crisis: I saw, firsthand, how addiction tore families apart, destroyed entire communities, and killed our most vulnerable people. In the first years of my recovery, I lost more than two dozen friends to preventable overdoses. I visited dozens of communities as part of a documentary project in 2016 called *AddictionXAmerica* and witnessed the losses sustained by ordinary families everywhere. I stayed in homes with parents who'd lost children to Purdue Pharma's bestselling painkiller, OxyContin. I ate at the tables of families that would never be the same. I vowed that I would bring justice to them and all the people who, like myself, had lost years of their lives to Purdue's rapacious hunger for profits.

I told these stories in testimony I delivered to Congress, in front of thousands of people calling for change, and at the gates of institutions with the Sackler family name emblazoned over them. I wrote my first book, *American Fix: Inside the Opioid Addiction Crisis—and How to End It,* which was published in 2018. I talked about the crisis on MSNBC, Fox News, and any other outlet that would listen to me. I met with leaders and politicians and tried to convince them to take emergency measures and to treat the crisis like any other public health issue. Few of them listened, and as a result things are not much better than they were when I wrote *American Fix.*

Let me make something clear. I will talk to literally *anybody* about finding a solution to the overdose crisis. And I mean *anybody.* I know what the cost of ignoring addiction is: it means that we'll keep losing our friends, family members, loved ones, and neighbors to a highly treatable health-care problem that is severely stigmatized. So stigmatized that America's 90 percent treatment gap (the inability to access treatment) has remained stagnant for decades. It's not enough to organize people individually. I had to go to the source, the company that gaslit a nation.

I thought taking on Purdue Pharma was enough. I had called them out for years, in the public domain and in the press. Our efforts slowly chipped away at the pharmaceutical giant. Within three years, institutions stopped taking philanthropic donations from the Sackler family. The Sacklers, who became billionaires from drug profits, struggled socially: they were no longer invited to black-tie functions, and former friends snubbed them. I watched the company's lawyers bluster through hearings, claiming that Purdue wasn't guilty of coordinated, state-sanctioned genocide in the name of profit. I thought I'd never crack the thick wall of glass that seemed to protect the Sacklers from the consequences of their greed.

Then, all of a sudden, the impenetrable shield opened and I walked through.

When a company such as Purdue files for bankruptcy, it's a major operation. Dividing the company's assets, paying its debts, and dismantling its internal structures is a huge undertaking. The process happened behind closed doors under the eyes of a judge, a ton of lawyers, state attorneys general, and a committee of creditors who have personal or corporate interests in the case. The general assumption is that whoever represents the state—usually a state attorney general—has the people's best interests in mind. I had thought that there were two teams: Purdue was the villain, and everyone taking them on were the good guys. But as I learned more, I found that there were way more questionable folks than I'd assumed. The folks I thought were good often had their own interests in mind, not the interests of the people they were allegedly helping. They were unintentionally causing harm because of their lack of information and unwillingness to see the overdose crisis for what it is. They undermined the victims—the survivors and their families—for political and institutional power.

Since nobody knew what happened in those meetings or what was said behind closed doors, I knew it was vital to make sure there was a public record of *everything* I could possibly get my hands on. No company that takes advantage of the public should be able to hide behind the uniquely American bankruptcy process. Every elected official who claims to "help" must be accountable to their constituents. I'm not writing this for any reason other than to share the truth. My contribution is putting my truth about this case in the hands of the people. The American bankruptcy process needs radical reform because it is shockingly easy for various actors—even some so-called helpers—to keep the truth hidden and turn an astronomical profit.

I knew from the beginning that a case of this scope wasn't something that should be dealt with in bankruptcy court. But that wasn't my call. Purdue Pharma had been sued before and gotten away with paying relatively small settlements compared with the damage they'd done. Little money, if any, made its way to survivors and victims' families. And no company executive or member of the Sackler family ever had to worry about dropping the soap.

I knew that this corporate bankruptcy case wasn't "real" in the way that bankruptcies are for ordinary people. Purdue wasn't on-paper bankrupt. They had assets, valuable patents, and more than $1 billion in the bank when they filed for Chapter 11. This case gave them an escape route, a way to walk away from the wreckage they'd created. So, after years of dogging them, I had finally caught up to Purdue. But tearing them apart wasn't as easy as you'd think.

In a way, I'd been preparing to participate since I first stepped into the ring. Prior to the company's bankruptcy, I'd been talking to different lawyer groups about how to get involved in a massive civil litigation against Purdue, representing myself and other groups and individuals whose lives were ruined by OxyContin. When the phone call came, I was more ready than I expected to be. Sean and I flew back home from New York, and Purdue declared bankruptcy two weeks later, on September 15. By then, I'd heard about the Unsecured Creditors Committee (UCC), looked into my options, and taken action to get myself a spot on the committee. When the news hit the national wire services, it spread so fast it was as though there were a national emergency. The next day, Monday, September 16, I wrote my letter to the US trustee at the Department of Justice. He alone would decide who was seated on the committee. The following week, I was invited to New York City to interview with the trustee. The process moved so quickly that I hardly had a moment to internalize what I was about to get myself into. For the life of me, I didn't expect to get appointed.

Above all, it was critical that Purdue and its lawyers not be aware that I was vying for an appointment to the entity that was charged with dismantling them. They all knew who I was. I'd made a point of making sure they all knew my name. The Purdue people had copies of my book, *American Fix,* and knew about the op-eds and protests. They never thought I could be impartial because of my activism. Just a few months before the meeting with the trustee, I'd been on MSNBC's Ali Velshi show, calling for the Sacklers to be cuffed and jailed. When I arrived at the committee interview, I wore the same clothes I'd worn on Ali's show: my black suit and light blue plaid tie. My friend Cheryl Juaire, who'd lost her son to an opioid overdose, was there. We walked around waiting with over seventy other people who'd applied to be on the committee. The trustee interviewed all of us in five hours.

Finally, after some deliberation, the trustee came down and

announced the nine members had been chosen. I was surrounded in the room by big insurance representatives, pharmaceutical CEOs, and powerful lobbyists. I was a small fish: not powerful, not an expert. I didn't think I had a chance. The trustee said that the names on the list were final and the choices couldn't be appealed or challenged: this was *it*. Upon the reading of the names, those people would be taken to a conference room on a different floor. They'd convene for the first time with lawyers and financial advisers, figure out bylaws, meet one another, and start work immediately.

They read the list. Ryan Hampton was the *seventh* name.

Within three minutes, I was whisked away and told I couldn't talk to the press. If I was going to participate and see justice done, I would have to keep my mouth shut for the time being. In those three minutes, I went from being *very* loud about Purdue to buttoning my lip. I was *not* going to be on television again anytime soon.

The first meeting of our committee was the same night. I was exhausted. My suit was rumpled, and my phone was almost out of juice. The selection process happened so fast that I wasn't prepared, and I felt unbalanced by how quickly things were moving. I was used to advocacy and vocal activism, where a single goal might take months or years to accomplish. Now, in a week, I was being rocketed into this world I was totally overwhelmed by.

Furthermore, the people I was supposed to work with *really* didn't like me. I looked at the list of other UCC members. My name was surrounded by those of folks I'd squared off with for years. I recognized the big insurance companies and hospitals, the pharmacies who were also on the list. The idea of working with them hand in glove gave me the creeps. But as we sized each other up, I also realized that I was one of the people in the room most prepared to take on this challenge. I'd been doing the research for years, staying current, and working with victims. I already knew more than the pension group or even the judge about the real impact Purdue had had on American lives. The others were all looking at this case through a lens of bankruptcy law, not public health.

A bead of sweat ran into my collar and I swiped at it. Cheryl and I were two people, vastly outnumbered by corporate and state interests. Our voices were going to have to be *loud*. Without us and the other victims on the committee (a small but powerful minority), every individual out there whose life had been ruined by Purdue was going to get ripped off. The "bankruptcy" would be a total scam: a way for government interests, corporations, lawyers, and the highest echelon of the one-percenters to divide the spoils of Purdue's assets and keep the settlement for themselves. Anyone who wasn't a victim or a survivor was acting on behalf of an institution, not human beings. I scanned the room again, noticing who was already getting friendly with whom. Yep. They were here to do business as usual.

Purdue was not happy about my appointment for a lot of reasons. I'd made it clear to everyone that I thought their company should be burned to the ground. They perceived me as a loose cannon or a firebrand who was interested only in getting people wound up. They saw me as someone who ran on emotion, not rational decisions. They didn't see what I was capable of, but the trustee clearly did. I did my best to lead with a sound mind and a level head. As hard as it was, I could somewhat detach emotionally and make reasonable decisions. My struggle wasn't between speaking up or sticking with the process. My struggle was between my head and my heart. Setting aside my personal feelings is hard for me: anyone who knows me knows I wear my heart on my sleeve.

My essential feelings haven't changed. I still think Purdue should be burned to the ground and the Sacklers should rot in jail, but as it became clear that was a near impossibility, it was more important to do right by the victims rather than fight a losing, ideological battle. In the beginning, I was against *any* settlement that didn't end in Purdue being dismantled and turned into charcoal briquettes, but then I got inside and realized it was a deeper rabbit hole than I'd imagined. Nothing was simple anymore. It was a political game of hot potato, and nobody wanted to take responsibility for the choices that had led us to this point. These are the facts that would never make it onto the news or be shared with the public. In spite of the black-and-white stories I saw in the media, people didn't understand that the Sacklers, Purdue, and many of the states and government actors were all hiding the truth from the American public. *All* of them are to blame. They all profited by maintaining the status quo, harming people—whether that was their intention or not.

I made it my mission to disrupt this case and do my best so that the money went to the people who were actually affected by the crisis. How easy would it be for each state, claiming to work in the "public interest," to hoard a few billion dollars for old-school scare tactics that squandered valuable resources on billboards and worthless pamphlets? Or tougher crackdowns on people with substance use disorder, funding police squads that targeted our community instead of helping people by lowering the barriers to treatment and giving them access to the full continuum of care? I imagined that many of these representatives weren't interested in radical change: they wanted to keep the status quo and still look like heroes. I knew exactly what that meant for real, ordinary people. It meant they'd get nothing—and that the epidemic would continue to spiral out of control.

Everyone knew that Purdue Pharma was the villain. What they didn't know was how the billion-dollar corporation was aided and abetted in their merciless assault on Americans by the systems and institutions that were supposed to protect us. Money, not justice, was calling the shots.

However, this time things were a little different. For the first time, the Sacklers were personally involved. They are not known to be at the table with *anybody* and had stayed out of court proceedings in the past, preferring to communicate through lawyers and publicity reps. The power dynamics of this situation had shifted: as victims/people impacted on the advocate side and pushing the envelope, we'd never had mutual power. We'd never sat face-to-face with them. There was nothing they needed from us. Now, they *did*. They begged for mercy. And I was the *last* person on earth they wanted to beg from.

In this book, you'll read the story of Purdue Pharma, the billionaire family that owned it, and the carnage they wreaked on unsuspecting Americans. You'll hear the conversations I had with members of the Sackler family and how they *really* feel about seeing their company's heyday end. You'll also hear the untold story of how a group of determined, motivated, ordinary people tried to see justice done against all odds—and in the face of a *lot* of opposition from so-called public servants. You'll see how the people who are supposed to serve and protect us exploit legal loopholes for their own political gain and let companies such as Purdue run amok.

My UCC appointment put me in a spot where I felt isolated and unsupported. I was uncomfortable working one-on-one with these players. What did I know about bankruptcy law? I'm not a lawyer. I'm not a CEO. I'm not a university professor. I'm just one person who wants to do the right thing. Having agreed not to discuss the case, I couldn't rely on the large group of people I would usually call on for advice and counsel. This experience drove me deeply into myself and my inner soul and sent me searching for answers. It would alter my perspective on the world and my place in it. It would change who I was. Suddenly, I was having to find myself again. I wondered, *What's best for my community? What would my past self, the loud advocate who protested outside Purdue in August 2018, feel about this? Was this a good decision or a terrible mistake?*

I turned down interviews and couldn't share what was happening with any of my allies in the community. In committee meetings, new information was exposed every day—but I couldn't say a word. In writing this book, the time for silence has passed; it's time to talk. We must make this process public or it will repeat itself, and big corporations will continue to exploit people in the name of profits, with the state's implicit consent and support.

I had unique access to documents, discussions, and budgets. My opinions are based on what I've heard and read. I'm writing this not just so I can sleep at night but because my first responsibility is to the people who deserve an honest answer.

In the past, I received my information from the public domain and believed what was told to me: Purdue was evil and everybody else was on the same team. Many of my trusted friends and allies had expressed zero tolerance about what should happen to Big Pharma. I was afraid that they'd think I was playing ball with the devil or that the committee position was effectively buying my silence at a time when our movement needed *more* voices, not fewer.

On top of this, I had to be honest with myself about the scope of committing to participating in the bankruptcy. Sean and I talked for three days about what it might mean for us, how my involvement in the case would affect our relationship, and how we wanted to handle it. I knew that I wouldn't be able to do this without his support, and I also knew it could potentially be a huge strain on our partnership.

To make it work, we had to agree about privacy and boundaries. So much was at stake, and I couldn't jeopardize any of it. Sean's community and mine overlapped pretty much everywhere. Mutual friends often asked one of us about the other. When Purdue was a topic, we agreed that Sean wouldn't answer for me. He wouldn't run interference. I am grateful for his unconditional love and his dedication to seeing this through. He thought it was the right thing to do, saying, "Somebody needs to be in there, and it needs to be you."

I took this journey knowing that the love of my life had my back. This helped put my heart at ease: at least we would go through it together. Travel, phone calls, me being pulled away, and the constant stress are what he signed up for when we decided to get married. I know it was hard for me, but in a way, I think it was harder on Sean.

For almost seven hundred days, the case consumed our time and also our conversations, meals, free time, and even our wedding plans. Yet, I wouldn't have wanted to face it with anyone else.

Sean has been my rock through this, which was essential when so many of my other relationships changed, seemingly overnight. I have learned whom I can trust and whom I can't. The worst were people who have been around for a long time and were resentful and condescending throughout the whole process.

In every instance, I chose to disengage instead of defending myself. What was I supposed to say? There wasn't much I *could* say, even if I wanted to. They were operating without all the information. What they didn't know, I couldn't tell them—until now.

This commitment represented a huge sacrifice, even within my own self. It's been brutal. It's been heartbreaking. It's been disappointing. But it was necessary. This shit was *hard.* It was all volunteer. It was not paid. It caused me to question everything I thought I knew. I felt a huge amount of self-doubt and feelings of inadequacy, from the first minute of the very first meeting. I'd never do it again. Even with the love of my partner and my closest friends, it's only *me* who internalizes this. That inner work has indelibly altered who I am. There's only so many times you can fire up your passion and hope to inspire institutional drones. They have money to make and a job to do. They don't have the same kind of empathy that a person who's lived through it does. Trying to change their mechanical minds every day was draining and discouraging. Try as I might, I often found it impossible to create any empathy or kindness. They don't get it because they haven't lived it.

The trek also built my confidence in what I *do* know and drives me to believe that I'm in the right place. When I felt weak, I still had faith. I knew that we had to exert our power—whether we thought we had it or not. We couldn't accept a pat on the head any longer. I fought behind closed doors for the right to say that we deserved more.

Justice means justice for *you.* That means *your* family. That means *your* community. You deserve to know exactly who is responsible for the losses you've sustained and what they got in exchange for failing to protect people over profits. You should know what a human life is worth to the corporations, the billionaires, and the lawmakers.

Unsettled is my truth.

I'll tell you who's really making America sick.

1

BILLIONS SERVED

Two months into the COVID-19 lockdown, I was busier than a church fan in the dog days. Although the rest of America and my home state of Nevada had come to a standstill, the bankruptcy proceedings against Purdue Pharma hadn't slowed down at all. If anything, they were even more intense: people had *time* to talk, and we all had plenty to say. My already-packed calendar stretched into seventeen-hour days of phone calls and Zoom meetings. The commitments that used to punctuate my schedule, such as air travel or in-person presentations, were gone, eliminating the brief hours when I could take a break, catch my breath, and recharge for the next sprint. My bedroom became a fortress where I sat at a makeshift computer station, blinds dimmed, drinking water and lots of coffee.

One afternoon, my fiancé, Sean, stuck his head around the door. "We need to get out. We haven't been spending any time together."

"I just have one more thing to finish."

There was *always* one more thing. He rolled his eyes, giving me a patient-yet-exasperated look I knew all too well. "I'm taking you for a drive. You need some air. Put your shoes on."

We slipped our cloth masks over our noses and got into the car. Sean drove: my eyes were weak from looking at screens all day, every day. I squinted at my phone, then switched to the radio, messing with the dial until I landed on the local news station. Body-count updates, transmission statistics, and the chants of angry anti-mask protesters filled the car.

"Relaxing," Sean said. His gentle sarcasm was well deserved. The night before, we had our first serious talk about the toll the Purdue case was taking on us. "This is exhausting," Sean had said, and although I wanted to argue, I knew he wasn't wrong. Every single part of me was tapped, and the end was still nowhere in sight.

The news changed to what sounded like a high-end *Better Call Saul* ad, and with a sigh I turned it down.

"If I never talk to another lawyer in my life, I will die a happy man," I said.

We pulled into the McDonald's drive-through. It wasn't a typical date for us: usually we went to theme parks, held hands at the movies, browsed bookstores, and caught live performances of our favorite musicals. But during lockdown, those things were on hiatus or closed indefinitely. McDonald's was all we had. We were trying to escape into our normal life, and this was the only thing left.

We ordered, shouting through our masks at the metal speaker embedded in the lit-up menu. I rubbed my eyes, grateful I hadn't insisted on taking the keys. Although Sean and I lived together, we were rarely in the same room these days. I was always working, even when I wasn't at my desk. The radio caught my ear.

"Sean, it's the ad!" I turned it up. That weekend in April was the first time I heard the radio commercial for the massive Purdue noticing campaign. I had helped advise on this huge campaign, supposedly the most expensive, at $23 million, and furthest-reaching bankruptcy noticing strategy in American history.

The deep, serious voice on the radio said, "File your claim if you've been harmed by a Purdue product."

I *had* been harmed. It wasn't lost on me that even with several years of recovery under my belt, OxyContin was still ruining my life, this time in court. The legal fight stole my waking hours, affected my relationships, and even intruded in my dreams. The obsession to bring down the Sackler family and their multibillion-dollar empire was as intense as my addiction had been. The motive was different, but so what? It was still consuming me alive. I found myself unable to completely rely on my lawyers' advice; although they had a passion for the case, no matter how much they cared, there was a profit motive. I couldn't ask my community what was best for us. The burden of making the best decision for the people I loved was heavy on me.

As Sean and I eased up to the window to pay and collect our food, I noticed that my mind was already wandering back to my unanswered emails and the meeting I had later that evening. I stuck a straw in my drink and stowed it in my armrest. As I bent down to retrieve a loose french fry from the floor, it hit me.

"Billions Served"—the McDonald's motto. The radio rattled on with the instructions on how to file a claim, and it was crystal clear: Purdue had been selling OxyContin like hamburgers, and Americans were still lining up to buy it. Not because we didn't know the risks but because the road to addiction was smooth, soothing, and paved with people we trusted. Purdue guided unwitting people into chemical dependency using advertising that distorted and obscured the true nature of their product. They effectively converted people into return business by getting them hooked and then lying to them about why they couldn't live without their daily dose. They didn't do this alone: doctors, federal regulators, states, lawmakers, and even lawyers and judges had upheld Purdue's right to do this. They were all supporting a system that killed Americans and decimated communities, and the survivors were the ones left holding the greasy bag.

"I've got to get home," I said, and Sean sighed, resigned.

If the Sackler family invented anything, it was an idea: that medicine could be marketed just like Coca-Cola, just like our McDonald's burgers. Arthur Sackler pushed pills more effectively than anyone else had before, *billions served*. He built his toxic empire through the magic of advertising, through the magic of repeating the name of the drug and a claim about the drug and a lie about the drug, over and over and over. His brothers did it, too, and their kids did it, and the company those kids owned, Purdue Pharma, built the world's most wildly ambitious marketing machine and sales force to push a single pill—OxyContin.

Every kingdom has its roots—and the Sacklers had humble beginnings, the realization of the American Dream. Isaac Sackler and Sophie Greenberg were Eastern European Jews who immigrated to Brooklyn before World War I and opened up a grocery store. They had five children, including two daughters and three sons: Arthur, Mortimer, and Raymond. Arthur was the oldest and as a young adult would perform the duties of the family patriarch. He went to medical school, then paid for his brothers to do the same. Later in life, Arthur became a psychiatrist and went to work at Creedmoor psychiatric hospital in Queens, an imposing building at the heart of a sprawling urban farm. (Lou Reed and Woody Guthrie are listed as former "notable residents," according to public sources.) His younger brothers also worked there. (They looked so much alike that they would fool the staff by pretending to be one another.) After leaving Creedmoor, Arthur became an entrepreneur in the field of pharmaceuticals. His brothers followed.

At the time, psychiatry was still dominated by the Freudian school of thought, which held that problems were "neuroses" that could be treated through talk therapy and by uncovering past trauma. But Arthur Sackler grew to believe that these mental health disorders were biological and could therefore be treated with medicine and other modern techniques. He identified some of the chemical causes behind schizophrenia and manic depression. Arthur was the first to use ultrasound for medical diagnosis and pioneered other techniques, such as using histamine to treat psychiatric patients. He authored or coauthored more than 150 papers, on subjects such as neuroendocrinology and experimental medicine. He was on the cutting edge, and if he had been content to be an honest leader and progressive voice in his field, history as we know it would be very different today.

But that's not what happened: Arthur's next step was advertising. While in college, he'd worked part-time at a small ad agency in New York, William Douglas McAdams. Its owner liked to boast that it was the largest medical-advertising agency in the country—a big fish in the very small pond known as Medicine Avenue. In 1944, Arthur returned to William Douglas McAdams, this time as its medical and creative director. He also bought a share in the company.

It was the start of a remarkable career. Arthur Sackler was the Don Draper of pills. Upon his induction into the Medical Advertising Hall of Fame (yes, there really is such a thing) in 1998, the organization wrote, "No single individual did more to shape the character of medical advertising than the multi-talented Dr. Arthur Sackler. His seminal contribution was bringing the full power of advertising and promotion to pharmaceutical marketing."

The New Yorker later quoted the psychiatrist Allen Frances with a different take: "Most of the questionable practices that propelled the pharmaceutical industry into the scourge it is today can be attributed to Arthur Sackler."

Arthur's winning strategy was to sell drugs through doctors. He targeted physicians relentlessly, both through sales representatives and through print advertisements placed in medical journals. His ads often featured other doctors. One, for a new Pfizer antibiotic, Sigmamycin, read, "More and more physicians find Sigmamycin the antibiotic therapy of choice," and showed a number of doctors' business cards. Those doctors didn't exist. *Surprise, surprise.*

This casual relationship with the truth wasn't new to advertising, but it was new to medicine.

Sackler's marketing genius—or perhaps his boldness—transformed Pfizer into the giant it is today. Pfizer, in turn, made Arthur and his firm rich. *Very* rich. Before the two crossed paths, Charles Pfizer and Company was a chemical manufacturer, the world's largest producer of vitamin C. Its new pharmaceutical research department had come up with a synthetic antibiotic called Terramycin. Sackler, the story goes, told Pfizer that, given a big enough advertising budget, he could make the company a household name. Pfizer's CEO took the gamble and approved a budget of $7.5 million, an unheard-of figure at the time.

The resulting torrent of advertising was unlike anything the medical world had ever seen: print ads, direct mail, and phone calls directly to doctors. According to Gerald Posner, author of *Pharma,*

"Physicians known as heavy prescribers received two to three direct mail pitches daily for nearly a year."

Thousands of doctors received postcards appearing to be from far-flung lands such as Egypt, Australia, and Malta, claiming to have successfully treated exotic diseases such as "milk fever" and "Q fever." They were signed, "Sincerely, Pfizer."

Other ads cited studies that had been paid for by pharmaceutical companies. According to journalist Katherine Eban, writing in *Fortune* magazine, "Arthur's philosophy was to sell drugs by lavishing doctors with fancy junkets, expensive dinners and lucrative speaking fees, an approach so effective that the entire industry adopted it."

Terramycin became an instant blockbuster. It did $45 million in sales in 1952 and completely rewrote the drug-sales playbook—a playbook that would remain unchanged for half a century, when Purdue would dust it off to launch OxyContin.

In 2003, while hiking just outside the Washington, D.C., beltway, I'd injured my ankle and knee. My life wasn't pain-free.

At first, it started at an urgent care center, where the doctor handed me a prescription, put me in a plastic boot, and said, "We'll order you an MRI."

I took the first slick yellow pill—Dilaudid, another Purdue product—and my pain went away. Four hours later, it came back, so I took a second pill. Like magic, I felt normal again—as though I'd never been injured. My focus and ability returned, and I was able to physically keep up with the demands of my job. At the time, I was working for a political committee headquartered in our nation's capital. I didn't have to choose between work and my physical pain. I never did get that MRI. But I was able to refill my prescription again and again—and *again*.

Purdue's playbook definitely worked on me. Shortly after my injury, I relocated back home to South Florida. Pills were everywhere. Every billboard, bus bench, newspaper, and cab marquee had a phone number on it: *Call us for a solution to your pain*. Ads ran on TV and on the radio, filling our eyes and ears with the tactics created by Arthur Sackler, refined by Purdue, and utilized for more than five decades. They claimed that back pain, depression, old injuries, and chronic pain could all be cured by a quick trip to the doctor. It was an attractive lie, and I was one of the millions of people who lined up to give the miracle cure a try.

As I look back, it seemed as if everyone was on pills. I knew nothing about Dilaudid, and I didn't know anything about OxyContin when it came around, either. Since we were told these medications weren't addictive and were safe for long-term use, many of us used them as though they were heavy-duty aspirin, to shake off a hangover or relax at the end of a long day. At work, colleagues would ask me if I had any painkillers they could borrow. I'd go to a friend's house for drinks, and she'd ask me if I wanted to split an Oxy.

Pills were all-purpose. And pain clinics were just like fast food: accessible, common, overmarketed. Palm Beach State Attorney Dave Aronberg once claimed that there were "more pain clinics in Broward County than McDonald's."

In 2009, I worked on Aronberg's campaign for Florida attorney general; I was at the peak of my pill addiction. I'd pop pills before I went to work and showed up high as a kite. Aronberg had taken on OxyContin as deputy attorney general. I was eating handfuls of OxyContin. When I was let go right before the election, the person who fired me said there was clearly an issue, pointing to my erratic behavior and shrinking waistline. But I was never directly called out, nor was my illness named. He lost that race for AG and later became state attorney. The stigma of addiction was so severe that, although I was dying in plain sight, nobody would call it what it was. The problem was all around us. I didn't have a name for it, but I could easily tell you the cause: Florida was awash with messages that assured everyone they were one pill away from being all better, forever.

Back then, you could hardly go six blocks without seeing a pill mill. By 2010, more than half of opioid prescription pills in the country went to Florida, my home at the time. I went to many of those pill mills. When one place wasn't convenient, I'd pick a new one from the back page of the *Miami New Times*. There were hundreds to choose from. Ads for pain management clinics literally announced, "We prescribe Oxy!"

I called one of them, and that's how I met Dr. Leah.

Her clinic lobby wasn't any different from most of the others I'd been in. The waiting room was the size of a small airport hangar and had the same sense of anticipation, the tension of a hundred people shifting in their seats, keeping an eye on the clock, and waiting for their turn to see the doctor in the back room. The clinic was solidly booked, and even though it had enough chairs for a hundred patients, every time I checked in for my fifteen-minute appointment, I had to jockey for a seat among the many other patients who crowded around the battered tables of kids' blocks and tattered magazines.

Each visit to Dr. Leah was $200. They didn't take a check or credit card, and they definitely didn't take insurance. I handed my cash over to the receptionist at the desk and found a seat in the cavernous waiting room. The walls were lined with flat-screen TVs playing the news or a new DVD release. Waiting to see Dr. Leah, I swear I saw the same ten minutes of *The Matrix* a thousand times. I held an old *People* magazine on my lap, though I couldn't bring myself to leaf through its ragged pages. I leaned back in the upholstered chair, trying not to notice whether the rough burgundy-and-teal cushions were warm or sweaty from a previous patient. The arms of these chairs were always sticky and had gold-leaf trim, like a Las Vegas cafeteria. In the middle of the room was a table; if I came for a morning appointment, they served bagels and cream cheese, watery cut fruit, and syrupy orange juice in a pitcher nested in a bowl of melting ice. Often, this was the only food I would eat: a Big Pharma breakfast, padding my stomach for the handfuls of pills sure to come.

OxyContin-branded pens, notepads, and Swiss Army knives were scattered around the food. A paper card on the table cheerfully announced which pharmaceutical rep had treated us to breakfast.

"Thanks, Mikayla," I muttered, snagging a bagel on my way into the back.

Dr. Leah was a former ob-gyn with the bedside manner of a person who knows what to do in an emergency. She was attractive, professional, and soft-spoken, greeting me with a friendly smile and a warm handshake. I trusted her. My first time at her clinic, she promptly wrote me out two prescriptions: 120 tablets of 80 mg OxyContin and 60 tablets of 30 mg oxycodone. Even to me, that seemed like a lot. She instructed me to take one OxyContin every twelve hours and, if I felt any pain in between those pills, to take an oxycodone to "fill in the gaps." I'd never heard of that before, but I was well acquainted with the sick, dizzy sensation when I reached the end of a pill's effectiveness—as though I were falling from a plane, spinning, counting my breaths as the ground rushed up toward me. I never wanted to feel that way, and Dr. Leah promised me that the oxycodone would break my fall and support me between the higher-dosage pills. I clutched the paper prescription as if it were a parachute.

She didn't warn me about overdosing or getting addicted. We had a plan, and Purdue's marketing materials claimed that if you were taking these pills *as prescribed*, there was no danger of addiction. They also said that if you had "real pain," the pills would act like a sponge, soaking the pain up and returning you to normal. Dr. Leah actually warned me not to *stop* taking them and said that I could easily taper off at any time—another Purdue promise.

As she gave me instructions, her demeanor was calm and nonchalant. She'd said these same things to a hundred other people that day. She bought the lie and passed it on to me.

I floated out of her office, past the breakfast table, waving to the receptionist. I filled my prescriptions and took the first pill in the pharmacy parking lot, just as the doctor had told me to. I felt myself gaining altitude. My ankle didn't hurt. Nothing hurt. My vision cleared, as though my car's windshield had been washed and buffed.

In that moment, my OxyContin use changed from "take as needed" to a necessity. Paired with oxycodone, it became a crutch. I *needed* it. I was addicted, though I didn't know what was on the other side of the looking glass. Dr. Leah didn't call it an addiction; she called it "dependence," which she said was totally normal. The Purdue marketing campaign that had "educated" my doctor had turned me into the ideal customer: one who kept coming back for more Purdue products and would eventually blow six figures on the pills I couldn't live without.

What happened to me wasn't a fluke, and it wasn't a onetime thing. This approach to pharmaceutical marketing, which converted patients into people with chemical dependency, was time-tested within the industry. The Sacklers had spent decades honing this simple process to perfection. In 1952, Arthur Sackler and his two brothers bought the Purdue Frederick Company, just as their new antibiotic Terramycin was taking off. Purdue Frederick started as a small patent-medicine company that mostly sold over-the-counter products such as antiseptics, laxatives, and an earwax remover. Nothing crazy. This little company was a tiny piece of the "Sackler empire." For decades, it just *existed,* turning a modest profit.

However, Purdue Frederick wasn't just selling medicine. They also had a publishing company; a newspaper called the *Medical Tribune,* which was sent out to hundreds of thousands of doctors around the world; the UK-based Napp Pharmaceuticals; the Basel-based Mundipharma; and dozens of other companies. The interconnected nature of Purdue Frederick proved to be the key to making billions off addiction. Like any good crime syndicate, the Sackler empire was a completely integrated operation. They could devise a new drug in their drug-development enterprise, then have the drug clinically tested. Next, favorable reports on the drug would be secured from various hospitals through industry connections. The company would conceive the advertising approach and prepare the actual advertising copy with which to promote the drug. They could publish the clinical articles as well as advertising copy in their own medical journals. Then, to take it a step further, they could plant favorable reviews in newspapers and magazines. Sounds like a racket to me! The company's sprawling structure made it difficult to determine what was reality and what was fiction. All the promotional copy was coming from within Purdue itself. Using misdirection and different names and identifiers, Purdue bamboozled outsiders by making it seem as if internally generated advertising was research from neutral, reputable sources.

One thing that I've learned later in life is to *never* trust a marketing company or a pharmaceutical marketing campaign. I've seen the best of the best. Purdue used advertisements, the media, and political influence to manipulate the market and mainstream their lie to the American people. OxyContin, the drug, is not inherently bad; the way it was marketed turned medicine into poison. Purdue took the truth and twisted it as far as it could bend.

In their prebankruptcy days, the Sacklers hired some of the biggest crisis-management companies to represent them. These PR firms had one job: to defend the Sackler name and continue perpetuating the myth that Purdue was blameless. Purdue, or their PR firm, wrote parts of Steve Miller's 2020 op-ed in *The Washington Post*. The piece, published under the name of the chairman of the board of directors for Purdue Pharma, painted their actions as ethical and lawful, when what happened seemed to be anything but. The Sacklers also seeded the media with misinformation that would make them look as though they were cooperating, or offered quotes to journalists. Anytime people negatively mention the Sackler family, somebody calls them, emails them, and pressures them, trying to convince them to change their mind. For example, Zachary Siegel, a well-respected Chicago-based investigative journalist, wrote an article that mentioned the Sacklers. He received an email within twenty-four hours to demand a "correction" to the facts he'd already cleared. You can't correct a fact, but that doesn't matter to these people. They don't care about the facts. They care about their client's image, and image only.

I experienced my fair share of "reputation management" calls from these PR firms as well. The only way I could give insights into my feelings was by sharing a news article relevant to the case that I agreed with from time to time. Periodically, I would post an article aligned with my beliefs on my social media accounts, just to give a hint to people about where my head was. I never explicitly called out the Purdue case or the Sacklers, but that didn't seem to matter. Within twelve hours of these social media posts, some Purdue PR hack would contact my friend Tim, who handled the publicity for *American Fix*. Their emails or calls made it clear that they were monitoring my social media. They quoted the post and challenged what I said, asking, "What does Ryan really mean by this?"

Every time this happened, Tim told me, and I got *irate*. Once, I was so fed up that I emailed my lawyer. I was furious. I wanted them to call Purdue and tell them to step off my First Amendment rights. I wasn't saying or writing anything: I could post whatever I wanted. It was telling that the Sacklers and their representatives were still trying to control the story. They could do nothing to change public opinion, but they could still run around harassing people for even a *suggestion* of criticism. These fucking people still believed that they could change the narrative around what had happened. They thought, even at this point, that they could change history.

Well, history doesn't belong to Purdue. And it certainly doesn't belong to the Sackler family. Nobody is allowed to re-create it. Once I was identified as a "potential addict," then converted into a return customer, I became a dollar sign. Even throughout the bankruptcy, that dollar sign didn't go away. My interest was still represented by a dollar figure: I'm a payout to them, not a person. That's how they see us. That's how it's always been.

For example, in the 1960s, the Sackler marketing machine set to work on a new drug from the Swiss company Roche. Librium was the world's first benzodiazepine—or "minor tranquilizer," as they were sometimes called. Benzos relax you; today, they're prescribed for such things as anxiety or seizures. I was once prescribed them to help me sleep, and to "take the edge off." They even gave them to me when I was in medical detox.

Detox was a novel concept to me in 2006, the first time I went to rehab. It was a nice facility, white-collar, a far cry from the county-funded places I'd end up in later. That first time, I was detoxed with a combo of buprenorphine and benzodiazepines. My mother took one look at the medication and did a double take.

"What?" she said, baffled. "Isn't that for sleep?"

I was withdrawing from OxyContin. This was years before I even started on heroin, before the days of injecting or smoking. My addiction took the form of snorting OxyContin. I lived on a combo of Oxy 80s and Roxy 30 mg, enough to kill a horse. I went through bottles of those pills every week. I knew I had a problem and had tried to detox myself, which was painful. I couldn't stick with it long enough to get through withdrawals. In July of 2006, in the middle of a hot, swampy Florida summer, I was trying to kick opioids during the midterm election for governor. I was working for the Florida Democratic Party, but not really "working" because I was mostly just getting high. I'd been dismissed, to put it kindly.

I ended up in Palm Beach County, where I was checked into

a "medical detox." I didn't know what that meant, but what I was trying at home wasn't working. I didn't know "medical" meant more drugs—just a different kind. I was ready to go at eight that morning, but they didn't get to me until eleven, after the intake. I was jonesing badly and didn't make it to the medical facility until 6:00 P.M. The hours leading up to withdrawal, when you know it's coming, are worse than the feeling itself. You suffer through the anxiousness, the nervous sweats, not being able to eat. You know it's coming, after the shaking and goose bumps, and you know it's only going to get worse.

When I was finally checked in, the first thing they did was dose me with Valium. A giant dose of benzos was the only thing that would keep me from climbing the wall. It was the only thing they could give me for the first twenty-four hours. The "medical" part of detox included comfort meds, a cocktail of Valium, electrolyte pills, and mild muscle relaxers. This mix is standard protocol. I was no stranger to Valium and Xanax. I'd taken them before, prescribed as part of my regimen with Oxy. Some of the first doctors I saw would include them in the prescription; the doctors seemed eager to pre-scribe those together because I was the type of user who wouldn't necessarily nod out when I was using opioids. Whether I was get-ting sick or trying to find help, the doctors had a pill for me. That was part of Purdue's playbook, too. Diversify, pathologize, and over-market, until America was saturated with pills and every person was convinced that he or she couldn't live without a prescription.

Valium had been around, in some form, as long as my mom. Librium was approved by the FDA in 1960, the same year the Ham-ilton Rating Scale for Depression was first published. The scale was a questionnaire designed to rate a variety of patients' moods and mood disorders, including suicidal ideation, insomnia, and anxiety.

Librium arrived at the perfect moment. As part of their marketing push, Sackler's firm spread around two studies, paid for by Roche. One reported that violent, psychotic prisoners in a Texas state prison who were given Librium became "placid and alert." The second involved animals at the San Diego Zoo and showed similar results.

The national press, including *Time, Newsweek, Esquire,* and *National Geographic,* dutifully parroted the results of these trials without skepticism. Sackler sent copies of the magazines out to thousands of doctors. The "facts" looked legitimate because they were in print, in distinguished publications. Armed with a $2 million budget, Sackler then copied the Terramycin strategy: glossy print ads, direct mail, and an army of sales reps (called detail men), all carefully coached, to talk the drug up to doctors.

Doctors wrote 1.5 million prescriptions for Librium in its first month on the market. Soon, Librium accounted for 70 percent of all tranquilizer sales in America.

Valium was the next generation of Librium: a tweaked version that was allegedly way more powerful but with fewer side effects. The FDA approved it in 1963—just as the Senate was holding hearings about the dangers of Librium. Undaunted, Arthur Sackler prepared for the first big drug launch of his career. While the Librium campaign was all about taming dangerous psychotics, Valium was touted as the drug for everyone. It was the drug for vague feelings of anxiety, nervousness, stress, boredom, and ennui. One advertisement actually read, "For this kind of patient—with no demonstrable pathology—consider the usefulness of Valium."

Ads promised, "No serious side effects." Previously, tranquilizers were considered the exclusive territory of psychiatrists, too heavy-duty for the average person. It's telling that most Valium prescriptions were written by general practitioners. Sales reps gave away millions of free samples of Valium to doctors, hospitals, medical institutions, and even the military.

The tactic worked, and it worked well. Valium wasn't just a bestselling drug. It was a cultural sensation. It was "a staple in medicine cabinets, as common as toothbrushes and razors," said historian Andrea Tone in *The Age of Anxiety*. Everyone took it, for every imaginable complaint, or maybe even no complaint at all. The Rolling Stones called it "mother's little helper," singing, "And though she's not really ill, there's a little yellow pill."

It's not surprising that Valium became the highest-selling pharmaceutical of its time, the first pill to generate $100 million in sales. It was as popular with bored housewives as it was with Wall Street tycoons, who called it "executive aspirin." *Fortune* called it "the greatest commercial success ever." It proved Sackler's theory right: marketing could push pills more effectively than science. Sackler's claims were supported by a built-in infrastructure of institutions—including the press, the FDA, and prescribers—who didn't have enough information to fact-check one another.

Because of this disconnect, Arthur Sackler's advertising copy became industry gospel. Only the manufacturer knew the truth, and with hundreds of millions of dollars coming in, they had no reason to ruin their cash flow by admitting the drug's real risks to the public.

Valium proved far more addictive than people first thought. It was misrepresented as safe and risk-free, and the consequences were severe for people who believed the lies they were told. The years following Valium's release were disastrous. Elizabeth Taylor got hooked. So did evangelist Tammy Faye Bakker. It was one of many drugs found in the blood of Elvis Presley when he died in

1977. The very next year, Valium passed a billion dollars in cumulative sales. The people who suffered from addiction became punch lines. It was easier to make fun of Elvis or Tammy Faye than acknowledge the truth: they were victims of a substance that was misrepresented as a magical cure-all.

In a 1979 Senate hearing, Ted Kennedy said, "These drugs have produced a nightmare of dependence and addiction, both very difficult to treat and to recover from." He warned, "I believe that what we will hear about today is the tip of the iceberg. Thousands of Americans are hooked and do not know it."

The Valium wave was only the beginning of the Sacklers' storm of addiction in America. The key elements were strategic distribution of misinformation by pharmaceutical companies, institutional blind spots, bad drug policy, and deeply held systemic biases. The drug's creation and launch set the stage for the modern-day American overdose crisis. Arthur Sackler had found a formula that worked, and worked well—eventually to the tune of billions of dollars.

Thirty-two years later, Purdue Pharma debuted their next megahit on the American market. This time, the Sackler family had fine-tuned the playbook that would change America—and my life, among millions of others—forever.

2

A SLEEPING GIANT

When Tiarra Renee Brown-Lewis died on May 17, 2020, she was alone in her bedroom, in an apartment littered with prescription-pill bottles. She had so many opioids in her system that she wasn't even able to push the button on her MedicAlert bracelet. An unopened box of naloxone, a lifesaving overdose-reversal medication, sat on her dresser. She was prescribed a number of multiple opioid painkillers, enough that the pharmacist gave her naloxone in case she accidentally doubled a dose. But, living all by herself, who was going to administer that medication in the event of an OD? Nobody. She died wearing a T-shirt that read "What's not to love about me?"

Tiarra's walker, with its neon-bright tennis-ball feet, was still next to the bed when her body was found. The vibrant twenty-eight-year-old was born with sickle cell anemia, an inherited red blood cell disorder in which there aren't enough healthy red blood cells to carry oxygen throughout the body. Pain was one of the symptoms of her chronic illness. Sticky, crescent-shaped blood cells jammed together in her small blood vessels, blocking blood flow and oxygen to different parts of her body. Some days, Tiarra was fine; others, she was so weak and inflamed that she couldn't stand without assistance.

When the EMTs responded to a caregiver's 911 call, they knew about Tiarra's sickle cell diagnosis. But the minute they saw the dresser covered in pill bottles, their entire demeanor changed. Suddenly, Tiarra wasn't a person anymore. She was an *overdose*. They went straight to the medication, commenting that Tiarra was "obviously drug dependent."

Her grieving mother, Tiffinee Scott, a recovery-support specialist and member of an ad hoc committee of personal injury victims, had to educate them about sickle cell and blood disorders over her child's dead body. She had to stand there and calmly explain to these so-called medical professionals that Tiarra was prescribed these medications to manage a somatic illness, that she wasn't an "addict." She was a lifelong patient who needed support for her symptoms. Tiffinee told the truth, but the prejudice was still there. It tainted the room, changing the way that the outsiders saw the situation. The respect Tiarra deserved was gone.

Her obituary was posted on Facebook, without fanfare. Friends and family members shared memories of her, tagging photos of Tiarra dancing, posing, and laughing. They commented about how hilarious she was, how bright. Her suffering, they said, was finally over.

What the posts didn't show was the king-size plastic bedding bag, filled with every medication Tiarra was given. After her body was taken away by the ambulance, her mother stayed behind to clean up the two-bedroom apartment. Tiarra was on nineteen prescribed medications, including psychotropics and physical health meds. Her regimen of narcotics included OxyContin, 80 mg pills she took multiple times a day, and oxycodone, at 30 mg and 20 mg doses. She was also given Toradol, Percocet, Dilaudid, morphine, and Seroquel. Tiffinee found notes in her own handwriting, the lettering big and bold so that Tiarra would be able to read it. The many, many pills interfered with Tiarra's cognitive function, causing her to lose track of her thoughts and processes. The bright, promising student who had navigated the health-care system from birth was reduced to a shuffling, confused child who needed to be reminded to feed herself. Tiffinee added Tiarra's asthma inhaler to the bag, along with the naloxone kit, still in its box. Her daughter was prescribed opioids from birth for her sickle cell diagnosis. She needed them.

Sickle cell anemia affects people of color almost exclusively: one in thirteen Black or African American babies is born with sickle cell traits. The disease is expensive to treat and has a high mortality rate. Even with access to medical care, the people who have it often live painful, unfairly short lives. Add to this the massive health-care disparities that affect Black people, thanks to institutional racism, generational trauma, economic inequity, and racist insurance policies, and what you have is a system designed to dampen pain that sometimes doesn't improve quality of life.

Tiarra had told her mother, "These meds are only putting me to sleep. They keep filling them so I keep getting them." Her mom noticed that Tiarra's condition changed significantly after being put on OxyContin.

Tiarra was following medical direction and doing her best to manage an incredibly challenging chronic illness. Yet, nobody seemed to consider the long-term consequences to her health. To understand why Tiarra overdosed, you have to understand how the pharmaceutical industry works hand in glove with doctors and other medical providers. You also have to understand institutional racism: Tiarra, a Black woman, was treated as a second-class citizen by the people who were supposed to help her, both while she was alive and after she tragically died. There was no outrage at Tiarra's passing. Nobody got sued. Her mother wasn't on the news. Without question, Tiarra needed opioids to manage her sickle cell anemia. However, her grave concerns about her treatment plan were essentially ignored by medical providers. Tiarra was swept aside as a "hopeless case," and that is largely the outcome of the "education" Big Pharma started giving providers long before she was even born.

Bear in mind that the health risks of long-term opioid use were well-known, studied, and documented; for years, those risks made it hard to sell heavy-duty opioid painkillers to people who weren't severe chronic pain or terminal cancer patients. That changed in 1987, when MS Contin was approved by the FDA. MS Contin was the precursor to OxyContin, and it showed up at a critical time for the Sackler family. The company structure changed when Arthur Sackler died, also in 1987. Control passed to his two brothers, Raymond and Mortimer. But they were no spring chickens and did not rule the roost alone: Raymond's son Richard was a growing influence in the company. He had followed the family tradition of training to become a doctor, joined Purdue Frederick as an assistant to his father, and worked his way up. Richard pushed his father and uncle to start a new company, which they would call Purdue Pharma. Purdue incorporated in 1991 and packed their board with Sackler family members, making it one of the few big family-owned drug companies.

MS Contin was the Sacklers' first major pill to go to market; a few years later, the company was already hard at work on their next product, OxyContin, which it hoped would be its breakthrough drug. They were certain they had the winning formula.

Up until the mid-1980s, the scientific consensus was that people who used opioids for more than a short period of time risked opioid dependency. When you give someone pharmaceutical-grade heroin, then suddenly take it away, they feel terrible. Sounds like a no-brainer, right? Even someone who wasn't an MD could understand that. It was common sense. Without considering psychological issues such as addiction, the physical effects were enough to convince most doctors to prescribe opioid medications sparingly, reserving them for severe cases. Part of medicine should be *whole body wellness,* which means that doctors make sure the treatment isn't going to kill their patients.

Some doctors departed from conventional wisdom and embraced the "heresy" Arthur Sackler identified as a force for market change. Going against the grain could put people's lives at risk— but if the Sacklers could turn a buck, so what? Money talked and doctors listened. Within the medical field, a quiet revolution was taking place.

In the 1970s, the World Health Organization declared "freedom from pain" to be a universal human right. Later, in the 1980s, a new kind of health-care specialty arose: palliative care. Seriously ill patients needed treatment for their stress and pain. Part of their care was therapy, counseling, and even spiritual practice. And, yes, they needed painkillers. Thus began a nuanced debate about the meaning of "pain." How was pain defined? How could we measure it? How could we treat it?

Although the FDA was the primary gatekeeper for drugs, their authority was essentially limited to approval or denial. "FDA-approved" didn't mean the government endorsed a particular medication or even that it was completely safe. It only meant that it was legal and had passed a bureaucratic review of its clinical trials. Just as not all organic food is healthy, not every FDA-approved drug rubber-stamped "safe and effective" is harmless. The FDA had no say over how a drug was used; that was up to doctors, who could be influenced by pharmaceutical companies intent on getting as many pills as possible into a medication-hungry market. Pain was a growth vertical, and Big Pharma was eager to cash in. Many doctors pushed pills to patients *not* according to FDA guidelines or even the instructions printed on the side of the box. They made use of "black box" prescribing, a loophole that allows doctors to give a medica-tion *as they deem necessary,* not exclusively as directed by the manu-facturer or FDA. A doctor could give unlimited pills to patients who still said they were in pain, no matter what the FDA said.

That black box rule was a billion-dollar opportunity for the Sacklers.

Over the next few years, the debate around pain gathered more support. In 1986, the WHO proclaimed "the inadequate treatment of cancer and noncancer pain is a serious public health concern." It encouraged doctors to prescribe opioids for cancer patients. That same year, the doctors Russell Portenoy and Kathy Foley published "Chronic Use of Opioid Analgesics in Non-malignant Pain: Report of 38 Cases" in a journal called *Pain*—a controversial paper with an earth-shattering argument: that cancer patients taking opioids weren't becoming addicted to them.

"There is a growing literature showing that [opioids] can be used for a long time, with few side effects," Portenoy told *The New York Times* in 1993. Drug manufacturers took note. From a mar-ket perspective, these cracks in conventional prescribing practices plus a newly declared "global pain epidemic" that made painkillers a vital part of any treatment plan represented an incredible commercial opportunity.

Significantly, the provocative claims in the *Pain* paper didn't need strong research supporting them to be perceived as reasonable. The statements got people heated. Doctors jumped in to argue and "well, actually" at each other. The controversy *was* the support. Portenoy later admitted that his conclusions were based on "weak, weak, weak data." He added, "In essence, this was education to destigmatize. . . . Clearly, if I had an inkling of what I know now then, I wouldn't have spoken in the way that I spoke."

But it was too late. The rebuttals and debate around *Pain* helped to weaponize the American medicine cabinet.

In 1996, the American Pain Society, a nonprofit advocacy group, recommended that pain be treated as the fifth vital sign. The first four signs of life were temperature, pulse, blood pressure, and breathing rate. Now, feeling pain, too, meant you were alive, and you got tested for your pain levels right along with your heart rate. It soon became standard practice for nurses to ask patients how much pain they were in on the scale of one to ten. The goal was to move the score lower, since less pain was always better. A series of subtle interventions, both government created and industry normalized, pushed clinical behavior for both doctors and the people they treated. The sliding scale, backed by the claim that everyone was entitled to a pain-free existence, acted as a nudge to doctors to prescribe more painkillers. If the patient pointed at the frowning face, it was a doctor's job to turn that frown upside down. The chart also trained patients to be more sensitive to pain, effectively putting a monster under the bed. Maybe it was there, and maybe it wasn't, but it *felt* real, and that suggestion was enough to bring on a nightmare. Patients started getting used to the idea that if you were in pain, you could tell your doctor and you'd probably leave with a prescription for Vicodin—which was perceived by many as a perfectly safe, nonaddictive substance.

Tiarra was taking those "perfectly safe," FDA-approved medications as prescribed, up until the day she died. She was driven by the prescriber; if she had pain, they offered her more pills, even though she was already concerned about her laundry list of medications. They were given to her by the hundreds by legitimate doctors, nurses, and pharmacists whose degrees came from accredited medical schools.

Some doctors, nurses, and pharmacists are trained to *not* take Black patients seriously when they talk about pain. In *Nursing: A Concept-Based Approach to Learning,* a table says, "Blacks often report higher pain intensity than other cultures. They believe suffering and pain are inevitable. They believe in prayer and laying on of hands to heal pain and believe that relief is proportional to faith." This racist garbage is printed in a fucking *textbook* that is used in hundreds of classrooms to train thousands of providers. From the beginning, providers are taught bigoted, false information about Black pain patients.

Tiarra's pain wasn't the enemy. The system was. Doctors out to "cure" Tiarra's pain didn't care to listen to a Black woman about her own body and her own needs. They used prescriptions to shut Tiarra up and get her out of their offices—and because of this, she died.

There are thousands of Tiarras, in countless Black families in America. The Sacklers preyed on them, lining their pockets from overprescribed meds pushed on people with chronic illnesses. Without the Tiarras of the world, there would be no Sackler empire. But without the Sacklers, we might still have Tiarra.

Tiarra's story isn't in any of the Sackler family's obituaries, though I believe they should be read side by side. When Arthur Sackler died in 1987, his obituaries focused on his role as an art collector, art patron, and "philanthropist." *The Washington Post* lovingly praised him as "an art collector of breathtaking scope and discernment, and a founder of various museums, wings, galleries and other institutions that keep his pictures and objects in the public eye." The piece made no mention of Valium or Librium. Instead, it mentioned Arthur's fascination with Asian art; he was one of the world's foremost collectors and often allowed galleries and museums to include in exhibitions pieces he personally owned. It is deeply ironic that many of the people who walked through these museums suffered from Sackler's products. They went out to see Sackler's art collection and went home to a medicine cabinet full of the pills that had made those purchases possible.

Reputation management was crucial in obscuring the connection between Sackler marketing tactics and the accelerating health crisis. Media initially chose to focus on philanthropy, omitting unsavory stories. The same pattern repeated when Arthur's brother Raymond died in 2017. His obituary in *The New York Times* named his survivors and alluded to the "brief illness" that killed him. It did not mention the ninety-one people who died that same day due to lethal overdoses of the pills that made the Sacklers billionaires. However, the obituary did include a biography of OxyContin, including the 2007 court settlements Purdue paid for misleading marketing, and the long list of institutions that benefited from the Sacklers' beneficence, including the Metropolitan Museum of Art in New York (home to the Temple of Dendur), the Freer and Sackler Galleries at the Smithsonian Institution in Washington, the Sackler School of Graduate Biomedical Sciences at Tufts University, the

Mortimer and Raymond Sackler Institute of Advanced Studies at Tel Aviv University, the Raymond and Beverly Sackler Gallery for Assyrian Art at the Metropolitan Museum, Leiden University in the Netherlands, Weill Cornell Medical College in New York, the Columbia University College of Physicians and Surgeons, the British Museum, and the Raymond and Beverly Sackler Medical Research Center at the University of Cambridge School of Clinical Medicine. And the list goes on and on and on.

Tiarra's name was forgotten by all but the people who loved her. Raymond's, on the other hand, was plastered across British cultural institutions, schools in Israel, and scores of scientific, academic, and cultural programs. The system held him up as a model citizen. When he passed, his beneficiaries mourned him. Their inability to see his role in the rising overdose crisis was an inability to see their own complicity in it. If they felt guilty for how they abetted the Sacklers' rise to power, they comforted themselves with the knowledge that they'd followed the rules. They hadn't broken any laws. Whether those laws were just, or whether the "legitimate" system that supported them was moral, was never debated. Raymond Sackler's dignity was unchallenged. Tiarra's was not.

The disconnect is jarring. Tiarra was one of hundreds of thousands of Americans who died due to a preventable overdose. There was no alternative treatment plan for her condition: prescribers just kept loading her up and sending her home. She was weakened by the pills that were supposed to help her, even though she took them only as her doctors ordered. Tapering off opioids with Suboxone or methadone wasn't an option, due to her primary diagnosis. The doctors always said the answer was more pills. Was it?

Opioids kill at a higher rate than guns and car accidents combined. They kill people who are sick and people who are healthy.

The systems that aided and abetted these deaths went unchallenged. Nobody suggested that human lives were more important than money or institutional prestige.

The New York Times didn't name the people who died of overdoses. Lauding Sackler for his generosity, when the dollars he donated came *directly* from his lethal marketing tactics, didn't make sense. The Sacklers were portrayed as respectable, cultured people who supported institutions that enriched the human experience. They were given respect, while the people who died because of capitalist greed—victims such as Tiarra—were instantly forgotten.

Yet, even in these whitewashed accounts of the Sacklers, the truth would still slip through. One anecdote was revealing. Arthur Sackler had a lot of famous friends, including Linus Pauling, the chemist who won two Nobel Prizes. The *Post* obit quoted Arthur Sackler as saying, "I once asked Linus Pauling, 'What is the role of heresy in science?' And he looked at me and said, 'Arthur, isn't heresy the source of all real progress?'"

The story was intended to frame Arthur as a disrupter and a hero who ignored conventional wisdom. Arthur Sackler was a pioneer, all right; he spearheaded a new, dangerous medical racket and made billions. The Sackler "heresy" continued after Arthur's death: there was nothing philanthropic or enlightening about it.

The drive to be the biggest, richest, and most powerful *made* the Sackler family. It also killed people who were at the mercy of the medications Purdue sold.

To understand why Tiarra lost her life, you have to look at the substances that killed her, and the people who kept giving it to her. (I know this is dry, but it's an important part of the story. This isn't just about Purdue: it's about where their products came from . . . follow along with me for a minute.)

One of the labeled bottles on Tiarra's dresser when she died was for OxyContin. Although this is one of the more powerful opioid medications on the market, it is not a completely synthetic drug. Its active ingredient comes from the seed pods of a beautiful red poppy plant, like the ones that put Dorothy to sleep in *The Wizard of Oz*. Opium is derived from the *Papaver somniferum* variety of poppy. One of the chemicals found inside the white, milky sap is morphine. It's named after the Greek god of sleep and dreams, Morpheus. That's the ingredient you feel the most when you use an opioid. Morphine gets you high, and morphine is more addictive than any other substance on the planet. Another chemical in the sap is codeine, also a painkiller and administered in cough syrups, among other medicines.

People have been using opioids for just about as long as they've been doing anything else. They've used them for medical reasons and for pleasure—sometimes both at once. Ancient Sumerians called opium the "joy plant." The Mesopotamians, Assyrians, and Egyptians all used it, as did the Greeks, who named it *opion*. Late in life, Roman emperor Marcus Aurelius was given opium by his doctor, who later lamented that his patient had become "habituated" to the drug. Sometime around AD 1000, a Persian doctor named Avicenna tried to standardize opium doses, making them the size of chickpeas. It may not have worked so well: Avicenna died of an opium overdose.

Long recognized as a treatment for pain, opium was industrialized and commercialized in the West. The morphine molecule was isolated by Friedrich Sertürner, a German pharmacist, who sampled it for himself to treat a toothache. Though lauded by the scientific community for his achievements, Sertürner suffered from depression and became severely withdrawn. He died dependent on morphine. His death was not considered a cautionary tale.

Unhappy endings abound throughout the history of opioids. For example, Alexander Wood invented the hypodermic needle in 1853. He thought it would make morphine less addictive. Boy, was he wrong. Wood's wife "developed a lethal fondness for morphine" and may have died of an overdose.

Morphine and other opioids tell the brain to stop caring about the pain our bodies feel; opioids block those signals, making physical discomfort manageable. Pain is not a substance that slushes around in our bloodstreams, although some crafty marketing campaigns suggested as much; I remember one depicting a pain pill as Pac-Man, chomping up "pain pellets." If there was no pain, these marketing posters suggested, the pills wouldn't work.

This deceitful approach to painkillers wasn't new. Despite morphine's obvious harms, "miracle cures" with folksy names proliferated in drugstores. Medicines of questionable quality such as Mrs. Winslow's Soothing Syrup were sold over the counter and even marketed for children. Then as now, there was a remedy for everything, and as long as the container looked clean and safe— and came with a doctor's or a pharmacist's stamp of approval—it couldn't possibly hurt you. Things got so out of hand that President Teddy Roosevelt appointed an opium commissioner, who told *The New York Times* in 1911, "Uncle Sam is the worst drug fiend in the world. . . . Our physicians use [opium] recklessly in remedies and thus become responsible for making numberless 'dope fiends,' and in uncounted nostrums offered everywhere for sale it figures, in habit-making quantities without restriction."

At the turn of the century, chemists had begun to tinker with the morphine molecule, changing it in tiny but important ways, making "semisynthetic" opioids such as oxycodone and hydrocodone. Later, they would invent fully synthetic opioids such as fentanyl. If you look back, it's hard not to notice a pattern: Someone invents a new opioid, thinking it less dangerous than previous kinds. It's marketed as such. Years later, a creeping realization: the new formulation is even *more* problematic. But the damage is done. Pulling the medicine off the market ensured that people who relied on it would find something else to use. Inevitably, that *something else* was a stronger substance. Tapering off wasn't commonly supported as a solution. The answer was usually a new painkiller, each one more powerful than the last.

That's how Tiarra Renee Brown-Lewis ended up with nineteen medications on her dresser. When one pill didn't work, she was given a new one. She had a port installed over her heart in case she needed emergency medication. The day she died, she went to the ER for pain but was turned away because she didn't have COVID-19 symptoms. Instead, the nurses sent her home to self-medicate. Hours after she got home from the ER, she died in her bed.

Tiarra was a lifelong opioid patient, due to her medical needs. She was given medications approved by the FDA at unusually high doses. At some point the body reaches a threshold: it cannot process opioids anymore. Doctors are always working against that threshold, trying to figure out how much is enough. The line between enough and too much is thin. Pharmaceutical companies on the hunt for higher profits push against that common sense, suggesting that patients can and should handle higher doses of existing medications. When that doesn't work, they just invent something new.

The endgame of this constant opioid leveling up was heroin. Invented in the 1890s by Felix Hoffmann, a German chemist working for Bayer, heroin was a semisynthetic opioid. It was a modified version of morphine, with one special feature: it dissolves in body fat more quickly than morphine. Since the human brain is 60 percent fat, heroin also had a profound psychological effect. It didn't just take your pain away. It felt *great*. Like, really great. Higher, better, faster. Yet, it was still marked as a safe, nonaddictive cough suppressant. Heroin was sold over the counter at pharmacies, like Bayer's other invention, aspirin. An unprecedented wave of addiction followed.

Eventually, good ol' Uncle Sam stepped in and cut off Americans' supply of heroin. It was a brutal, overnight detox. In 1914, after over fifty years of unlimited access to opioids at any corner drugstore, the United States passed the Harrison Narcotics Tax Act, a law regulating and controlling cocaine and opioids. Products containing opioids disappeared from store shelves. Doctors were arrested for giving them out, even though this act was passed only six months after the beginning of World War I, when many more Americans would return home with battlefield injuries and the pain that accompanied them. The Harrison Narcotics Tax Act identified certain substances as illegal and dangerous. Heroin, once a common medication that could be found in the average person's medicine cabinet, became a street drug. The people who relied on it sought out prescriptions or resorted to using now-illicit substances.

Addiction was seen as a moral failing back then, too; seeking help as a heroin user was nearly impossible. There were no resources for people who struggled.

Regulation ranged from prohibition to arbitrary labeling for substances. In 1971, Congress established the Schedule I through V labeling system that still exists today. Schedule V meant the drug had "low potential for abuse" and could pretty safely be prescribed by a doctor; for example, cough syrup with codeine. Schedule I meant "a high potential for abuse" with "no currently accepted medical use in treatment in the United States." This category included heroin, LSD, GHB, MDMA, and marijuana. (Yep, *marijuana*.) Opioids such as morphine, oxycodone, hydrocodone, and fentanyl were all assigned to Schedule II, meaning they had "a high potential for abuse" but could still be prescribed by doctors, albeit with restrictions.

Although heroin, morphine, oxycodone, hydrocodone, and fentanyl were all opioids and shared the same ingredients, they were split into separate categories. Heroin was grouped with other drugs that had ties to the hippie counterculture movement as well as racial discrimination. Just as opium was a "Chinese" drug, marijuana was "Mexican," and crackdowns on these drugs were undeniably linked to racist anti-immigration sentiment and the public policies that sanctioned racial stereotypes. This was a cornerstone of the War on Drugs, which incarcerated millions of mostly Black people and other people of color for minor infractions such as marijuana possession. They were forced into a new kind of slavery, working for fifty cents an hour at manufacturing jobs, and charged insanely high prices for basic items such as soap or tampons.

Marijuana was "dirty" and could land you in prison for decades. Lab drugs such as morphine and fentanyl, on the other hand, were considered acceptable in comparison. The entire DEA scheduling of drugs, like so many other guidelines around substances, was completely arbitrary.

In 1987, the Sackler-owned company Napp Pharmaceuticals introduced a new kind of morphine pill with a patented coating that released the drug gradually. The drug was MS Contin. Its sales were good, but it was far from a blockbuster. Doctors were reluctant to prescribe morphine for anything but bad pain. MS Contin became a niche painkiller for cancer patients and terminally ill people. The pill's time-release coating meant essentially that opioids could safely be administered at home, like a morphine drip without any need for medical oversight. No needles, no IV bags, no nurse checking your vitals. You could take that pill and feel its effects for hours as the opioid slowly moved through your bloodstream. This drug was a boon for the people who needed it—a comparatively small population of patients with specialized care needs. However, for people who *didn't* need it, that delayed-release opioid was about to become a real problem. *I would know.*

In late 2007, I was prescribed MS Contin as a cheaper replacement for OxyContin. Demand for Oxy was so high that pharmacies couldn't keep it on the shelves; the ones that carried it marked it *way* up, making it too expensive for someone such as me. I stayed on MS Contin for two or three cycles of medication before moving back. The pain doctor I was seeing just switched me from one Purdue product to another; even though I changed pills, Purdue was still making money off me. Other clinics were doing the same, using MS Contin as a filler med for Oxy patients. I wasn't much of a fan of MS Contin. It didn't do the trick. I was eager to get back to Oxy, which was the only pill that made me feel semi-okay anymore. I was so addicted that when I didn't have my drug of choice, I felt *more* pain. And pain was a symptom doctors were motivated to treat. Boy, were they *eager* to treat it.

The normalizing of pain as a symptom was an enormous cultural shift. Under the surface of the pain debate, commercial interests assessed the landscape and discreetly guided the conversation in ways that would benefit their bottom line. Pharmaceutical companies such as Purdue were major donors to the American Pain Society and other pain advocacy groups. And though Dr. Portenoy did come to his conclusions in *Pain* honestly, he would later receive a ton of money from Purdue. That research made Purdue billions of dollars.

Dr. Andrew Kolodny, an outspoken critic of Purdue and the codirector of opioid policy research at the Heller School for Social Policy and Management at Brandeis University, says, "Purdue, I think, played a leading role in changing the culture in opioid prescribing. At first, leading experts in the field of pain treatment were the biggest critics of aggressive opioid prescribing. Even in the 1980s, people with chronic pain ended up being stuck on opioids. They knew opioids were the worst thing they could treat pain with. When money came into professional societies to advocate for opioids, they changed their tune."

The influence that Purdue had over the pain movement and doctors' willingness to prescribe opioids would tighten like a vise throughout the 1990s and well into the 2000s, even as serious concerns about OxyContin were raised. In 2001, Purdue executive Robin Hogen wrote in a memo later unearthed by *Mother Jones* that if nonprofits such as the American Pain Society "want our bucks (and they honestly cannot survive without industry support) they are going to have to learn to live with 'industry' reps on their board. I don't think they can expect huge grants without some say in governance." That same year, Richard Sackler wrote, in an email, "Our goal is to bind these organizations more closely to us than heretofore, but also to align them with our expanded mission and to see that the fate of our product(s) are inextricably bound up with the trajectory of the pain movement."

This meant big business, and Purdue cashed in by using the

same marketing and distribution strategies that had worked on Valium. By 1990, MS Contin had become a favorite of oncologists. Purdue tried to market the painkiller to noncancer patients, but with limited success. Now, with just two years left on their patent, they faced the prospect of being undercut by generic versions. Purdue needed a new drug.

Dr. Robert Kaiko, Purdue's vice president of clinical research and a key figure in the creation of MS Contin, outlined the problem in a memo to Richard Sackler and two executives: "Other pharmaceutical firms are thought to also be developing other controlled-release opioid analgesics. . . . While we are 'going laterally' with MS Contin to non-cancer pain indications, it would be unwise to 'put all of our eggs into the MS Contin basket' in the face of the prospect of generic MS Contin competition that would 'crush all of the analgesic eggs.'" The metaphor properly driven home, Kaiko proposed that instead of coming up with a new morphine-based painkiller, Purdue should try a different Schedule II opioid: oxycodone.

Oxycodone was the active ingredient in both Percodan and Percocet, though both were heavily diluted with aspirin and acetaminophen, respectively. Although plenty of people did misuse those drugs, you could only take so much of them before you got a stomachache or developed a liver problem. Kaiko quoted a doctor who called oxycodone "a 'sleeping giant' in that among all the opioid analgesics utilized in fixed combinations, oxycodone is the only one with an analgesic potential comparable to that of morphine." In other words: oxycodone was just as powerful as morphine, but a lot of doctors didn't know that, so they weren't afraid to prescribe it.

"Purdue capitalized on a misunderstanding," says Dr. Kolodny.

"Many in the medical community thought oxycodone was weaker than morphine. That morphine was for cancer, and oxycodone was more like codeine. In fact it's the opposite. There is very little difference in oxycodone and heroin. They are both semisynthetic opioids that are highly addictive."

Two weeks to the day after Tiarra died, I talked to her mother over a Zoom video conference. She asked if she could show me something. When she held up the package, I wasn't sure what I was seeing. It was massive. Photos of Tiarra were taped all over it. It rattled when she picked it up, as though it contained a snake. It was the king-size bedding bag from Tiarra's room. It was packed with pill bottles, hundreds of them. Tiarra took these every day, day after day. Up to the day of her death, Tiarra struggled to find a place where she felt as if she belonged. She was ostracized for so many reasons, cut off—and finally victimized by a system designed to take advantage of her and her family.

I looked at that bag of pill bottles. Our lives get so small after we pass on. We go from larger-than-life to fitting in a little plastic bag. It wasn't right that such a vivacious, sharp, and funny young woman should have such a bleak memorial, packed by her mother. Tiarra and her family deserved so much more.

Justice, I knew, had to be big enough for everyone affected by Purdue's nefarious actions. A single doctor could give one person more pills than they would need in a hundred lifetimes. Purdue raked in the cash as many people who used their products suffered in silence, struggled with addiction, and died. Even people who *needed* pain relief were at risk. We had proof of the ways Purdue products wrecked communities nationwide. As I learned more about the influence the Sacklers' products had on our economy, health-care system, criminal justice system, and policy decisions, in addition to the colossal number of deaths linked to Oxy, I saw that we had to do *something*.

I always thought it was us versus Big Pharma, but this was a much bigger problem than one bankruptcy could solve. It wasn't just about fixing a broken system that failed to protect us. It was about making sure the survivors weren't left behind. Purdue might be as American as apple pie, but we could change that. They were only a symptom. The real problem was that America put the almighty dollar at the center of its guiding principles. As Vinay Krishnan, field director at the Center for Popular Democracy says, "Capitalism kills. That's not hyperbole. It's not a metaphor. Literally, capitalism kills."

I was witnessing a total system failure, and the deeper I went, the more complicated things got.

3

THE BLIZZARD WAS COMING

My new view from the inside showed me that I was a chess piece for the industries, institutions, and laws that conspired to turn a profit. Before, I believed that my addiction was a moral sin and I was deeply ashamed of how far I'd fallen. I went from a bright, promising political career to shooting up in a pill mill bathroom. I couldn't make the connection between the pills and the pushers, but I could certainly see how the drugs themselves affected every area of my life, destroying me.

As my addiction progressed, I lost my apartment, couldn't hold a job, and survived by couch surfing. Sometimes I got lucky and found a room at a trap house—some of them were even "sober living homes," run by people who were only interested in quick cash. I stayed in one of these flophouses for almost a year, as my habit got worse and worse. There were never any spoons in the kitchen since everyone there was shooting up. My room had a queen-size mattress on the floor, no linens, and a single battered pillow without a cover. The only window was a small single pane right next to the bed, which I could slide open and closed, like a drive-through window. I had a small TV with a built-in VCR that was so old that it only picked up air cable and one local broadcast station. I owned one VHS tape: *Body of Lies,* starring Leonardo DiCaprio. Other than the short clips of *The Matrix* that I saw in Dr. Leah's waiting room, this VHS was the only movie I had. I watched it on a loop on the days I was sick, receiving deliveries of pills through the tiny window with one hand when I was too weak to sit up in bed.

Over the bed, I had my only prized possession: a movie poster from Blockbuster Video. It featured a big picture of President Barack Obama giving his election-night speech. Underneath, it had a quote that I committed to memory: "Where we are met with cynicism and doubts, and those who tell us that we can't, we will respond with that timeless creed that sums up the spirit of a people: Yes, we can."

I didn't have much spirit left in 2009. I had a closet full of loose shoes, clothes, all too small, too big, or too dirty to wear. My only light came from a small bedside lamp on the little drawer table next to the bed. Nothing matched. The bare tile floor held its chill even in the Florida summer, seeping through the mattress and making my dope-sick shivers worse. I was afraid of getting robbed, so I stashed my kit in the closet under layers of dirty clothes and trash bags. I'd get high, hide it, forget, and end up digging through the trash like a crazed raccoon, positive that someone had stolen it from me. My greatest fear was withdrawal. As long as I had my prescription, I could get through the day. I could always get more pills, although by this time I clearly wasn't using them as prescribed anymore.

I rotated clinics, sticking with the ones that were freest with their dispensing. The black box loophole helped me bypass prescription restrictions, and since much of my use predated the databases that kept track of opioid patients, I could collect pills whenever I needed them—which was frequently. The looser the doctor was with pre-scriptions, the more money the doctor made. The loophole was incentivized, and doctors willing to bend the rules, bypass FDA guidelines, and follow Big Pharma's yellow brick road could make tens of thousands of dollars a day. My most reliable clinic was run by Dr. Stephen Brown. To get there, I would walk a mile from the trap house to the main bus line and take two transfers. It took about seventy minutes and $1.25. I got the money either by panhandling or cribbing some change from a friend, offering to pay the person back when I got home. If I couldn't come up with anything, I would just tell the bus driver I was going to the hospital so I could ride for free. They didn't pay attention. There were so many of us, all sick, all going nowhere.

No matter how many times I took the route, I always timed it wrong and left late. Nothing is worse than riding a public bus when you're sick. I sat in the handicapped row in the front because there was more space, and any strong odor or harsh sound made my nausea unbearable. I could sit down as soon as I got in, and they were the only seats that had a tacky fabric covering on them, mak-ing them about 1 percent more comfortable than a regular seat. I opened the bus window an inch and tried to take deep breaths as I fought to keep myself from vomiting. My head pounded and I sweated through my shirt, even though I was shivering. It was hell. Once, a woman sat in the bench row facing me. Her belongings and bags were on one side, and a massive oversize bucket of fried chicken was on the other. She was going to town. The bus smelled like chicken and grease, turning my stomach. She was eating, eat-ing, eating. Halfway through her meal, she looked at her hands, which were coated in fat, breading, and stray flecks of meat. She looked at me, then moved her bag to one side, wiped her hands all over the seat, and went back to eating. I couldn't help myself. I threw up in my mouth, swallowed it, and had to sit there for another hour anyway. That was my normal.

There are two kinds of pain. One is a neurological event; it's a physical sensation that signals that your body is in trouble. Hit your thumb with a hammer? Pain. Bite your tongue? Pain. Everyone experiences physical pain, some more severely than others. The other kind of pain is *suffering*, which is much more complex. Suffering is physical pain with an emotional component. I didn't just hurt. I *ached*.

Ironically, pain and suffering became indistinguishable from each other for me. When I was using, I suffered. I felt pain every day. After a while, I couldn't tell if I was using OxyContin for my body or for my mind. I was trapped in a cycle that destroyed my ability to tell the difference. In some recovery programs, they call this "pitiful and incomprehensible demoralization." It's the feeling that you've gone as low as you can possibly sink.

I had plenty of help staying down, too. Dr. Brown re-upped my prescriptions regularly, providing extra pills to "cushion" my use. Oxy wasn't like other pain pills I'd taken. It was way better. The pills energized me as much as they numbed me, like a shot of espresso and a bath of novocaine. One small problem: my prescription was supposed to last one month. It lasted three weeks. Then two. Then only a few days. I began to collect physicians, a rotating cast, each one shadier than the last. Dr. Brown was the best of the bunch; at least his clinics pretended to be reputable. But once I was in the back room, it wasn't any different from seeing a regular street dealer. I didn't have to lie. We both knew why I was there. It was like any other transaction in America.

"What do you want?"

"Well, I like OxyContin. . . ."

"Okay, we'll start you off at eighty milligrams."

When I couldn't get a prescription, for whatever reason, I could easily buy Oxys on the street or from one of the people I knew from the waiting rooms. Addiction can be such a long and gentle slope. You make one little compromise, cut one little corner, at a time. You make deals with yourself—*I won't take this much, I won't eat one before breakfast, I won't smoke it, I won't shoot it.* Those aren't hard rules, though. They're just another *yet.* I broke those deals one at a time, never worried about the consequences. In the moment, they were just minor infractions, but those broken promises add up. Along with the physical dependence came shame, shame at my lack of fortitude and willpower. I started to think, *This is just who I am.* Just like that, I was putting a needle in my arm.

While I was under the influence, I could pretend to myself that I was a different person, but hiding my addiction on the outside was impossible. I always wore beige cargo shorts so I could carry my rig, and a white T-shirt. All my shirts had tiny pinprick bloodstains on them. I was sprinkled with blood; I didn't have new clothes, so I used shirts to wrap my arm when I was done. I lost weight rapidly and my shorts were baggy on me. I had to hitch them up when the pockets were loaded from a trip to the pain clinic. I either had no appetite or nothing to eat. I would literally fall down from not having food. I would go three or four days without eating, stand up, and collapse. No matter where I was, I just passed out. Sometimes, I would fall facedown on the cement, splitting my lip or bruising the side of my face.

Any reason was a good enough reason to add another pill. Some of my doctors even claimed that opioids could be used to help people with depression, as well as pain. The pills weren't just supposed to help with physical discomfort: they were designed to eliminate suffering. And they did, but it didn't last. The thing was, they actually made things worse—creating pain that didn't exist before, or forcing me to go through the hell of opioid withdrawal. Purdue pushed the narrative that more pills meant fewer problems and conveniently ignored the growing number of people such as myself—onetime pain patients who couldn't stop coming back for more. Nobody saw the doctors, pharmacies, hospitals, pharmaceutical executives, FDA commissioners, lawmakers, research scientists, distributors, police officers, judges, or lawyers that conspired with Purdue. If you looked at me then, all you would see was a sick, underweight, profoundly unhappy man with bloodstains on his clothes, an empty stomach, and a cell phone full of people to call when the pills ran out. You wouldn't see the system around me that was making me sick with one hand and depriving me of help with the other. Once I was in that system, I was screwed—and I knew it. And I could feel it, *hard*.

I was hyperaware of the consequences of being a person in active addiction. I knew I could face jail time if I was caught with pills—unlike the executives at drug companies and distributors, who were rewarded for moving product, to the tune of billions. The system that punished me was always present in some way. It supported the existing people in power while it dehumanized and degraded people such as me. At Dr. Brown's office, I had to creep past the armed security guard with my rig stuffed into the pockets of my cargo shorts. The guard had a Broward County badge and a gun—an off-duty cop from the sheriff's office, picking up extra hours on the side—and he was clearly there to protect the pills, not the patients.

I brought a spoon and a lighter to the clinic and an empty pill bottle with cotton in it. I twisted them together with grocery-store twist ties; if I didn't tie them together, someone would hear me jingling. On my way to the waiting room, I passed a room in the back that was filled with a massive safe where they were supposed to keep the controlled substances, but there were so many pills that boxes were just sitting around. The holy grail of opioid manufacturers was represented in those stacks: Purdue, Actavis, McKesson, Mallinckrodt, and others. I slunk to a seat in the waiting room and fidgeted until it was my turn with the doctor.

Dr. Brown prescribed the meds and dispensed them at his office. He was also getting high. He would fill the script in the back room, come back into the office, and sit down as he was nodding off. He'd dump out one bottle, which was sealed, so the count was obviously correct. Each time, he gave me six bottles of oxycodone and three bottles of OxyContin. He opened one of each and got the nail file–shaped pill counter.

"One, two, five, seven," he slurred as he pushed the pills around on the tray. He couldn't even count them correctly because he was so high. He would take the first ten and slide them across the desk into a little bag he had in his drawer. He kept the ten pills and put the rest back into the bottle. Then, he gave them to me and said, "See you next month; call if you need anything else." Usually I *would* call: I always ran short and needed more. He prescribed me Oxydose or Oxyfast, the liquid form of OxyContin. I could get that as a holdover for "breakthrough pain." Funny, I always had that kind of pain—anytime my supply was low. And all I needed to do was call Dr. Brown and tell him I was hurting, and I'd get some more relief prescribed. Pain meant I was sick. Pills helped me stay well.

Although I couldn't see my part at the time, I was a cog in a massive moneymaking scheme. As long as I was hooked, I was profitable. My addiction fed the powers that be, bought them second summer homes, put their children through Ivy League colleges, and paid for their political contributions. It financed lobbying efforts, put judges on the bench, and paid for questionable research. Although I didn't realize it then, I was paying the system to exploit, demean, incarcerate, and miseducate. I wasn't just paying for a pill. I was paying for a whole corrupt system that wanted to drain me until I was dead, then blame me for killing myself.

Sourcing my pills was more than full-time. It was round-the-clock, 24–7. It never took a break and was so strong that I wasn't able to work. Any potential employer could take one look at me and see that I had a problem. I relied on trading my extra pills so I could keep a roof over my head, eat, and keep the Oxy flowing. Honestly, I didn't have any other options. It was sell the pills or sell my body, and I wasn't that good-looking.

I rationalized with myself: It wasn't as if I were on the streets, standing on the corner slinging Oxy. I was doing what Dr. Brown and Dr. Leah did, just without a medical degree. There was an inside network of patients of these doctors. I had twenty numbers on my phone, and when I was flush or running low, I'd start hitting people up. One friend, Matty, was selling to me when I was out; I sold to him when he was out. We both saw the same doctor, getting our pills from the same supplier. The setup wasn't a scam. It was more like a circular firing squad. My use was so high that I would eventually have to buy my pills back. It was like a check-cashing-store arrangement, where I was always going to be upside down. When I picked up my script, I wasn't thinking, *In ten days, I'll be dope sick again and pass out and not eat for four days.* There's no such thing as rationing when you're hooked. It's so easy to go from "take as prescribed" to "take whenever you don't feel right."

There was a pill for everything, and companies just kept adding more to the roster. The pain market was booming, and the FDA kept approving medicines that often overlapped in purpose and function. When one pill didn't work as well, it was easy to switch to another one, double up, or add a new prescription. Purdue spent $40 million developing OxyContin. In presenting the drug to the FDA for approval, it highlighted one feature that set it apart from previous painkillers: it would last for twelve hours. Patients experiencing pain would have to take just two pills a day. They wouldn't have to get up in the middle of the night to take another one.

Two pills a day would be enough. At least, that's what Purdue *said*. But the company knew otherwise. Purdue's own studies, undertaken before the FDA approved the drug, showed that not all patients got twelve-hour pain relief from OxyContin. For some, it was closer to eight, especially after taking the drug for more than a few days. But because the majority of patients in Purdue's studies got pain relief for twelve hours, they were allowed to make the claim.

The FDA approved OxyContin for 10, 20, and 40 mg pills in 1995. (It later added 80 and 160 mg.) Despite there being little research into how addictive OxyContin was, the FDA allowed Purdue to claim, on the product's insert, "Delayed absorption, as provided by OxyContin tablets, is believed to reduce the abuse liability of a drug." Although the insert contained numerous warnings, including that it was a "potential drug of abuse," the FDA allowed Purdue to claim, in its marketing materials, that their new drug was less addictive than other narcotic painkillers. Purdue had pushed the idea that because of OxyContin's time-release coating, patients would experience fewer "peaks and troughs," or highs and lows, just a steady stream of narcotics. But it was just a theory. The FDA examiner, Curtis Wright, wrote a medical officer review (MOR) of OxyContin's new drug application (NDA) that concluded that OxyContin was "as good as current therapy, but has not been shown to have a significant advantage beyond reduction in frequency of dosing." His MOR made two key and misleading statements that became the basis of Purdue's aggressive OxyContin marketing campaigns:

1. "Delayed absorption, as provided by OxyContin tablets, is believed to reduce the abuse liability of a drug." This is known as the Delayed Absorption Statement.
2. "When the patient no longer requires therapy with Oxy-Contin tablets, patients receiving doses of 20–60 mg/day can usually have the therapy stopped abruptly without incident." This is known as the Stop Therapy Abruptly Statement.

The Stop Therapy Abruptly Statement had mysterious origins, and Dr. Wright originally wrote, "The reaction to abrupt withdrawal of oxycodone was typical for opioid analgesics." Dr. Wright could not recall when, how, or why the Stop language was included in his report, or why he came to that conclusion when the research demonstrated a different effect on opioid patients. However, Wright solicited Purdue's help in writing his reports—the same ones the company needed to legally sell their product.

A confidential memo revealed that Dr. Wright told Purdue that he was willing to work with them; he told the company that their application review "could be accelerated" if the company traveled to the FDA's location in Rockville, Maryland, rented a room nearby, and spent three to five days helping him write up his reports for the agency. Inviting Purdue meant that they suddenly had a voice—and a *lot* of input—into Wright's reviews of the clinical study reports and OxyContin's integrated summaries of efficacy and safety. This secret meeting happened between January 31 and February 2, 1995. Interestingly, on March 24, 1995—within three months after the submission of the NDA and nearly nine months before it was actually approved—a Purdue employee said that Dr. Wright "has confirmed that we will receive an APPROVAL letter for OxyContin (NDA 20–553) by the end of December 1995." Dr. Wright and Purdue were working hand in hand, and both sides got what they wanted out of the deal. On October 9, 1998, a year after he left the FDA, Purdue offered Dr. Wright a job as an executive medical director, with a first-year compensation package of at least $379,000. Wright started on December 1, 1998.

Any petty dealer can tell you that drugs don't come from nowhere. It takes a huge organization to move product. Legal or not, all drug-dealing operations work the same. If you follow the money, you find out how they work. Purdue worked like any other kingpin. The company co-opted doctors, FDA officials, law enforcement, regulators, and federal and state electeds. They won over people who cashed in their integrity. It was a multipronged attack.

In 2018, years after I'd gotten sober and people were calling for reparations for the death and destruction OxyContin had unleashed on our country, states and municipalities sued Big Pharma. The multifaceted assault on our cities and neighborhoods was turned back on the drug companies. Purdue Pharma, Johnson & Johnson, Mallinckrodt, Endo International, Allergan, Teva Pharmaceuticals, McKesson, Cardinal Health, and AmerisourceBergen were some of the companies named as perpetrators. Distributors, pharmacies, and manufacturers were also called out.

The list of plaintiffs in this multidistrict litigation (MDL) was huge and included more than twenty-five hundred cities, counties, and tribal authorities. The impact of opioids was so far-reaching and profound that it brought people together for the first time in a meaningful way. The judge overseeing the case, US district judge Dan Polster, pushed to consolidate the lawsuits into "global settlement" deals so rather than negotiating each individual claim, the claims could be bundled and settled. According to the judge, that would keep the case from going on forever and help the parties come to an agreement faster. With tens of billions of dollars in play, the judge approved a plan to create a "negotiation class." That would permit lawyers representing a single group of forty-nine local governments to hammer out any settlement deals. Individual cities or counties could opt out of the arrangement and go it alone if they thought they could get a better deal. The lawyers would be paid a percentage of the settlement, an impressive sum. (More on that later.)

With the whole supply chain of opioids in the hot seat, it was hard to separate companies from one another. Clearly, it would be difficult to divide settlements up. Which company was most at fault? Whose products killed the most people? The moving parts of the industry were so deeply connected that singling out one company as "guilty" would be almost impossible. So, consolidating the defendants and the plaintiffs made sense to some. At least that way, Judge Polster thought a settlement could be reached sooner rather than later. Most important, it would avoid an ugly litigation where the plaintiffs would air out Big Pharma's dirty laundry in discovery. The plaintiffs and pharmaceutical companies were complicit in this, and both were willing to work toward a deal that avoided any unnecessary embarrassment in favor of a few billion dollars trading hands.

The cost of the crisis was estimated at $2.5 trillion for the period from 2015 to 2018, with overdose deaths hitting another historic high. At the time, many advocates thought the combined settlement payout could potentially be hundreds of billions of dollars—more than Purdue or the Sackler family had made during their lifetimes. By the end of 2019, as the MDL was gaining steam, Purdue pulled the plug. They declared bankruptcy. Although they were anything but bankrupt, filing for Chapter 11 removed Purdue from test trials scheduled for the MDL, meant to gauge whether the plaintiffs' allegations were valid. It also moved them behind closed doors, where they would be protected from full transparency. Dividing the company's assets, paying its debts, and dismantling its internal structures would be a huge undertaking, conducted largely in secret. The process would happen under the eye of a judge, a ton of lawyers, state attorneys general, and a committee of private creditors. Purdue Pharma had been sued before and gotten away with relatively small settlements compared with the damage they'd done. I knew that the bankruptcy case wasn't "real" in the way that it was for ordinary people or normal mom-and-pop businesses. Purdue wasn't on-paper bankrupt. They had assets, valuable patents, and more than $1 billion in the bank. They were getting sued, and this case gave them another escape route, a way to walk away from the wreckage they'd created. They were dodging responsibility yet again—and the American justice system was eager to help.

I never had any doubt that Purdue was culpable in the overdose crisis. When I set out to bring them down, I was convinced they were public enemy number one. I was one of many activists who set their sights on Purdue. I couldn't see anything bigger than them. The evidence against the company was so overwhelming that I didn't think I needed to look any further.

Purdue had a rap sheet that was longer than my arm. The Drug Enforcement Administration would describe Purdue's marketing of OxyContin as the "most aggressive campaign for an opioid in US history." The goal of that campaign was to get more patients to take OxyContin, at the highest doses possible, for the longest time. They were successful beyond measure. At a launch meeting in the spring of 1995, Purdue executives laid out the company's ambitious sales strategy. According to a memo summarizing the meeting: "We do not want to niche OxyContin just for cancer pain. OxyContin will be positioned into Step 2 of the W.H.O. Analgesic Stepladder (the opioid to start with), but we will also move Oxy-Contin into Step 3 of the ladder (the opioid to stay with)."

OxyContin would be for everyone, for "mild to severe" pain. Any pain! No matter where the patient was on the suddenly ubiquitous pain scale, the patient qualified for Oxy. Purdue's target demographic wasn't just patients. It was *everybody*.

A big part of the pitch was that opioids weren't addictive after all. A typical claim appeared in a promotional video: "There's no question that our best, strongest pain medicines are the opioids. But these are the same drugs that have a reputation for causing addiction and other terrible things. Now, in fact, the rate of addiction amongst pain patients who are treated by doctors is much less than one percent. They don't wear out, they go on working, they do not have serious medical side effects."

Serious medical side effects such as—for example—a life-threatening heroin addiction. *No biggie.* The "one percent" factoid, repeated over and over in videos and brochures sent out to doctors, was based on a 101-word letter to the editor written by Dr. Hershel Jick in 1980. Jick had observed medical records of some forty-thousand-odd hospitalized patients given Percodan and hydromorphone. Jick wrote, "The development of addiction is rare in medical patients with no history of addiction." But these were hospitalized patients under supervision of medical professionals. It said nothing about average people sent home with a bottle of OxyContin—or, in my case, half a dozen bottles and no oversight. No matter; the finding was cited numerous times by Dr. Portenoy and others, until most people forgot just how limited the finding was. To Dr. Jick's great regret, his letter to the editor became the seed from which a great lie grew.

When Purdue's sales team fanned out across the country, they targeted not just pain specialists but doctors of all kinds, especially general practitioners, many of whom had little experience with opioids. These doctors saw that OxyContin's active ingredient was the same as Percocet's and assumed the drugs were similar. The sales team did nothing to dissuade doctors of these misconceptions. Quite the opposite. As one salesman told *Esquire* in 2017, "We were directed to lie. Why mince words about it? Greed took hold and overruled everything. They saw that potential for billions of dollars and just went after it."

Sales reps were rewarded handsomely for those lies. They got the best bonuses in the business, paid by the milligram prescribed. That gave salesmen every incentive to push not just more but stronger doses of OxyContin to doctors. One district sales memo— under the subject line "$$$$$$$$$$$$$$It's Bonus Time in the Neighborhood!"—urged the sales force, "Talk Titration, Titration,

Titration. . . . He who sells 40 mg will win the battle." And: "We know there is a strong correlation between sales calls and the usage of OxyContin."

In 2001, Purdue paid out $40 million in bonuses. Follow the money, right? These drug dealers weren't hustling in front of convenience stores, pushing baggies of mystery powder. They had offices, name badges, and white-collar jobs. They got paid for every doctor they hooked, and those doctors turned around and pushed pills to their patients.

Doctors were urged to prescribe OxyContin for things that opioids hadn't typically been used for in the past, such as arthritis, back pain, and fibromyalgia. Purdue targeted certain groups, such as geriatrics and veterans, because of the special health benefits they received. And they targeted first-time opioid users—the "opioid naive," as they were called in internal documents. Purdue gave away coupons for free seven- to thirty-day supplies of OxyContin. Doctors deemed likely to prescribe opioids were visited by sales reps weekly, or in some cases almost every day. According to the lawsuit Massachusetts would file in 2019, "Purdue salespeople asked doctors to list specific patients they were scheduled to see and pressed the doctors to commit to put the patients on Purdue opioids. By the time a patient walked into a clinic, the doctor, in Purdue's words, had already 'guaranteed' that he would prescribe Purdue's drugs. Purdue rewarded high-prescribing doctors with coffee, ice cream, catered lunches, and cash."

At the launch party for OxyContin, Richard Sackler, then the senior vice president for sales at Purdue, made a brash prediction: "The launch of OxyContin Tablets will be followed by a blizzard of prescriptions that will bury the competition. The prescription blizzard will be so deep, dense, and white . . ." and so on. By the year 2000, Sackler had become president of the company and OxyContin was earning Purdue more than a billion dollars a year. "There is no sign of it slowing down," Richard Sackler told a team of employees in 2000. In the combined years of 2001 and 2002, doctors wrote more than 14 million prescriptions for OxyContin, generating $3 billion in revenue for Purdue.

Sackler's prophetic blizzard had come to pass. It would bury more than just the competition. In the decades to follow, hundreds of thousands of Americans would die from overdoses related to OxyContin and other prescription drugs. Countless others had addictions unlocked by OxyContin and either died or went through hell.

The seeds of the overdose crisis weren't just sown by Purdue, or a few rogue doctors, or the FDA, or the state medical boards. By the turn of the millennium, it was heresy not to treat any type of pain with opioids. Doctors could actually be disciplined for *not* prescribing painkillers. In 1999, Dr. Paul Bilder of Roseburg, Oregon, was ordered to attend a physician's education program and undergo psychiatric treatment after the state medical board determined that he had "not prescribed enough drugs to alleviate pain in six patients between 1993 and 1998," according to *The New York Times*.

In Oxy's heyday, five states—California, Idaho, Illinois, New York, and Texas—had a program that tracked when doctors wrote prescriptions for narcotics. Called triplicate programs, they kept a paper record of every time a doctor issued a prescription for a Schedule II substance. Purdue's own focus groups showed that doctors in those states "did not respond positively to the drug, since it is a Class II narcotic which would require triplicate prescriptions. Therefore, only a few would ever use the product, and for them it would be on a very infrequent basis." Another report recommended, "The product [OxyContin] should only be positioned to physicians in non-triplicate states."

Seeing the reduction in prescriptions, other states rushed to institute their own tracking programs, but it was already too late. By that time, ripping pills away from people was impossible and pushed many of us out of the system toward illicit drugs like heroin. I can remember following the news when Florida was getting ready to launch its own tracking database. I was terrified at the thought of being cut off.

We used to call Dr. Brown "Old Faithful." He wasn't deterred by the impending tracking system, and it certainly didn't seem to disrupt his network of seven pain-management clinics. He went to jail for a little bit after being caught with a pill bottle with someone else's name on it. He was arrested and released the same night on bail; one of the other pain patients I knew sent me the article. I remember feeling a total panic, like, "Fuck! I have an appointment in two days, where am I going to get my pills?" I thought I was going to die since this guy was my connection. The next day I called and they were open, as if nothing had happened. Still, Dr. Brown showed up at work and kept on writing scripts. The same Broward County Sheriff's Office guard was right outside the building when I got there, and Dr. Brown was in the office, legally dispensing and prescribing medication. A later investigation triggered by the arrest led to the suspension of his license.

Not long after the OxyContin launch, stories began to circulate that OxyContin wasn't lasting twelve hours. Patients told doctors, who told the sales reps, who told their managers. The reports were passed up the corporate ladder. Doctors often told the patients to take the pills more frequently. Enterprising people bought Oxys on the street and removed the time-release coating to make the pills work faster. Elderly pain patients were selling their pills for something that wasn't time-release. Pharmacies were getting robbed. Purdue's blockbuster drug was showing up in the pockets of arrested drug dealers and in the toxicology reports of overdose victims. Small, rural newspapers began to write articles about Oxy misuse. *The blizzard was coming.*

In November 1999, a sales rep named Jim Speed emailed Purdue executive David Haddox to warn about OxyContin's rapidly deteriorating reputation: "Many physicians now think, 'OxyContin is obviously a street drug all the drug addicts are seeking.' Issues like purposely crushing the 40 mg and 80 mg tabs to 'get high' have been expressed. I have heard from physicians and pharmacists that on the streets people are finding ways to extract the oxycodone from the tablet and are using a cotton ball to filter the talc as they draw it up in a syringe for 'mainlining.'" In 2000, an internal report by Purdue's Medical Services department found "this type of question, patients not being able to stop OxyContin without withdrawal symptoms, has come up quite a bit here in Medical Services lately (at least 3 calls in the last 2 days)."

Then in 2001, *The New York Times* published its first story on what it called "a growing wave of drug abuse."

"Heck, we already know it's pretty epidemic down here," a police captain in eastern Kentucky told *The Times*. "Abuse of this drug has become unbelievable in the last year, with probably eighty-five to ninety percent of our field work now related to Oxys." If *The Times*' first piece focused on people misusing OxyContin, a follow-up, the next month, began to cast blame on Purdue's aggressive sales tactics. The story quoted a doctor who threw a sales rep out of his office, saying, "They were pushing it for everything." A narcotics investigator said, "Nobody is immune from this. . . . I'm seeing housewives; I'm seeing loggers, nurses, mechanics."

You could imagine a different world, perhaps a saner world, in which this was the end of it. But that's not at all what happened. Instead, Purdue doubled down and went on the offensive. Richard Sackler had been appointed president of Purdue in 1999; in February of 2001, he sent a now-infamous email outlining his strategy.

"We will have to mobilize the millions that have serious pain and need our product. This we will try to do." But then he added, "Meanwhile, we have to hammer on the abusers in every way possible. They are the culprits and the problem. They are reckless criminals."

He wanted pain patients to become Purdue's advocates, and he wanted to pit "good" pill users against "bad" ones. He wanted to preserve Purdue's reputation and let the stigma of addiction protect the company. Who would listen to a bunch of "junkies," anyway? He guessed right: it took hundreds of thousands of deaths before "those people" and their families started organizing against drugmakers.

Michael Friedman, then the chief operating officer of Purdue, testified before a congressional subcommittee in 2001. The hearing was supposed to be about misuse and addiction to OxyContin. But Friedman avoided the question of addiction, and chose to focus on legitimate pain patients: "Unfortunately for those patients, concern generated by the abuse of OxyContin has mushroomed to the point that in some locations, some patients are asking their doctors to switch them to less effective medicines, some doctors are refusing to renew patients' prescriptions for OxyContin, and some pharmacists are no longer willing to carry OxyContin for their patients."

And what about me, a user who did become physically addicted to prescribed OxyContin? Actually, I was told that I wasn't addicted at all—I was only "pseudoaddicted," a term Purdue executive David Haddox had coined in 1989. "Pseudoaddiction," explained a Purdue pamphlet, "seems similar to addiction, but is due to unrelieved pain. . . . Misunderstanding of this phenomenon may lead the clinician to inappropriately stigmatize the patient with the label 'addict.'" Fortunately, pseudoaddiction had an easy cure: more opioids. It was like the Tom Waits line, "I don't have a drinking problem, 'cept when I can't get a drink."

In 2001, the FDA stepped in and changed the label for Oxy-Contin. Among other things, it removed the claim that OxyContin's time-release coating was "believed to reduce the abuse liability of a drug" and added a new black box warning that stressed that Oxy-Contin was "a Schedule II controlled substance with an abuse liability similar to morphine." Drug companies generally want to avoid a black box warning, so the move was seen as the FDA cracking down on Purdue. But one change actually worked in Purdue's favor. The new label was allowed to claim that OxyContin was for "the management of moderate to severe pain when a continuous around the clock analgesic is needed for an extended period of time."

It was yet another astonishing gift from the FDA, and Purdue executives knew it. "The action by the FDA . . . has created enormous opportunities," read one internal memo. "In effect, the FDA has expanded the indication for OxyContin. . . . This broad labeling is likely to never again be available for an opioid seeking FDA approval."

Just when the FDA should have been reining Purdue in, it had given it a license to print money. Purdue wasn't about to allow that opportunity to pass by. Roughly three-quarters of the $400 million Purdue would spend on promoting OxyContin came after the year

2000. The Purdue sales team continued to push doctors to prescribe more patients higher doses for longer periods. Physical dependence, sales reps were instructed to tell doctors, was "a normal physiologic response," "an expected occurrence," no more dangerous than "many classes of medications"—such as, for example, blood pressure drugs. Doctors were told that "data supports the use of opioids beyond ninety days and maintained through fifty-two weeks." *A whole year.* Most of the time, it didn't stop after a year. According to the Massachusetts lawsuit, "Purdue's campaign to 'extend average treatment duration' succeeded. A national study of tens of thousands of medical and pharmacy claims records published in the *Journal of General Internal Medicine* found that two-thirds of patients who took opioids for ninety days were still taking opioids five years later."

In the two years after the FDA's action, OxyContin sales tripled. When crooked doctors were arrested, Purdue still paid out bonuses to their sales reps. The strategy remained the same: target the doctors who prescribed the most—the "super prescribers" or "whales." According to Posner's *Pharma,* in OxyContin's thirteen top markets, a few hundred super prescribers wrote more prescriptions than there were people in that area. In the United States, the majority of all opioids were prescribed by just 3 percent of all physicians. Yet, those prescriptions were enough to flood the entire country with highly addictive—and profitable—pills.

What was the real truth? Doctors washed their hands of the problem, saying they were misinformed. Pharmaceutical executives claimed to have bent the facts, but took no responsibility for the devastation their products caused. When we spoke up, we were dismissed as "addicts," morally bankrupt criminals who should have known better than to take that first pill. The only way to solve the riddle was to follow the money. As in any other racket, that money talked—and it told the truth. The financial connections between doctors, CEOs, distributors, and lobbyists spoke volumes. When Purdue was sued in the MDL, they had so much liability that bankruptcy was their only option to protect themselves and their assets. *Un-fucking-believable.*

In the beginning, I was so convinced that Purdue was the only bad guy that I lost sight of the bigger issues, the many other complicit systems. The night that Purdue filed, I was up late watching the news. My phone lit up with notifications. MSNBC was the first alert on the list, with breaking news that Purdue Pharma was filing for Chapter 11 bankruptcy. Chapter 11 is a form of bankruptcy that involves a reorganization of a debtor's business affairs, debts, and assets—the debtor being Purdue. It is known as "reorganization" bankruptcy. Corporations generally file Chapter 11 if they require time to restructure their debts; in this case, Purdue was trying to get ahead of the massive number of payouts it would have to make. The expense of the bankruptcy filing and fees, not to mention lawyers, was worth it for them. They could afford to tap out. The bankruptcy would also protect the Sackler family and the company's existing assets. It was a shell game and it was set up to work in their favor.

"Those fuckers got away again," I muttered to myself. I wanted this case to be as simple as revealing the villain at the end of *Scooby-Doo.* I imagined myself pulling the mask off and showing the face of the Sacklers underneath it. I wanted to show the world what greed did, and who was responsible for the daily death toll. I wanted not just justice, but revenge. Whenever I could, I spoke out against Purdue. I was likely one of the people they hated the most: every Sackler knew my name. I dogged them tirelessly.

My immediate concern was, Where was the money going to

go? Would it support victims and fund the massive disparity in services for people who need help? Was it going to support harm reduction? Would it support families who had lost their children? Would it provide for people whose lives were ruined by Oxy-Contin? Would the Sacklers ever truly be held responsible? Would this process have any shred of transparency or justice? I had so many questions.

The company wasn't broke, by a long shot. The bankruptcy filing worked in their favor. Filing for bankruptcy allowed Purdue an "automatic stay," which freezes litigation against the company. Once plaintiffs' claims were moved to bankruptcy court, Purdue could negotiate or litigate over the amount they would pay. They'd negotiate with each party making a claim and set terms for how long they'd have to pay it—which could be *years*. Purdue's segment of the mega-case was moved out of unfriendly Ohio into bankruptcy court and overseen in capitalist-friendly White Plains, New York, under the extraordinary power of Judge Robert Drain. The system continued to work by design. The bankruptcy judge accepted the case as separate from the rest of the MDL. That decision was entirely up to him, not any of the other defendants, the company, or the plaintiffs. According to the website STAT, this is because bankruptcy cases were designed to produce a resolution in a faster, more focused manner than would be the case in civil court. The judge's job is to get the settlement over with, which doesn't necessarily work in the plaintiffs' favor. In fact, when these cases are rushed, plaintiffs often receive a fraction of what they are owed. Bankruptcy aims to get everyone a piece of the pie—but it's not a big slice, and it's nowhere near what we deserved.

Bankruptcy means that plaintiffs might have to compete against one another for the now-limited pie. Some plaintiffs might try to take the full amount owed to them, leaving little for other plaintiffs. Since it's a finite amount, bankruptcy escalates competition between groups instead of offering a fair, equitable settlement. It becomes a land grab to see who can get the most.

"If [a company] has to pay cases as they were finalized, the plaintiff that had reached a resolution in its case earlier might get paid in full, but there would be nothing left for anyone else," said Jesse Fried, a professor at Harvard Law School, as explained to STAT.

Once a company files for bankruptcy, it's basically frozen in time. It has to provide all of its assets and debts to the court. Also, there's a specific order for payoffs: the first creditors to get paid are the so-called secured creditors, who might have invested money in the company or provided a loan that needs to be repaid. Once those creditors are paid, the leftovers are doled out to whoever is left.

Purdue entered Chapter 11 with zero secured debt; all creditors were "unsecured creditors." Unsecured creditors included victims and families whose lives were harmed by Purdue products; states and municipalities; the Department of Justice and federal government; hospitals; insurance companies; neonatal abstinence syndrome (NAS) babies; pension funds; and, yes, even pharmacies. The bankruptcy judge or an appointee, such as a mediator, generally decides how much each of those creditors is owed. Again, that is *one* person's decision, made without public input. The judge tallies up all the unsecured creditors' claims and divides the company's remaining assets among them proportionately. The smaller the pie, the less everyone gets—and there's nothing anybody can do about it.

The entire bankruptcy process is built to favor the corporation, not the interests of people such as Tiarra Renee Brown-Lewis's mother. For example, if a judge decides a particular creditor is owed

$10, but the whole pie of unsecured creditors' claims amounts to $100, and the debtor only has assets of $10, that particular creditor might get fifty cents, or nothing. And once the creditors receive payment, the case is closed. No further action can be taken against the company—or, in this case, the Sackler family as well.

With Purdue, the company's profits are inextricably tied to the Sackler family's wealth. Some states said the family should be charged separately because the family absorbed the bulk of the company's profits. Shortly after the bankruptcy filing, the New York attorney general's office said it had uncovered $1 billion in wire transfers by the Sacklers, alleging the family was trying to hide its assets.

Keeping things behind closed doors never worked in my favor. Whether I was concealing my issues with addiction, suffering in silence, or being told to keep my mouth shut, I knew that hiding was not the answer. Much of the progress I made was from the *opposite* of hiding. If I chose to engage in this hush-hush undertaking, would that result in justice? Would that be just as meaningful as calling Purdue out in public? I wasn't sure. All I knew is that I had to find out.

4

FLESH AND BLOOD

Even before getting a front-and-center seat at what would be the closest thing to Purdue's murder trial, I held the belief that the bankruptcy was a gross miscarriage of justice. Seventy-two thousand Americans died of a preventable overdose in 2019 (that number would surge to a historic high of eighty-seven thousand just one year later). The process shouldn't be put on hold: lives were at stake, and delay meant death. Why should the lawsuits be paused? I thought we should just barrel through and demand that the Sacklers be held accountable in court. I was naive because my only lens was through activism. A successful action or campaign could be measured in protesters, signatures, and wins you can *see*. Bankruptcy, which mostly happens out of the public eye, is another story. It's not about cooperation. It's about concessions—usually to the people you like the least.

Before, I had the luxury of ideological purity. But being on the inside meant that I had to work with people I despised. It meant I had to consider decisions that I would, in the past, have deemed beyond the pale. Justice, like the truth, is subjective. It's not black-and-white. It's an infinite number of shades of gray. Although I came to the Purdue case thinking I knew what justice meant, I quickly realized that I was in a completely different league, playing by a set of rules that made no sense to me. I realized that my definition of that word was at odds with the court's. There's pure justice, the kind we read about in books and see in movies. Balance is restored to the galaxy, the bad guys are vanquished, and all get what they deserve. Then there's *legal* justice. That kind of justice means "law-abiding," and how it's interpreted is up for debate.

Legal justice was created by lawyers, interpreted by lawyers, and argued in courts. The law, as I learned, isn't necessarily ethical, moral, beneficial, or even reflective of how the people who are governed by those laws want to live. There are plenty of examples of how something that is legal is evil and wrong: slavery, for example, was legal. Stealing land from Native and Indigenous people was legal. Beating your wife was legal. I quickly found my core beliefs at odds with the way the justice system was set up to work.

Once I was on the inside, it became clear that I had to get right in the middle of things. Participation was the only possible way we could get anything done. I had to sit across the table from people I had spent years squaring off against, in the media and on the streets. I was fighting to win—on behalf of so many that had been harmed. I had to get a front-row seat or I had no chance of changing the outcome in our favor. My hands were tied by the greater good, and even if I was the only person who believed in that goodness, I had to represent it. The Sackler family, the case, and American bankruptcy law didn't care about justice the same way I did.

They were ready to eat our lunch from day one, not leaving a single crumb.

"Tell me a little bit about yourself."

On September 26, 2019, we were in a conference room, high up on the executive floor of the Hyatt hotel in Times Square. The floor was eerily silent; it had been rented out to the US trustee (UST) from the Southern District of New York for the purposes of the appointment of the Unsecured Creditors Committee (UCC) for the bankruptcy. The committee would have a fiduciary responsibility to all creditors, including state and local governments, hospitals, pharmacies, insurance companies, a bunch of other entities, and tens of thousands of individual victims, all of whom claimed to have been harmed by the pharmaceutical giant.

The UCC's job would be to advocate for the creditors throughout the bankruptcy, like a mega-plaintiff. The committee would serve as a watchdog for the case. Through discovery and depositions, they'd try to figure out just how much money Purdue and the Sackler family had. They'd advise on a plan of reorganization and present a case for how the money should be divided up, although the final decision would lie with the judge. The committee would have broad powers: it could subpoena records, take depositions, even cross-examine witnesses. It was an extraordinarily powerful voice in the case, and I needed to be part of it.

I couldn't afford a hotel room in Manhattan, so I spent the night before in New Jersey, driving into the city the next day in a rental car. That morning, I couldn't get near the hotel, because the United Nations was in session and the streets were blocked off for Donald Trump's motorcade. So I had to walk a sweaty mile and a half in my suit. I was feeling out of sorts as I sat face-to-face with Paul Schwartzberg, the US trustee for the Southern District of New York, for what was to be the shortest, but one of the more consequential, job interviews of my life.

"Tell me why you want to serve on this committee," he said.

I told him my story—the abbreviated version—and I said I thought it was important that victims have a voice. I had two minutes, and anyone who knows me knows that I can barely say my name in less than five. I tried to keep it brief. The trustee knew I was an activist, and that I had made public statements about the Sackler family. I had, for example, written that Purdue entering bankruptcy was "a prime example of Purdue literally getting away with murder" and that "the states must go after the Sackler family personally if we have any hope of getting them to pay." I had, in effect, said there shouldn't be a bankruptcy at all: we should just empty the Sacklers' bank accounts, lock them up, and publicly shame them for the rest of their lives.

I told the trustee that I would do my best to be levelheaded and impartial.

"Usually we wouldn't sit victims on a committee like this," Schwartzberg said. "But this is a very different case."

Most creditors committees are composed of lawyers representing banks, investment firms, and other large corporations. Only when a company is caught up in some horrible scandal and has harmed dozens, hundreds, or even thousands of people do victims get appointed to the creditors committee, because actual victims make up such a large percentage of creditors. For example, when Harvey Weinstein's production company declared bankruptcy, two women who accused the movie mogul of sexual assault were given seats on the creditors committee.

The Weinstein bankruptcy was dwarfed by the Purdue case,

both in terms of its sheer size (the company claimed to be worth billions) and the number of alleged victims. The whole country had been touched by the overdose crisis. As Judge Robert Drain would later put it, "One could conclude . . . that every citizen of every state in the United States is a claimant, in one way or another." Everyone wanted a piece of Purdue. In some ways, this wasn't a bankruptcy so much as a piece of public policy. It was political. The trustee had to decide how much weight to give the opinions of people directly affected by opioid addiction.

Most of the lawyers in the room were predicting that Schwartz-berg would appoint one or two victims—a person in recovery and the parent from a family of loss, perhaps. So it was a surprise to all of us when, of the nine members chosen for the committee, *four* were victims. The committee's statement announcing our selection was succinct, to say the least.

The victims were:

Me, Ryan Hampton, described as "a staffer at the White House in the Clinton administration who became addicted to OxyContin and other prescription opioids."

My friend Cheryl Juaire, whose son Corey became addicted to prescription painkillers and died of an overdose at age twenty-three.

Kara Trainor, a prescription-opioid user, whose son Riley was born dependent on opioids. Riley "faces a lifetime of latent medical and emotional conditions, including brain damage, muscular-skeletal developmental disorders, speech and language disorders, cognitive developmental disorders,

psychiatric disorders, emotional development disorders, be-
havioral disorders, and increased risk of addiction."

Walter Lee Salmons, a grandfather of two opioid-affected
children he was helping to raise. Walter and Kara were there
to represent relatives of infants born with neonatal abstinence syndrome (NAS). In 2014, there were around thirty-
two thousand babies with NAS.

The other five seats were filled by institutional representatives.
They were:

CVS Pharmacy, one of Purdue's biggest creditors, claiming
they were owed money from unpaid rebates the drug company
pledged to pay pharmacies to entice new Oxycontin users. *CVS
was as complicit as Purdue and was a defendant in the MDL.*

West Boca Medical Center, a Florida hospital that had sued
Purdue, claiming "RICO violations, deceptive and unfair
trade practices, misleading advertising, breach of implied
warranty, negligence, nuisance and unjust enrichment."
WBMC was there to represent all the hospitals with claims
against Purdue. *They'd kicked me off their doorstep more than
once when I was in desperate need during my Florida days.*

Blue Cross Blue Shield, which provides health insurance to a
third of all Americans. The company claimed that it had been
charged "excessive amounts" for Purdue's drugs, and that it
had been forced to pay for the treatment of "illnesses, injuries,
and addiction" caused by the overdose crisis, which Purdue

played a role in setting off. *BCBS denied me medical coverage many times and refused to pay to send me to treatment. They should be a defendant but were claiming to be harmed.*

The Pension Benefit Guaranty Corporation, "a wholly owned United States government corporation and agency," to which Purdue owed money in pension contributions and insurance premiums.

LTS Lohmann Therapy Systems Corporation. They make medicinal patches, such as the nicotine patch and a naltrexone patch, which is used to treat opioid addiction. LTS Lohmann had a contract with Purdue to make a Butrans patch (another Purdue product). Purdue still owed royalties for these patches.

What a lovely bunch. We had to work with these corporate creditors, many of whom were just as guilty and had made billions from the same corrupt system that made Purdue rich. The actual victims were a minority on the committee, and I knew our voices would have to be loud to keep from being overwhelmed by corporate interests. But whereas the other creditors had different kinds of claims and were competing with one another, the victims immediately recognized one another as allies. We would attempt to form a cohesive voting bloc. The trustee knew what he was doing. He'd given victims an incredibly powerful voice on the committee. But it was up to us to figure out how to use it.

I believe in the power of voting. I believe in the system, as flawed, broken, and unequal as it can sometimes be, because I've seen firsthand that it can work. I believe in justice, by and for the people. Up until this point, my participation in the system had always been *near* the decision-making table, as a contributor. I gave congressional testimony in the Capitol to support new policy. I lobbied the White House. I spoke at statehouses all over the country. But I'd never been in the room where it happens. I was used to agitating, lobbying people with *actual* power. Now I had a vote— one vote out of nine that could move billions of dollars one way or another. One vote out of nine that could decide the fate of a family. Did I feel I was in over my head? Some days, you could say that. I think the other victims felt the same way.

The conference room where we convened for the first time was large and antiseptic. Everyone had a lawyer. The lawyers had lawyers. I've never seen so many lawyers. Even I had a lawyer: Anne Andrews, the woman who got me into the hot seat in the first place. Anne was a well-respected lawyer who looked more like an actress than a legal maven. She wore red lipstick and had curly dark hair that she tamed in a chic chignon. She was professional but feminine, and one of the toughest women in her field. She focused on representing people harmed in catastrophes or disasters of all kinds related to commercial products. Anne made her mark doing silicone breast implant litigation; she noticed that thin-walled, leaky implants failed within seven years, hurt people, and made them sick.

Anne was passionate about representing victims, which was what drew me to her. She had her own firm and had in college used Ruth Bader Ginsburg's first textbooks. Anne advocated for other women who wanted to get into law. She told me that from day one, as a baby lawyer, she knew she was never supposed to work for a man or be defined by male orders from the top. She was quickly noticed as a force, who had a gift for figuring out how to organize the type of litigation we faced with Purdue. Anne viewed the victims' participation in the Purdue case as a mass tort, not a bankruptcy. To her, it was comparable to the Big Tobacco suit or the Firestone tire lawsuit. A mass tort acknowledged that Purdue's victims were all poisoned by the same root; the same opioid molecule affected millions of people. Anne looked at the overdose crisis and saw that an addictive drug changed our entire culture and belief system, as Purdue's marketing mesmerized people into accepting OxyContin as a cure for any type of pain. Purdue was Anne's seventeenth bankruptcy case.

One of the lawyers—it was impossible to tell anyone apart at this point, with their near-identical pin-striped suits and mono-grammed briefcases—stood up. He said the committee needed to draft bylaws and elect a chair.

Surprise, surprise: the reps for Big Insurance, BCBS, practically leaped out of their seats and hollered, "Yeah, we'll serve. We do this all the time. We'll do it."

Maybe I was just annoyed at all the lawyers and their friendly chatter. But I was quickly getting the impression that the five corporate entities on the committee, along with their lawyers, thought they could control the process. For them, this was just another walk in the park. These guys probably played golf together and met for barbecues in the Hamptons. Though their interests may have been at odds, they were all part of corporate America; who cared what team they played for because they were all on the same side—and they were all going to make a *killing*.

For me, the Purdue bankruptcy was about more than just balance sheets. It was about reparations, about trying to mitigate the unimaginable harm the company caused. I couldn't let this lawyer club compromise any chance of the victims getting justice. So, before I knew what was happening, my hand shot up.

I said, "I'll do it."

"Yeah, there should be a cochair, and we should actually have a victim as a cochair," someone said. It was Ed Neiger, who was sitting in the corner of the room, apart from everyone else. Ed had worked on the Enron bankruptcy and was now representing the ad hoc committee of personal injury victims. Ed was one of the loudest and most important voices for victims and their families throughout the entire process.

"Should we have a vote?" he said.

It was unanimous. BCBS and I would serve as cochairs. Afterward, one of their lawyers came up to me and said, "Oh, congrats."

It sounded a bit patronizing.

"For what?" I asked.

"Well, it basically just means you're just going to have to sign a lot of stuff."

"I don't understand what you mean." I was pissed, but I let it go. This was the first of many hints at what all the bankruptcy attorneys really thought of us. To them, the four victims, whose lives had been torn apart in various ways, were there to lend the process legitimacy. We were supposed to make the proceedings look fair, even though they were inherently skewed. The creditors committee needed to appear to represent *all* creditors, not just CVS and BCBS. But did they want to actually hear from us? Not really.

The next thing we had to do was to choose the committee's legal counsel. Six or seven of the top law firms in the country were there, all hoping for a piece of the action. We asked them questions about possible conflicts of interest, such as, "Do you represent any pharmaceutical companies or potential defendants in the opioid litigation?" Most of them did. They all had an explanation about why it wasn't a problem. They said they had firewalls, they'd brought in some former governor to consult, and so on.

By far the most impressive was Arik Preis, who was a few years older than me. Unlike a lot of the other lawyers, he seemed guided by a moral conviction to do the right thing. It wasn't business as usual for him. His firm, Akin Gump, was one of the most profitable law firms in the country. Not only were they conflict-free, but they came in with an interesting idea: an emergency relief fund.

"People are dying," Arik said when he was questioned. "This is an unprecedented case, so it calls for unprecedented measures. This has never been done before, but what I'd like to suggest is that we ask for several hundred million dollars to come off the balance sheet right now. That can go into on-the-ground services that are going to save lives right now. This case is going to take a year and a half to two years, and it would be a shame if we have money going toward consultants and lawyers, while the people who actually need it aren't getting it."

I thought it was a novel idea, and it sounded like the easiest thing in the world. But nothing about this dumpster fire was going to be easy. Every step of the way, our humane suggestions were battered within an inch of their lives by lawyers who didn't want to grant a single penny to victims. Every measure that would support people who were harmed faced half a dozen objections. I realized quickly that whatever victims got, we'd have to fight for it tooth and nail against trained litigators who were going to get paid millions of dollars either way. Justice had plenty of competition.

Thousands of lawsuits had been filed against Purdue by states, municipalities, private companies, and some regular people. The opioid litigation was like a scene in a Quentin Tarantino movie, a circular firing squad where everyone was pointing a gun at someone else.

"The opioid litigation is probably the most complex litigation in the history of the world," Ed Neiger told me. "There are so many parties, and there are so many levels of wrong. In a certain sense, everyone in this society has been wronged. We are all still paying the price of the opioid epidemic in higher taxes, resources that are siphoned off from education. So in a way we're all victims."

When Purdue was in negotiations to settle these lawsuits, the company made an offer. Purdue would declare bankruptcy and become a "public benefit corporation," with all future profits going toward the settlement. This would emerge as a grim irony throughout all of this: to pay reparations to victims, Purdue would continue selling OxyContin. In addition to the company's value, the Sackler family offered to put in another $3 billion of their own money. But that was just to seem sympathetic: they would get that money back when they sold off other assets, such as Mundipharma. The $3 billion seemed beneficial to some because it would give creditors an instant infusion of cash. That money was desperately needed; as Arik Preis pointed out, some people had urgent medical needs that were the direct result of opioids and had to pay for medical bills, housing, and other necessities.

The $3 billion offer from the Sacklers included an unspoken but potentially crucial clause for the term sheet: immunity for both Purdue and all the members of the Sackler family. That meant they couldn't be prosecuted in a civil court or even possibly criminally charged.

That was what their power could buy them. They'd front a few billion, walk away scot-free, and make the money back within a few years. They would continue living untouched by the consequences of their actions.

About half the states in the suit wanted to take the deal. (These states would later be known as the "consenting states.") The other states wanted more, particularly from the Sackler family, and because of this disagreement, negotiations stalled. Some people, including me, wondered if the elected officials of these "dissenting states" were simply posturing, in an effort to score political points and look as if they were being tough on Big Pharma, or if they were just holding out for more money. The rumor I heard was that most of the dissenting states prebankruptcy wanted somewhere in the range of $5 billion from the Sackler family. Massachusetts's lawsuits alleged that the family took out between $12 billion and $13 billion from Purdue over the years; it was fair to assume the Sacklers could afford to hand over more than $3 billion. But the family held firm, and clearly no amount of toughness or appeals would change their minds.

Because the Sacklers weren't willing to budge, Purdue declared a "free fall" bankruptcy, without a prenegotiated deal. It should have been pretty cut-and-dried, except for the deal that half the states had agreed to. This deal, a "term sheet," represented what a lot of lawyers involved thought was fair for everyone. It was the elephant in the room. What was "fair" and who was "everyone"?

Twenty-six hundred lawsuits were still pending against Purdue when it declared bankruptcy. The first plaintiff to win a judgment would be first in line to pick over Purdue's rotting carcass. When Purdue filed Chapter 11, Judge Robert Drain issued an injunction (also called a stay) against all ongoing litigation, effectively pressing the pause button on all suits. This happens in nearly all bankruptcy filings. The bankruptcy process, in theory, provides a venue for an orderly distribution of remaining resources.

At the end of 2019, I traveled to New York again to formally meet the representatives of the states, counties, and municipalities. At that meeting, I truly understood the depth of power I was up against. They all put their cards on the table: what they wanted was in plain sight. I wanted money to get out the door as quickly as possible to people in need. Nobody pulled any punches. We were all there to stake our claims. I sat next to Anne at the conference table, trying not to fidget.

On the other side of the table, men in expensive suits talked shop, balancing a fruit cup in their free hand. These were rich, powerful men, with longtime relationships and rivalries. Joe Rice, a tall guy with handsome salt-and-pepper hair, was holding forth with a few friends. I caught a few words as he bragged about the settlement he expected from the case. He smoothed his yellow silk tie and announced, "Purdue needs to open up the kimono. Ha! The last thing I wanna see is Sheila Birnbaum's kimono."

Anne was furious. She leaned over to me and whispered, "These motherfuckers. I disagree with Sheila but I respect her, and I have to deal with this shit every time I get in a room with these guys. Beyond the case, this is what we're up against. You're an addict and I'm a fucking woman."

Sheila Birnbaum was one of Purdue's chief attorneys: a grandmotherly, petite woman with a high, gentle voice. Despite her warm demeanor, she was a stone-cold killer, a hired gun. She was a liberal to the core, and despite Joe's shitty "kimono" joke, she commanded a lot of respect. She had won three Supreme Court cases and had overseen a special trust created by the state of New York for 9/11 victims. She sounded like a sweet little old lady, but there was more to her than met the eye, as I would see when I met her several months later. I pretended I hadn't heard Rice, who got up to refill his cup of coffee. All the other attorneys sat around chatting quietly. I caught murmurs from their little side conversations, and it seemed as if they all knew one another or had worked together in the past. Corporate law at this level is highly specialized; these lawyers were like the climbers who'd summited Everest. They were used to breathing the same thin air, swapping tips, and keeping their eye on the mountain's rapidly shifting conditions.

In spite of the fierce competition for Purdue's assets, we still went through the motions of a respectable case. Judge Drain would preside over the bankruptcy proceedings for its duration. A stern, serious presence on the bench, he was a former bankruptcy attorney who became a federal bankruptcy judge in White Plains, New York, in 2002. There was more to the judge than his outer appearance. Drain had once written an absurdist comic novel, entitled *The Great Work in the United States of America,* about the founder of a new religion in the late 1800s. He also worked at the New York firm Paul, Weiss, Rifkind, Wharton & Garrison—a law practice connected to Purdue—until he was appointed to the bench.

One of the weird things about bankruptcy law is that debtors can pretty much pick any court they want. Delaware, Manhattan, Houston, and Richmond are well-known hubs for large corporate bankruptcies. Courts compete with one another for cases, leading certain courts to be more and more pro-debtor. Top courts compete to attract large Chapter 11 cases, a dynamic that undermines the integrity of the bankruptcy system. Some companies go a step further and set up shop in a state that is likely to give them a favorable outcome. They rent short-term office space at suite 101 in the modern, white-columned office building at 777 Westchester Avenue in White Plains, New York, as a safeguard. According to *The Wall Street Journal,* "Some law firms have incorporated limited liability companies in White Plains months before their clients filed for Chapter 11 protection to make sure their cases wind up before Judge Drain."

The rules say companies can pick their court, but not their judge; judges are assigned at random. Judge Robert Drain is the only bankruptcy judge in White Plains, and until a recent rule change made during the coronavirus pandemic to shift some cases to Manhattan, corporate restructurings filed in the suburb went only to him. That sets White Plains apart from other popular bankruptcy venues: there's no chance another, less sympathetic judge will oversee the case. In White Plains, the judge is a sure thing. Since 2016, there have been 116 bankruptcy cases in the Southern District of New York involving public and private companies listing either assets or liabilities of $50 million or more, according to BankruptcyData. Judge Drain has overseen twenty-five of them, the most of any judge in the district, which has courthouses in Manhattan, Poughkeepsie, and White Plains. Judge Drain also has overseen more Chapter 11 filings by large public companies than his peers in Manhattan—eight since 2015, according to the UCLA-LoPucki Bankruptcy Research Database.

Purdue chose White Plains. What Purdue was really choosing was Judge Drain.

"This system is a very corrupt system," according to Professor Lynn M. LoPucki, of the UCLA School of Law. "If you are the debtor, you can put a pin in the map, and you can take your case to that court."

Drain had a reputation for being somewhat pro-debtor. An Associated Press story quoted a law professor and former colleague of Drain's saying, "If he thinks the debtor is in good faith attempting to reorganize, he will, on balance, support that when he can. . . . The tie goes to the debtor." The AP story also noted, "In 2012, he let Hostess shut down over the objections of employee unions. Earlier this year, he allowed Sears to be sold to a hedge fund despite opposition from creditors and landlords who wanted it liquidated."

Yet, I could see that the judge recognized that the Purdue case wasn't a normal bankruptcy. This was about more than just numbers on a balance sheet. It wasn't just about chopping up a company for parts, paying people off, and moving on. At the beginning, it seemed that Drain could be mindful of the human cost and the lives at stake. He made numerous references to victims of the overdose crisis being real people or, as he liked to say, "flesh and blood."

Yet, I was still hesitant about Drain. My opinion was that he was batting for Purdue; from time to time, he'd make some heartfelt statement to move the case along, but this was lip service that made no difference in the outcome.

I knew nothing about bankruptcy law. I was an activist, not a legal expert. I was coming to this with good intentions but almost no understanding of the process. I'd read some John Grisham and seen a few white-collar thrillers, but that wasn't exactly the same thing as decades in a courtroom or a legal library. The Purdue case was a crash course. The creditors committee had a teleconference every day for the first few weeks. The lawyers talked and talked and *talked*, and I took notes and discreetly googled terms I didn't understand. I didn't say anything during those calls because I had no idea what anyone meant.

But I knew what they weren't talking about: human beings. Death. Life. Addiction. Recovery. Lawyers weren't concerned with people; they cared about *legal stuff*. They cared about themselves. They talked about balance sheets, bottom lines, ad hoc committees, and mediators. I swam in the alphabet soup of their acronyms: TPP and PEC and the UCC. My head hurt. I started to get pissed off. I couldn't help but think, *I'm the chair of this fucking committee. Why am I sitting here feeling stupid? I'm not in the dark—they are. None of these people know what we've been through.*

"Listen," I said, interrupting one of our first UCC calls. "I need you all to slow down for a second. I don't understand a lot of what you're talking about because I didn't go to law school. I do have a feeling that some of these things you're mentioning are going to have a massive impact on what happens to this company, and more importantly, what happens to my community. So I need you to start explaining things to me—piece by piece, slowly, and in layman's terms."

I paused. No one said anything. So I continued, "So next, I'd like you, our lawyers, to please make a cheat sheet for me of what the fuck you're talking about when you say certain acronyms. And who these different players in the case are. I'd like you to put together some members from your team to do a quick 101 with us, the victims on the committee, so we can understand this process a little bit more."

Another pause.

Then Arik said, "Absolutely."

From then on, Arik made sure I understood what was going on and made sure I got access to documents that I wouldn't necessarily have gotten to see. He once told me, "It's important what victims want to do here."

As for the other committee members and the other lawyers, they realized they were going to have to placate me. One thing they did was put me in charge of the emergency relief fund. They said, "This is your project. You run with it." I think they thought that they could give me that, like a little toy, and that would pacify me for a while. But it didn't quite work out that way. Tension between me and the lawyers on the committee grew. After my minor outburst, they thought that I just needed things explained better. Their constant refrain would be "This is a bankruptcy." Or "This is how bankruptcy works."

But to me, this was bigger than a bankruptcy.

This was the closest we were going to get to a murder trial.

Without an injunction, the race to the courthouse would be back on. The states were likely to get all the money, and they would use it however they wanted to. I knew they'd blow millions on more gyms for their police departments, to pay down their debt, to give themselves a few tax breaks, you name it. There'd be no oversight on how the money would be spent. It would be a free-for-all. Individual plaintiffs wouldn't see a dime.

The injunction delayed the states' grab for a settlement and also gave us leverage. In exchange for pausing litigation, Purdue and the Sackler family would agree to hand over all sorts of documents, including emails, internal records, and financial statements. They would agree to a formal deposition and discovery. That would help us make a better judgment on just how much money they had socked away. What a tall order—more on that later. We knew they had billions, but getting our hands on an honest balance sheet was going to be like fighting a greased pig. The injunction would be contingent on the family's cooperation. If the Sacklers didn't play ball, the lawsuits would be back on.

The agreement to delay would also allow us to get the ball rolling on the emergency relief fund, which was $200 million right away to help people suffering from the overdose crisis. It was a good deal, made with despicable people. Without it, there would be no bankruptcy process. Without it, we may as well have all gone home. So we recommended that the judge extend the injunction for six months, with the option to end it and let litigation continue if the Sacklers and Purdue weren't compliant.

The dissenting states opposed that. A calm, orderly process didn't necessarily suit the attorneys general of these states. It's easy to forget that state attorneys general are elected officials. They're politicians. Many are in it for political gain, what they can get. Most of them are eyeing their next job. How they behaved in the bankruptcy was a career move, sensitive to the optics of their next campaign. Almost all of the dissenting attorneys general were from blue states with left-leaning electorates. Castigating corporations, blaming pharmaceutical companies—that stuff plays well in blue states. The best political move those attorneys general felt they could make was to fight Purdue every step of the way. They didn't seem to mind if, in the end, it meant less direct money for victims, or for the people who needed help—as long as it appeared that they put up a fight.

On the outset, the dissent looked like a good thing, and I agreed with the attorneys general's talking points; but once we were behind closed doors, I realized they were driving money away from the people who needed it most. Anybody who wasn't behind the scenes wouldn't see what I saw; no politicians should have their hands on a settlement that should have put victims before state interests.

This all led to a fairly testy hearing in October of 2019. The attorney for the dissenting states, Andrew Troop, argued that a successful lawsuit, a decision against Purdue, would act as a legal determination that what they did was wrong. Judge Drain disagreed. He responded that a trial "results in a ruling, not the truth."

Drain said that since the Sackler family was already giving up their company, they were in effect admitting guilt.

"Liability's acknowledged here, in essence, by giving up the company," he said. "You know what? They're paying everything. So I'm assuming that pretty much acknowledges they owe it. They're not saying that, but that's the path we're on." A trial, he said, would be little more than an "autopsy."

Earlier, the dissenting states had asked the judge to block Purdue from paying out $34 million in bonuses to top executives, a move that Drain approved. Now the judge used that against the dissenting states, saying, "Why spend anywhere close to that amount of money in a trial that will probably lead to other trials, when you could actually sit back and look at the facts?"

Drain added later, "And, of course, you could lose, just as the plaintiffs in the Triangle Shirtwaist fire lost."

Troop said the injunction, however temporary, was simply a stalling tactic on the part of Purdue. This argument irked Drain, as if it was a challenge to the authority of the court.

"I disagree completely," he said, his voice rising with an anger I hadn't before heard. "And I would expect each other, including your group—if I grant this injunction—to engage in good faith as fiduciaries, to make the most of the time." Then he added sternly, "No one wastes time in front of me in an injunction. *Ever.*"

"Of course they will," said Troop.

"In any case. Period."

"Of course they will, Your Honor."

"Oh, no, I don't think so."

Drain then took aim at the states' ability to spend the money the right way: "If you get a judgment, I'm sure the attorneys general here would say, 'It's going to be devoted to this public health crisis, that's where the money's going to go.' Very good attorneys general did that with the tobacco litigation, including the attorney general of Ohio. Within a matter of just a few years, that money was taken away. I believe it is the goal of all of the public servants that they address the public health crisis, that it is asserted with some credibility, this debtor helped start, and probably more than helped start. That the money goes to solve that problem.

"That could happen under a bankruptcy plan because a plan is binding on all of the parties. It didn't happen with cigarettes, even though there were statutes passed, trusts created, et cetera. Within years the money was used for general purposes and even for such things as seven hundred thousand dollars for refurbishing a golf course."

Drain's point was clear: he thought the bankruptcy process was the best way to figure out how to dismantle Purdue and distribute the money in a way that would help undo the great harm the company had unleashed. What the states were asking for would have allowed them the money with no oversight or restraints on how to spend it.

But just when it seemed as if Drain was about to give Purdue everything it was asking for, he compromised, issuing an injunction for just a few weeks, with an option of extending it further. That kept Purdue on a short leash. The injunction, he said, worked "both ways." It barred Purdue from promoting opioids and funding pain-management groups, as it had done in the past. But the injunction also extended legal protection to the Sackler family. *This was total, complete, and utter bullshit.* This was perhaps the most controversial part of the ruling, because accountability was how many of us envisioned justice. It was hard to let go of the fantasy of the Sacklers finally getting what was coming to them. But, according to the court, it was necessary.

This was the court's first big decision in the process. Though not covered widely in the media, the case was being obsessively followed by a small group of activists, most of whom wanted to see the Sacklers rot in jail for the rest of their lives. Minutes after the court filing was uploaded onto the online docket, I began to get angry texts and emails. The activists saw any concession to Purdue, no matter how small, as a capitulation. On social media, they worked themselves up into a lather. They called the $200 million emergency relief fund a "payoff," implying that the money was somehow going to the committee. (It wasn't.) These were people whom I knew personally, whom I had worked with. They were reacting as so many of us do on social media, without all the facts, driven by the emotion of the group, with a tiny online riot. They acted as I would have if I'd been on the outside instead of in the front row.

At the time, I couldn't defend myself or correct any misconceptions. I had to sit there and take it, quietly doing what I thought was right while my former friends slandered me.

The handful of newspaper stories about the decision didn't offer much clarity. *The Washington Post* headline read "Judge Grants Purdue Pharma, Sackler Family Pause in Civil Lawsuits." *The New York Times:* "Judge Orders Pause in Opioid Litigation Against Purdue Pharma and Sacklers." Both quoted the attorneys general as being "disappointed" with the ruling, and *The Post* quoted Purdue's lawyer saying, "Continued litigation harms everyone." So there they were, the two sides, Purdue and the attorneys general. None of the other creditors were quoted, so they didn't appear in any stories.

The one story that even mentioned my committee was from the Associated Press, which wrote, "Just before the hearing, a committee of unsecured creditors that includes opioid crisis victims said it would support pausing the lawsuits.

"That deal came at a price. The company agreed it would put $200 million into a fund in the next six months to pay for emergency relief of a crisis that has been linked to the deaths of more than four hundred thousand people in the US since 2000."

If you were reading quickly, you might be forgiven for thinking that the creditors committee had taken Purdue's side, and that we had done so in exchange for the vague promise of a $200 million slush fund. If I hadn't had all the facts, I probably would have thought the same thing.

We couldn't get our side of the story out there. I tried to explain myself to a couple people. It didn't go well.

One mother called me up in a rage: "How could you let this happen?"

I told her, this is what it takes. This is the process. Otherwise it's just a feeding frenzy. She was skeptical, still burning with anger at Purdue and what her son had to endure. She didn't care about the money, she said, not really. She just wanted to see the Sackler family suffer. It was a respectable point of view. I identified with this perspective but couldn't act on it, if that makes sense. My heart and head were divided, and I hurt from all the things I couldn't say.

We spoke for about an hour. Before we hung up, she told me, in the most motherly way possible, "I know you're doing the best you can. But it's not good enough."

Advocates such as that mother saw the bankruptcy in black-and-white, Purdue versus the attorneys general. From the outside, it was—it boiled down to David and Goliath, the evil corporation and its victims. But from the inside, the case was anything but simple. Each side was fractured. The states were divided, as were the other creditors. Besides the official Unsecured Creditors Committee, which I was the cochair of, other "ad hoc" creditor committees had standing to make arguments in front of the court. There was the ad hoc committee for personal injury victims; there was the ad hoc committee for NAS babies; there were ad hoc committees for hospitals, for ratepayers, for Native American tribes.

In May 2020, another committee appeared: the Ad Hoc Committee on Accountability (AHCA). This was formed by parents and activists whom I knew well and respected, such as the artist Nan Goldin and parents Ed Bisch and Cynthia Munger. They were there to argue for accountability and transparency. If I hadn't been on the UCC, I would have been right there with them, shoulder to shoulder, locked in arms. Instead, I had my hands tied. One of the delicate things in my position was figuring out how we could work together. They could say things I couldn't; I could take actions that were inaccessible to them. Working in tandem, we could be a louder voice and call out other parties on conflicts of interest.

One filing by the AHCA in June 2020 illustrates just how much animosity there was between all the different creditors. The filing rightly singled out CVS and BCBS as being complicit in the overdose crisis and said, "For years, big pharmacy companies, including CVS, were keenly aware of the illegal oversupply of prescription opioids. CVS collected sales information and maintained a prescription database in its role as a retail seller of opioids. The pharmacy giant was slow to take meaningful action to stem the flow of addictive drugs in the communities it serviced. Instead, CVS profited in the oversupply of Purdue opioids, such as OxyContin."

As for insurance companies: "Based on profit motive, carriers pushed patients toward opioid use instead of steering them toward safer pain treatments. Insurers cut reimbursements for non-opioid pain treatments or not covered them at all. According to Dr. Stuart Schweitzer, a professor of Health Policy and Management at the UCLA Fielding School of Public Health, if insurers 'don't allow us to treat pain effectively, then this is what you get. You go down to the lowest-cost option that is authorized, and it is painkillers.'"

Those insurance and pharmacy lowlifes were my honorable co-chairs and committee members, whom I had to deal with every day.

The AHCA urged the judge to "consider the role corporate creditors played as co-debtors and examine how various insurer and pharmacy benefit policies may have been influenced by Purdue." In other words, don't give any other parties money because they've made their billions; save the money for the victims.

I was more than sympathetic to this sentiment. But I understood that holding out for one ideal solution, in which every penny went to the people OxyContin harmed, was a surefire way to sink the whole case. Judge Drain would never go for that; and anyway, that's not how bankruptcy law was set up. Bankruptcy, at its core, wasn't about right and wrong. It was a corporate autopsy, performed by a group, according to a set of rules that looked at facts and figures and rarely considered morality. There was more than one kind of justice, I was learning. The most powerful kept their power, and the least powerful hoped to collect from their scraps. Representation and a seat at the table was progress but it certainly wasn't justice—which would have required a complete overhaul of a deeply corrupt and convoluted system that continued to serve the people at the top and starve those at the bottom.

One thing was for sure: injunction or not, the Sacklers would be walking away with their wealth intact. But I wasn't willing to let them go without a fight.

5

UNCHECKED POWER

How much money is a billion dollars? Let me put it this way: if you saved $10,000 dollars every day for two hundred years, never spending a penny of it, you still wouldn't come close. Billionaires aren't made from pinching pennies; their wealth is an aggregate that results from interest rates, the stock market, and corporations that can turn astronomical profits in a single quarter. For the Sacklers, OxyContin was the golden goose that made their family fortunes. Those painkillers transformed the family from regular rich to dirty rich, rocketing them into the top 1 percent of the world's wealthiest people.

Extreme wealth doesn't usually come from doing the right thing or helping other people. It's inherited from previous generations or collected from people who have less, turning someone else's income into your own. Landlords are one example of this: they own property and tenants pay them to live there. Collecting a monthly rent check transfers the money earned by the tenant into the pocket of the landlord. Housing is a basic need, which makes rent inescapable for people who don't own their homes. People will do almost anything to stay housed, and the more desperate they are, the more power the landlord has over them.

That desperation is the same force that drove me to pay thousands of dollars a month for OxyContin in Dr. Brown's office, risk arrest and imprisonment, and endanger my life every time I used. Any drug dealer will tell you the same thing: it's about supply and demand. The more urgent the demand, the more expensive the supply. When I was dope sick, I would pay *any* amount of money and make absurd promises to whoever was holding. Anything to get well again. The doctors, pharmacists, and white-collar dealers who fed my addiction made millions off people such as me. I was as powerless as tenants handing over their paycheck to the landlord every month. I *had* to use. My addiction made those decisions for me.

Every drug deal has at least three parties: the user, the dealer, and the supplier. Although I saw my dealer several times a month—in the medical office, wearing a white coat, with degrees framed on the wall—the dealer was getting the pills from higher up the supply chain. The boxes I saw stacked nearly to the ceiling in Dr. Brown's supply room were labeled with their manufacturers' names. Purdue was well represented in that room, and each pill inside each thin paper carton translated to money on the company's bottom line, and a payout for the Sacklers. Every time I traded cash for an OxyContin prescription, a direct line led from me to the Sackler family.

My addiction, and the addiction of millions of Americans, made that family rich.

Now, I may not know what it's like to be a billionaire, but I do know some things about people. Where there is money, there's conflict. And I knew that the more powerful an individual, family, or corporation, the more attached they are to that power. They'll do *anything* to keep what they have, and they don't fight fair. They fight to win.

Unfortunately for them, so did I.

I was convinced that the Sackler family should be held to account along with the multibillion-dollar company that lined their pockets. Without the Sacklers, there was no Purdue; without Purdue, there was no OxyContin. In my mind, it was straightforward. I wasn't satisfied with dismantling the pharmaceutical giant. I wanted to go further up the chain. The real culprits, I thought, were the people who knowingly pushed hundreds of millions of pills into unsuspecting markets, flooded every community with OxyContin, and authorized cutthroat marketing techniques that targeted prescribers. Those who could do that weren't just cold-blooded. They were evil.

My public statements, including an obituary excoriating Raymond Sackler in *The Huffington Post*, made no bones about it. In a just world, Purdue would be a handful of dust, the Sacklers would be stripped of their holdings, and all money would be given to the people whose lives were ruined by the company. I wasn't alone in this opinion. The advocates on the Ad Hoc Committee on Accountability shared my feelings and were vocal about zipping the Sacklers into orange jumpsuits. However, as the case progressed, I began to wonder if this was a real possibility or just a revenge fantasy.

Purdue and the Sacklers to me, or any other reasonable person, were one and the same. The two were interchangeable. Emails and financial statements showed that the family used Purdue and their other shell companies as piggy banks, withdrawing money to their personal accounts. Sackler family members had dominated

the Purdue board, but only a couple of them had ever been employees of the company. They all benefited in one way or another:
the ill-gotten blood money fed all of them, directly or indirectly.
In my mind, that meant they should all be held responsible for the
pain and suffering of millions of Americans. Yet, the legal system
makes a fine distinction between a corporation and an individual.
In some ways, corporations have more rights than people because
they can afford more rights; corporate personhood allows companies to hold property, enter contracts, and to sue and be sued just
like a private citizen. Corporations enjoy Fourth Amendment safeguards against unreasonable regulatory searches, but they do not
have a Fifth Amendment privilege against self-incrimination. More
recently, they can also make unlimited campaign contributions and
exercise religious preferences under the First Amendment. Suing a
company is not the same as suing a family, but in the Purdue case,
it certainly felt that way.

Even Purdue's lawyers saw that the company and the family
were one and the same. "Litigation against the Sacklers is litigation
against Purdue," Ben Kaminetzky, an attorney for Purdue Pharma,
told Judge Drain's court during the injunction hearing. The family's
willingness to put $3 billion of their own money in the settlement
was notable, too; the lines between Purdue and the Sacklers were
conveniently drawn. When a problem threatened the Sacklers, it
was easy to pin it on Purdue and disavow personal responsibility.
Yet, it was also impossible to overlook that the family owned the
company. Their fates were intertwined.

Let me put it this way: If Purdue was a rabid dog, running
around biting people, you wouldn't just shoot the dog. You'd blame
the owner for letting such a dangerous animal into the community. You'd question why that owner was negligent and hold him

accountable, even if he wasn't the one doing the biting. Every person bitten by that dog, every victim, would have something to say about it. The owner and the dog aren't the same, but like Purdue and the Sacklers, the harm they did couldn't be one entity's fault and not the other's.

The bankruptcy wasn't Purdue's first brush with the law. Looking at former legal settlements, the Sacklers were notably absent from the dealings. Purdue faced litigation related to OxyContin in 2001, 2004, and 2007. Each time, Purdue paid a fine, settled the case, and walked away promising to change its ways. Spoiler alert: few changes (if any) were actually made. The Sacklers were kept out of court and out of the newspapers, thanks to their powerful PR firms. They were portrayed as separate from the company, innocent of what executives were doing, and therefore blameless. They simply kept collecting billions, and where that money came from was none of their business.

Throughout the case, that fallacy was revealed. For example, in a deposition on Wednesday, September 2, 2020, that I attended, Marianna Sackler claimed not to know much about the business. She worked there as a "crisis manager" consultant in the R&D group from 2008 to 2009 working on OxyContin reformulation. The reformulation was a reputation saver for Purdue: a special coating on the pill was supposed to prevent misuse via injecting or snorting. (In my personal experience, it just added an extra step to the process—but what do I know?) Ten years after the allegedly "safer" pill hit the market, a panel of FDA experts and health advisers determined that there was no clear evidence that a harder-to-crush version did what Purdue said it would. The FDA panelists overwhelmingly ruled that data from Purdue and other researchers did not show that the reformulation curbed misuse overall or led to fewer overdoses. But it made Purdue *look* as if they cared, and that's what counted. Cover your ass and keep collecting a check: it was the Sackler family motto.

For example, although Marianna is a beneficiary of the family trusts, and almost her entire lifestyle has been funded and continues to be funded by such trusts (which have been funded by Purdue money), she claimed to know little to nothing about where the money comes from. Documents showed she received $4.4 million around 2010, but she claimed she doesn't know if she got it or not. Her answers about her finances were basically that, if she needs money, she goes to her dad, Richard Sackler, who kept her on a budget. She was also paid by Stephen Ives, the president of Cheyenne Petroleum Company and a trusted family friend. Ives has been employed by the Sacklers since 1984 and serves as the CFO in charge of their family office in Oklahoma City. Included in his duties is the management of the family investment portfolio; he also serves as trustee and board member of various family entities.

When the family held its annual-or-more-frequent Beneficiary Meetings, Marianna claimed she attended only one in person and one on the phone; her only recollection of any of them was the lunch she had and the room it was held in. She denied remembering anything from the two years she worked at Purdue and claimed to be ignorant of anything that happened there after 2009. Her answers in this deposition seemed well coached; unless an email was in front of her regarding something she wrote, she claimed not to know, not to remember, and not to be certain, other than for things that were obvious and nonconsequential, such as where she lived, her marriage, and so on. In a particularly Sackler-ish manner, Marianna responded coldly to questions about the drug epidemic. Her answers were that she didn't think Purdue is responsible for anything, and that while she feels remorse for those who have been harmed by opioids, she would not admit that Purdue did anything wrong. She wondered what the word *crisis* meant, finally saying she did not know enough to answer the question.

Her title at Purdue was *crisis manager*. How could she not know what that word meant?

I quickly noticed that, just as the state attorneys general fell into several camps, the debtors were also divided. There was Purdue, and there was the Sackler family, who were at pains to remind everyone that they were *very much separate* from their company. While this was patently untrue, the Sacklers invested millions of dollars and great effort into preserving their reputation while Purdue did the dirty work to make them even richer.

The Sackler family itself was split into two sides. The lawyers referred to them as the A Side and the B Side, as if they were dusty old 45 records. The split fell along familial lines. The A Side included the children of Mortimer Sackler (who died in 2010), including Ilene, Kathe, and Mortimer D. A., as well as Mortimer's widow, Theresa Rowling. The B Side was composed of the descendants of Raymond Sackler (who died in 2017), including his widow, Beverly Feldman; their children, Jonathan and Richard Sackler; and Richard's son, David, who had become the de facto spokesman of the Sackler family.

The family released an awkward statement addressing the split: "In any family or business grappling with important choices, it is normal for a range of opinions to be discussed and options presented. This internal discussion is necessary for reaching the right decisions in a collaborative way, and in no way signifies a split within our family."

As they say, a hit dog hollers, and the family was howling. Although the family presented a unified front to the public, privately they were divided.

The family rift happened before Purdue declared bankruptcy, when the company was fending off lawsuits and desperately trying not to look like the most evil company in the history of the world. Some of the Sackler family members apparently disagreed over legal tactics. They fought over whether to settle certain lawsuits and perhaps even whether to declare Chapter 11. Another bone of contention, according to the news service Reuters, was over whether Richard Sackler should apologize for some of his emails, such as the "hammer on the abusers" one. Although older family members, such as Jon Sackler, thought there was no basis for the family to be sued, younger ones had fewer illusions of immunity.

"Under logical circumstances, I'd agree with you," David told his uncle in a May 2007 email—the same month Purdue pleaded guilty to misleading the public about OxyContin's risk of addiction and agreed to pay $600 million in one of the largest pharmaceutical settlements in US history at the time. "This is the land of the free and the home of the blameless. We will be sued."

Over a decade later, David was proved right. After years of dodging responsibility, the Sacklers were shoved into the limelight by the Purdue bankruptcy. The dysfunctional family dynamic intensified as the A Side and B Side pointed fingers at each other.

After seeing some of the emails between B Side family members, I concluded the drama was Netflix-worthy. Greed intensified old grudges. Who took how much money out of what trust, who got a larger allowance, and whose financial needs should take precedence caused frequent arguments. David, who left a highly profitable position at his hedge fund, Moab Capital Partners, to run the Sackler family affairs, felt put-upon and unappreciated.

According to David, his father placed enormous pressure on him; but David felt he wasn't adequately compensated for his time or shown the respect he thought he deserved from the other family members. He and his wife, Joss, complained about the money they missed out on when David switched careers. The trustees, mostly other family members, were less generous with them while also demanding more attention. At one point, David was convinced the family underwrote the cost of a new swank house for his sister—a consideration not extended to David and Joss. It seemed that David himself believed the family was toxic, writing to his parents in 2015, "When my kids were born I made a promise to myself to break the cycle of manipulation that exists in our family." He went on to discuss "a pattern of behavior that is very hurtful" by "holding money over people's heads" and being able to "exert a huge amount of control."

Richard and his ex-wife Beth seemed to be at odds on how to deal with Joss and David's marriage issues; they contemplated ways to protect the family wealth if David were to divorce his wife. David struggled with issues related to excessive gambling and alcohol. Although Joss stuck with David against the rest of the Sacklers, their unhappiness was notable. Others had their own travails, including Richard himself, who had a relationship with a woman named Josephine Hoh while he was married to Beth and after the divorce. Hoh was an associate professor of epidemiology and public health at Yale University School of Medicine. Richard pumped millions into funding Hoh's research at Yale. In a series of secure WhatsApp chats described to me by counsel in the case, Richard would playfully refer to Hoh as Slips, and she called him Stix. He lavished gifts on her, exorbitant presents that included a multimillion-dollar house, which we suspect could have doubled as a way of hiding assets. (Yes, they're still together.)

But the press never got to hear about most of this. As ever, the main PR issue wasn't whether OxyContin was killing people; it was whether the Sacklers would look bad. Paying a settlement was a tacit admission of guilt, and nobody wanted to do that. In a doozy of an interview with *Vanity Fair* in 2019, David said of the lawsuits, "I really don't think there's much in the complaints, frankly, that's an issue that's not just, 'Oh, you shouldn't have marketed these things at all.' Right? And I guess that's a hindsight debate one can have."

If there wasn't much in the complaints, the family presumably wouldn't have seemed so concerned about its own members using OxyContin. Beth Sackler, Richard's ex-wife, wrote in a January 2, 2017, email (that I reviewed) that her mother was "really struggling" with Oxy. Beth wrote, "It's the same thing she had when she was on/off opioids . . . total confusion, feeling like she's losing her mind (her companion indicated it was better yesterday), but she sounds like she's struggling again (maybe more worried about it than confused). She also has no appetite. I reminded her that she had the exact same symptoms last time when she had been on OxyContin for her back pain, and that she was both confused and was never hungry. I told her to keep reminding herself that all of this is because of the medicine. How in the world are they going to control her pain post surgery?????"

Outside the family, the Sacklers downplayed the risks of their products. In an email exchange between Richard Sackler and Dr. David Alan Schoenfeld, a top researcher at Massachusetts General Hospital's Biostatistics Center and an emeritus professor of medicine at Harvard Medical School, Dr. Schoenfeld mentioned an epidemiologist friend who was having trouble quantifying the extent to which prescribed opioids led to addiction.

"If I had severe but bearable pain and I had an 80% chance of becoming addicted, I would bear the pain," Dr. Schoenfeld said. "If I had a 3% chance, I would take the opioid."

Richard Sackler's response was cold as ice: "Are you certain [the epidemiologist] isn't conflating physiologic dependence with the psycho-social-behavioral problem of addiction. Addiction might be said to be a compulsive seeking, hoarding and taking of opioids unrelated to any somatic pain, and it is my view that although it may be difficult to do the research, the frequency is below 1% after long-term therapy. Perhaps the true number is 0.1% or 2%, but it isn't by any means common in the general population. Of course, for the rarely addicted patient, the situation is 'important.' I'm sure that if you, for example, needed opioids long-term, you wouldn't become addicted in the sense described above, although physiologic dependence would follow weeks of use. BTW, physiologic dependence and abstinence syndromes are common to a majority of chronically used Rx drugs and even some OTC and unregulated drugs."

The Sacklers stuck to marketing slogans and unsubstantiated claims when they talked to the press, doctors, or anyone who wasn't a family member. Richard Sackler's choice of words, distinguishing "good" pill users from "bad" ones, or "addicts," was straight out of the Purdue playbook. Every time, they downplayed the risks of the pills and emphasized that *normal* people wouldn't have an issue stopping. Yet, they knew OxyContin was dangerous. That's why they may have been concerned about their own family members taking it. Apparently, it was fine for *other* people to suffer from substances, but not the Sacklers. Any hint of family issues with addiction were hushed up. They kept their problems private, zipped up, and out of the public eye.

In my recovery program, some will say, "You're only as sick as your secrets." The more I learned about the Sacklers, the more fucked-up I realized they were. Some secrets cost more than others, but the Sacklers weren't paying the price: we were. Totally dependent on the money from Purdue, jealous of one another, and raised to believe they could do no wrong, this billionaire family was not just sick. They were bent on taking the rest of us down with them by making *us* foot the bill for *their* damages.

The two sets of Sackler family lawyers wanted to make it clear that $3 billion of the Sacklers' family money was more than generous. The original offer was about one-fourth of the total settlement, valued at $10 billion to $12 billion. Some states objected, citing deposition testimony stating that the Sackler family took $12 billion to $13 billion in cash out of Purdue Pharma.

"The problem is that the Sacklers, who have thirteen billion dollars, fourteen billion dollars, are getting a free pass by putting in three billion dollars," said Beth Kaswan, an attorney for twenty municipalities, including thirteen in Massachusetts. "I would like to see financial statements for all of the shell companies. [Otherwise] how will I know if they are further transferring assets that are already in shell companies?"

To encourage the creditors to accept the offer of $3 billion, the Sackler family's lawyers made a presentation to the creditors in late 2019, a preview of the defense they planned to make should the lawsuits against them come to trial. The presentation was meant to convince all the creditors, including me and the states, that a case against the Sackler family was far from a sure thing, and that the deal on the table was good. The family made it clear they were more than willing to give up ownership of the flailing company so long as they could be left out of any future litigation. They would preserve their reputation, and as many billions as possible.

I watched the presentation from my home office via secure webcast. (Little did any of us know that months later the entire proceedings would move to Zoom and telephone, thanks to the COVID-19 pandemic.) I could have gone to New York to participate in person, but the thought of flying six hours to go eat bagels and muffins with the Sackler attorneys in some plush law firm's conference room made me sick to my stomach. I just couldn't bring myself to do it.

Gregory P. Joseph, one of the country's leading litigators and the former president of the American College of Trial Lawyers, was representing the B Side of the Sackler family (the Richard Sackler side). Joseph opened with an argument and a PowerPoint presentation. I expected to hear all the usual song and dance, the lies that were told over and over, in court and in the media: how the Sackler family had nothing to do with the marketing of OxyContin, they had no idea, they just wanted to help people, and so on. And, oh, by the way, the Sacklers don't have any money.

That's basically what Gregory P. Joseph said. He said Richard Sackler had been completely misrepresented by the media. Joseph said that it was difficult to prove causality, difficult to say that Purdue fueled the drug epidemic when so many other painkillers were out there, and difficult to prove that OxyContin caused individual people to become addicted when there were so many other factors. *Yeah, like the mislabeling and bad marketing the company was convicted of,* I growled to myself.

"You've won the PR war," Joseph said scornfully. "We haven't started the legal war."

I had to fight the temptation to shut off the webcast and throw my computer through the window. But as the presentation wore on, Joseph started to make a few points that surprised me. He said that since all the states had signed on to the 2007 State Consent Judgment, the Sacklers could no longer be sued for anything prior to that year. Anything *after* 2007 was fair game.

"No one is going to try to excuse the behavior prior to 2007," he said. He made the point that after that year, Sackler family members were no more than board members, as opposed to officers. He said there was "not a shred of evidence that the board was involved" in any misleading marketing claims or practices. Also after 2007, the board was given quarterly reports on compliance and was repeatedly told that its vast sales force was following the laws by regulators and government authorities. The board members claimed they were told everything was fine—and chose to believe it. That was something I didn't know.

But obeying the laws is the ultimate out for wrongdoers. "I was just following the rules" doesn't mean anything when the rules are morally and ethically deficient. Those same laws were designed to protect the interests of the rich and powerful. Throwing their hands up and claiming ignorance was not the same thing as actually being innocent. It was yet another legal loophole that exonerated the Sackler family from taking responsibility for their product's devastating impact on America.

There was more. The 2007 State Consent Judgment forced Purdue to set up an Abuse Detection and Deterrence Program (ADDP), and reports from the program were sent to the states. In

2016, an auditor approved by the New York attorney general concluded that Purdue had been operating the ADDP "conscientiously and in good faith" and that Purdue's "determinations whether to continue marketing were reasonable." Furthermore, the consent judgment gave the state attorneys general the right to request "records and documents . . . that relate to Purdue's compliance with each provision" of the judgment.

In other words, from 2007 on, the attorneys general were empowered as watchdogs. They were clearly deceived by the company and the Sacklers, but many of them were asleep in their doghouses. That's how the states found a way to position themselves as the ultimate victim—worse off than the people who died. After all, only ten years after the 2007 decision, in January 2017, the City of Everett, Washington, sued Purdue based on increased costs for the city from the use of OxyContin. They blamed Purdue for not intervening when the company knew of, and was tracking, odd OxyContin sales patterns. The city stated that Purdue was in violation of its 2007 legal agreements to track suspicious excess ordering or potential black market usage. Yet, in that 2007 decision, state governments, as well as Purdue, were supposed to be keeping score *together*. Who should really be held responsible for the overdoses? It's a heartbreaking riddle because the end result was the same: the dead stayed dead, and nothing really changed.

As soon as the five-hour presentation was over, I picked up the phone and called Cheryl Juaire.

"I didn't know a lot of that," I said. "If I was a juror in a court trial and I had just heard that presentation—man. They're really working that loophole."

"I agree," she said. "It really makes you think, doesn't it?"

It made both of us sick. The entire system all seemed to be on the same side—and it wasn't *our* side. Nausea leaked into my stomach as I realized the case went deeper than Purdue Pharma. The company was just a symptom of systemic injustice, the twist that turned our legal system away from the people it was supposed to serve. The so-called guardians of the people deprioritized American lives, and as a result millions of us were sick, dying, or already dead. It was a setup, a rigged game, from the beginning.

By the turn of the millennium, anyone with half a brain knew an overdose crisis was brewing. What did state lawmakers do to combat the burgeoning epidemic? Well—not a whole lot. Most states failed to pass laws regulating pharmaceutical companies or to increase funding for harm reduction, treatment, recovery supports, evidence-based prevention, or diversion programs. (Decriminalization wasn't even on the table.) Many states (with Republican-controlled legislatures) chose not to expand Medicaid; many states continued to have harsh prison sentences for drug possession. After 2007, states knew how many OxyContin prescriptions were being filled, and they began to understand the gravity of the ballooning overdoses. Yet they failed to treat the problem like the emergency it was. Advocacy groups and individuals, including me, pushed for federal and state governments to treat the epidemic like a public health crisis. We asked them to release emergency funds that would address the overdoses, widespread addiction, and related issues as in a flu outbreak. We asked for infrastructure, social change, and policy to back it up. (Ironically, a few years later, we'd see the COVID-19 pandemic destroy our economy and shut down our nation because that same infrastructure we asked for years earlier wasn't in place.)

States' inaction on the addiction crisis was due, in part, to the powerful influence that pharmaceutical companies have in Washington, D.C., and in state legislatures. In 2016, the Associated Press reported that Big Pharma had spent more than $880 million on lobbying and campaign contributions from 2006 through 2015. The news service wrote, "The makers of prescription painkillers have adopted a 50-state strategy that includes hundreds of lobbyists and millions in campaign contributions to help kill or weaken measures aimed at stemming the tide of prescription opioids."

Purdue hired people such as Rudy Giuliani, former Maine US attorney Jay McCloskey (who was one of the first officials to ring the alarm bell about OxyContin misuse in his state) and former US attorney in Kentucky Joe Famularo to defend the company from lawsuits as well as to fluff up its PR strategy. Figures such as McCloskey and Famularo could credibly claim that they cared about opioid misuse and knew of the dangers posed by OxyContin while at the same time defending their new employer. McCloskey told *The Boston Globe,* "Taking it off the market won't stop the larger problem of prescription drug abuse."

In 2007, he told Congress, "Even during the time OxyContin was getting all the attention, it never caused the most overdose deaths—methadone did. The drug diversion problem was not caused by OxyContin, and it will not be solved by going after Oxy-Contin as a whipping boy."

They made it sound as if OxyContin and the tactics used to promote it weren't a real threat—and even if they *were* harmful, there was no point in going after Purdue. McCloskey's words seemed to echo David Sackler's comments in *Vanity Fair.* Halting the aggressive marketing of OxyContin was a legitimate solution, but not one that Purdue would consider. It was the family's primary source of income.

With its high-profile supporters and the well-compensated

loyalty of key allies, Purdue was spending money to be the biggest fox in the henhouse. Companies such as Purdue Pharma have used their money to avoid taking meaningful responsibility more than once. Lobbying and campaign donations figured front and center in their strategy. I was no stranger to that, but when Big Pharma bombarded grassroots addiction recovery advocacy groups with big-money offers, I was horrified.

What I'm about to write makes me feel absolutely sick, because it happened to some of my closest friends and collaborators—the people who stood by me on the front lines of the crisis. I don't want to blame anyone for taking the check, because $25,000 is a lot of money when you're used to working eighty-plus hours per week on a shoestring budget. I want to put the blame where I believe it belongs: on people such as Jessica Nickel and the Addiction Policy Forum (APF). The APF is a "public charity" that was uber cozy with pharmaceutical companies, under the guise of the public good. The group exerts significant influence behind the scenes in Washington, D.C.

In 2017, the Pharmaceutical Research and Manufacturers of America (PhRMA) approached Jessica Nickel, who was the founder of a patient / family-of-loss organization while also representing a pharmaceutical company with a specific interest in the opioid epidemic. That's an instant conflict of interest to me. With her lobbying expertise and the appearance of "neutrality" she maintained as the APF's leader, Nickel was in the perfect position to influence city and state officials in states hardest hit. Working with APF could make PhRMA look good at a time when many cities and states were suing some of their member companies for billions. It felt like it was straight out of the reputation management handbook.

PhRMA's multimillion-dollar gift to the APF was announced with little fanfare in December 2017. The day the gift was announced, the only PhRMA member who publicly commented on the gift was good old Purdue Pharma. Purdue also took out full-page advertisements in *The New York Times* and *The Washington Post* that same month.

Nickel started calling small SUD (substance use disorder) non-profits, informing them they might be eligible for a grant from APF. Philanthropic giving in the SUD space is abysmal compared with that for other disease groups, so this type of grant would be a lifesaver to many of these organizations, who often struggle to keep their doors open.

The "tasks" the APF asked for seemed random: grants were offered for everything from starting a state APF chapter, developing a "warm line" for individuals and families who were in crisis from a substance problem, or developing and implementing a data platform. Sounds harmless, right? Well, it depends. Were the APF's motives pure?

Because Purdue was the only company that actively touted the gift, some advocates in the field who either take no or limited pharmaceutical money thought Purdue's paid media during this time was questionable and potentially linked to the PhRMA gift. Curious about Purdue's involvement, many advocates asked if there was any direct coordination with Purdue attached to the massive donation.

Funny story: I wasn't offered any money because they knew I wouldn't take it. I smelled a rat from the beginning. I can't accept a check from APF and then turn around and console people whose partner died in their arms of a preventable OxyContin overdose. I can't compromise myself like that. And, yeah, I made sure Jessica

Nickel knows I think she's full of shit. I think she's just as bad as anyone else in PhRMA because she allows them to whitewash their bloody, filthy hands. She seems to provide a veneer of respectability that I believe delays real change and enables Big Pharma to avoid meaningful responsibility.

I always suspected her relationship with Purdue went beyond taking PhRMA money, but I never had any evidence. While reviewing Purdue's documents, though, her name came up (shocker). In one set of documents, I saw an email that mentioned me. On July 20, 2017, Burt Rosen, an executive at Purdue, forwarded Nickel the scathing Raymond Sackler obituary I wrote for The Huffington Post. He asked, "Do you have a couple of minutes in the morning to talk about this?"

Nickel, from her APF email address, promptly replied, "Sure. Free before 9 a.m. That's not a helpful article . . . their group is tricky."

Tricky? I wondered what that meant. Sounded to me as if Nickel was acting as a private PR consultant for these executives, coaching them on the players and massaging their messages. I wonder if she was advising them on how to handle me, and all I can say is, good fucking luck.

In other emails that I reviewed, Nickel proactively approached Purdue as early as 2017, asking them to "participate" in a family-resource project. Purdue circulated the announcement of PhRMA's partnership with APF later that year; shortly after that, they invited Nickel to join the now-infamous Pain Care Forum—another shill Purdue project—according to Purdue, at her request. Purdue executives corresponded several times internally about APF and commented on how they should coordinate messaging with Nickel. It seems she solicited them for support and was looking to collaborate on a more formalized basis. In another email dated

August 30, 2018, Jonathan Sackler forwarded Nickel's biography to other Purdue executives, encouraging them to consult with her. The email exchange commented that Purdue execs were "already in touch" with Nickel and "knew her well."

But the real kicker for me was a December 4, 2017, email from Burt Rosen to another Purdue employee, regarding "staying apprised of the Addiction Policy Forum activities and how we can align our targeted states and activities to complement theirs." When I read that, my heart sank. I know many of the family members who helped organize APF chapters in states. They thought they were doing the right thing and making an impact. Now, it seemed that all along Purdue may have been helping to guide those efforts.

Jessica Nickel, how do you sleep at night?

With the help of groups such as the APF, Purdue had perfected the art of making itself look as if it cared about doing the right thing. For example, it funded an "education campaign," giving four states $125,000 for "public service announcements and educational materials." A *Portland Press Herald* article quoted the director of the Maine Office of Substance Abuse, Kim Johnson, who said, "I've never heard of another drug company that has funded prevention efforts or put as much energy into prevention efforts as Purdue Pharma has."

A whopping $31,250 for a few billboards in Maine? The bar, as they say, was on the *floor*.

Many state officials played along with Purdue's act, agreeing that only "addicts" misused drugs and that the company itself wasn't responsible. Even after 2007, when a number of mechanisms had been put into place by the legal settlements to make Purdue's actions more transparent, many state officials abdicated their roles as watchdogs. Then, in the late 2010s, when the overdose crisis became a campaign issue, they all piled on Purdue.

The second paragraph of Massachusetts's lawsuit against Purdue reads, "Purdue Pharma created the epidemic and profited from it through a web of illegal deceit." New York's complaint charged that Purdue and the Sackler family "deliberately betrayed [its] duties through a persistent course of fraudulent and illegal misconduct, in order to profiteer from the plague they knew would be unleashed."

But what about the states' duties? That question gnawed on me. After all, nefarious billionaires don't happen because of luck, ingenuity, or even innovation. Some of the greatest inventors and brightest minds in human history didn't crack a million dollars in their lifetimes. Money on the scale of the Sacklers' fortunes was the result of *collusion*. With its power unchecked by government, which was supposed to protect people, Purdue was free to rake in the cash. The FDA empowered them to mis-market and make addictive pills seem as safe as candy. Regulatory agencies failed to keep track of where boxes of Oxy turned up, who was prescribing them, and how many people ended up hooked. This beautiful friendship was fatal for many innocent people and lucrative for Purdue's bottom line.

"States and municipalities, they are in some ways responsible for the opioid epidemic," said Ed Neiger. "They were the only parties that had the prescription numbers and overdose numbers. They were the only ones that had the ability to find these clusters of overdose deaths. They just either turned a blind eye or they were negligent. They also had the authority to monitor Purdue, and they failed to do that."

By February 2020, I was running out of patience with the process. People around me were dying. Money was going out the door left and right for consultants and lawyers. I was disgusted with the wastefulness and delay, as well as the Sacklers' continuous disavowal of their part in the crisis. I decided to throw my cards on the table as a key player in the case. I saw how the Sacklers would talk to attorneys and even a few members of the press, but never say a word to the victims. I'd had enough. I told Arik, the committee's lawyer, that I wanted to meet with Richard Sackler.

"Yeah, I don't think that's going to fly," said Arik.

"Arik, you have to make this happen."

So Arik went to the attorneys for Richard's side of the family. A few days later, they told Arik that Richard wouldn't meet with me. Arik said, "Richard's attorneys are worried that you and Richard will end up killing each other by the end of the meeting. At the very least, someone's going to throw a punch." (Fair.)

However, there was another option. Richard's brother, Jonathan, who was also a former Purdue board member, was willing to meet.

The Sackler family lawyers laid out some ground rules. Nobody could be present except me and Arik and Kara Trainor, another victim on the committee. The meeting had to be a secret. I couldn't even tell my personal lawyer. They were afraid that the attorneys general would find out and get pissed off, because none of the Sacklers had had any direct communications with any of the other creditors during the bankruptcy. We scheduled the meeting for the second week of March in New York City. I bought a plane ticket.

Only days before our meeting, COVID-19 hit the United States. The pandemic upended just about everything in the world, and the Purdue bankruptcy was no exception. Everything went virtual—all the negotiations and mediations went to video conferences or telephone. My meeting with Jonathan Sackler was postponed. At first I just assumed, like most people, that stay-at-home orders would last a few weeks, maybe a month, and we'd return to business as usual. But as the pandemic wore on, I started to worry that I would never get my sit-down.

I told Arik, "This meeting is one of the most important things I'll probably do in the duration of this case. It's a big fucking deal. It has to happen. I need to look this guy in the eyes and call him on his bullshit. I need to tell him that this might be business as usual to him, but it isn't to me. These are our lives. The Sacklers have to pay for the damage."

Arik called the Sackler lawyers to relay my message.

"You can't tell anybody this," he said when he called me back. "Jonathan is really, really sick. It's not that he doesn't want to do this meeting. If they put him in front of a Zoom, you won't even understand what he's saying."

"Boo fucking hoo," I said. "He's probably faking because he changed his mind."

"Be nice. Have some empathy."

Okay, whatever, I thought. In fact, Jonathan Sackler wasn't faking. He died a few weeks later "after a long battle with cancer," according to a court filing. If he was given OxyContin for pain, it was not noted by the court. His death was part of what I had started thinking of as the Sackler family curse. One by one, in the middle of the case, a shocking number of the Sacklers and their closest supporters disclosed to the committee's counsel their excruciating health issues, the kind of illnesses that torture you physically before slowly ending your life. Things such as Alzheimer's, strokes, dementia, terminal cancer, throat cancer, concussions, multiple sclerosis, and more.

It seemed to me that being a Sackler was pretty high-risk, though I had trouble summoning a sense of empathy. After all, they'd gotten rich from the corporate genocide of my friends. And even at the last, when they could have redeemed themselves and done the right thing for victims, they were still acting like fools.

"But," Arik added, "David will meet with you."

David was Richard Sackler's son, the family spokesman, husband of Joss, chief executive of Summer Road LLC, the company that manages the Sackler family fortune.

I told Arik I'd take what I could get. A third-generation Sackler was still a Sackler. We scheduled a call for May.

Getting this meeting was almost an obsession for me. Was I curious what he would say? Sure. Thirsting for a fight? Definitely. Hoping for some kind of catharsis? Maybe. Hoping to gain some sort of strategic advantage in the negotiations? You bet. But I was also struggling with what I felt was the most important decision of the bankruptcy: the impending release, which I wasn't supporting because it would give the Sacklers immunity. I had to look one of the Sacklers in the eye, even if it was through a laptop screen. I wanted to see if David had anything meaningful to say to me or Kara, and if he could find it in his heart to apologize for himself or his family.

David Sackler was close to my age, a bear of a man. On May 26, 2020, he appeared on my screen with a blank white background, and a crisp white button-down shirt.

His lawyer sounded weary, eager to get the ordeal over with. "Let's begin."

David listened politely as Kara told her story. Her son Riley was born with neonatal abstinence syndrome (NAS) and would have lifelong health issues.

"He's now nine," Kara told David. "He is still in a diaper. He uses a sippy cup. His official diagnosis is low-functioning autism. They just don't really know because the first year was so bad."

I struggled to hold back tears. I could hear the pain in her voice, the weight of caring for a special needs kid whom she adored. She showed Riley on the screen. He waved at the camera, not realizing he was saying hello to the person who was quite possibly responsible for his physical disability, neurodivergence, and family's suffering. He was born dependent on opioids. Like David, he inherited the legacy of OxyContin. Unlike David, Riley didn't get the profitable runoff that goes with Oxy.

The Sacklers got billions of dollars. Riley got a sippy cup.

Then it was my turn. I started off nice and easy, telling David a bit of my story, about how I was prescribed OxyContin for pain, and I wasn't told it was addictive. I told him about people I had known and loved who had died from opioid overdoses. Then I asked him, quasi-innocently, "Do you know anyone that's ever struggled with addiction?"

"Uh," he stammered, caught off guard. "I have a number of friends who struggled with alcoholism. One died recently."

"Do you know anyone that's struggled with opioids?"

"No, I don't."

That surprised me because I'd seen emails that gave me a different impression. I thought, *Either he's lying, or he's just that far disconnected from reality.*

"How has this affected you personally?" I asked.

"I'm heartbroken to hear about the devastation and the stories. The medications have done a tremendous amount of good and alleviated suffering."

"Do people treat you differently because of your last name? Do you know what it's like to be stigmatized?"

"I certainly know what it's like to be stigmatized. But I'm not here to cry 'poor me.'"

"How do you think your family is going to be remembered?" I asked.

"I don't know what the future holds. I know how we feel about the facts and our conduct. I hope that as time goes by, public opinion about us will change. Frankly, I'm not concerned about that reputational side of things."

Then I got down to brass tacks. "There's four victims that sit on the UCC. We're a minority, but we're a very vocal, strong minority. In my opinion—the way the claims are adding up, the victims are going to have an extraordinary amount of power. The biggest question in my head is this three-billion-dollar number—"

"Sorry to interrupt you." He didn't sound sorry at all. "I gotta stop you. The total number for the settlement is—"

"—from the Sackler family."

"I gotta stop you." He waved his finger like a gospel singer prepping for a high note. "This is how we feel about it, and this will be instructive for you. It's all Sackler family money. We're giving Purdue over to the public benefit. But we don't have to do that. That doesn't have to happen. That was our company that we built over seventy years. We know how we feel about the facts. And we could, you know, without a settlement that both sides think is fair, we could all fight about the equity of Purdue all day, and you may win and we may lose, but tremendous value would be destroyed. And we're giving that over. So please, you know, understand, this is ten billion dollars—not three billion dollars."

"I'm talking about how much money the Sackler family is putting into the settlement."

"I just told you, it's ten to twelve billion dollars. That's how we see it."

"That's how you see it," I said, treading carefully. "I feel a little differently. We feel that the three billion dollars is just a number. The proportion of that money that's going to go to victims, and the amount of claims, it just feels like it's pennies of what it should be. And I know we differ on the death and destruction that the product has caused."

David told me he agreed with me about the proportion of the money going to the victims, as opposed to the states, should be higher—but that wasn't his department, was it? He said that the family was prepared to let the suits go forward in court and let the chips fall where they may—but nobody was going to win. He said, "It's going to destroy the company, it's going to destroy our personal fortune. And it will guarantee that almost no money goes to the people affected, where, as you say, it's so needed. Because it's going to take a decade to go through all the appeals. Huge fees will have been paid to lawyers along the way. We think we put the best we could do on the table. So whether or not you decide that's fair . . ." He trailed off.

"How did *you* decide that three billion dollars was fair?" I said, a little more sharply than before.

"We believe that this is a fair settlement for a number of reasons. The ten-billion-dollar number is more than the family received from OxyContin out of Purdue. That includes the taxes we paid, the money that went to other companies overseas that are being sold for this settlement. That right there says it's an incredibly fair number. We're not keeping the company, we're giving that up and all the value therein. We're giving up a huge amount of our own personal net worth. We're doing that, while maintaining we've done nothing wrong. We do not agree with the media's characterizations. But we want to help."

I was now convinced he wanted only to help himself. He must have been getting annoyed, or tense, because he shifted to bad cop.

"We've hit a point at which, for us, it feels like we've gone to the end of our rope, where fighting might be the better alternative for all of us, getting the facts out there, defending ourselves in court, letting the chips fall where they may. It would be destructive for us. It would be destructive for the stuff *you say* you care about. . . ."

It was a misstep, and we both knew it. He stopped himself and said sheepishly, "I'm sorry for what I said. You *do* care about it."

I let it go. But I said, "In my mindset, that number, it's going to be impossible. And I think we're going to have a very vocal minority on the UCC, and I believe we're going to have a strong constituency in terms of personal injury claims that I think are ultimately going to have to vote on this process and are going to be with us."

"There isn't a larger number out there," he said angrily. "It's not there. It's not going to happen. As far as the distribution, I can commiserate with you. The family doesn't have much control. Given our background in science and medicine, we don't want to see a bunch of money going into lawyers or state coffers. I just don't know how much control we have. It's being done in mediation that doesn't include us. Unfortunately. But when you say there's going to be way more money—it isn't there."

I couldn't believe what I was hearing. One of the richest men in the world was telling me the Sacklers didn't have money. Or, it's not that they didn't have money—they didn't have it *for this*. They had money to buy lobbyists, pay for their PR firm, woo prescribers with fancy dinners and free breakfasts, and cut $4 million checks to family members who didn't even remember cashing them. I'd noticed a news article on David pouring $14.2 million of Sackler family money into Palm Beach County real estate shortly before Purdue filed for Chapter 11. He'd bought right in the epicenter of the pill mill industry—my old stomping grounds. The Sacklers had money for new houses and first-class flights to Australia. But they didn't have money to make amends for the colossal tragedy they'd caused. Maybe we agreed on one minor point, which is that we didn't want states and other entities eating up the settlement for ineffective "awareness" campaigns or plugging up potholes. But that was where our similarities began and ended.

I took a deep breath. I wanted to say so many things in that moment, things I knew I would have to leave unsaid. This could not be our final confrontation. I nodded and reached for the mouse.

Again, I experienced that sickening sense of powerlessness. Was the epidemic David's fault? Yes and no. He could not have done it alone—but he wasn't willing to admit that he was implicated in the system's enablement of Purdue. In a justice system built on capitalism, the Sacklers would always be protected. The drug epidemic wasn't the work of one family or even one corporation. It was the work of many hands, the outcome of many choices. We ended up with an epidemic because, in the moment of truth when gatekeepers and government watchdogs could choose human beings, our safety, and our communities—they went with Purdue instead. In every one of those moments, life was not deemed as valuable as capitalism and the right of a company to turn a buck.

In this unjust system, David Sackler could cry "broke" to me and I could do nothing about it. In the middle of a pandemic, when I knew people who couldn't keep the lights on, couldn't access medical care because ERs were flooded with severe COVID-19 cases, couldn't get N95 masks or other safety measures because they were homeless or serving sentences for minor drug offenses—David Sackler was still choosing to play the victim. His family, not my community, would be protected. His life, not ours, would be valued. His opinion, not mine—or any other survivor's—was what mattered.

I locked eyes with David one more time. *So this is what evil looks like,* I thought to myself. He was so ordinary. It was hard to believe that his whole life was soaked in human blood. *The law is where you buy it and what you pay for it.* The Sacklers could afford to buy the whole system. They inherited it at birth, one generation from another. What kind of justice was possible for the people left behind, such as Kara and Riley? To people such as David, Riley was nothing: a simple claim on paper. I gritted my teeth. *This is unchecked power in America in 2020,* I thought.

I hit the Leave Meeting button on my screen and let it go to black.

6

THE DEATH CURVE

Being a person with substance use disorder means not just paying for substances, such as OxyContin; many people also pay for doctor visits and pharmacies, too. Addiction is an expensive illness, and it can be even more costly to get help if you need it. If you don't have insurance, it's even pricier. For example, if you have an accidental overdose but get 911 assistance in time, you will pay up to $1,200 to ride in an ambulance to the hospital for an ER visit that could cost around $3,000. (Or more. Always, more.) If you don't have insurance, you pay out of pocket.

Some of your money goes to the individual providers, and some goes into the pharmaceutical company's bank account. They all pay fees to the state, whether it's licensing, certification, taxes, or other costs. The state gets a cut of Big Pharma's business, which means the state has many reasons to stand aside while corporations collect on the front end, keeping people sick, or collect on the back end, such as with disreputable-but-perfect-on-paper rehabs fleecing scared families out of millions of dollars. Addiction is *big business*. Anytime someone makes a buck off your sickness, your fear, and your family, a percentage of it is paid to the state or federal government. Over time, "guardians of the public" stood by, collected taxes on Big Pharma products, and watched as the death curve skyrocketed. The Sacklers grew their wealth off the overdoses they turbocharged, while ordinary people were driven into debt and despair. It often feels as if the government did nothing; when they finally showed up, it seemed as if they were years late and billions of dollars short.

If I sound cynical, it's because I have so many times seen how these same government institutions preach one thing and practice another. They say they want to end overdose deaths but divert funding from resources such as syringe exchanges and harm reduction. They give lip service to our community but crack down on mutual aid that helps save lives.

In spite of state pushback, some brave people put themselves on the front lines to support our community. One of them was my friend Jesse Harvey, founder of Portland Overdose Prevention Society in Portland, Maine. Jesse, in recovery from opioid addiction, saw firsthand how the state persecuted struggling people. He wanted to expand access to harm-reduction services in Maine to save lives, providing clean needles, fentanyl test kits, and condoms to anyone who needed them, no questions asked. Maine had only half a dozen syringe-exchange programs back then, and their limited hours and locations made it nearly impossible for most people to access services that could keep them from dying or contracting a fatal illness. According to *Mainer*, "Jesse's group operated out of his red Honda hatchback, making home deliveries and parking after dark in places where active users were likely to find them; some clients would be notified of their schedule via Facebook."

The state of Maine, which at the time provided half-baked, ineffective recovery services through hard-to-access institutions or created barriers to entry for substance users, was *not* happy about Jesse Harvey. They cracked down on his organization, using the law as a way to discriminate against people in need. (So what else is new?) State health authorities required Maine's syringe-exchange programs to be licensed, which meant person-to-person harm-reduction aid was illegal. Maine's police hunted Jesse, ostensibly enforcing Maine's draconian law banning any individual from possessing more than ten needles at a time. Jesse, in his desire to help others, was labeled a criminal and an enemy of the state—a common experience for those of us who minister to people who use drugs in our community.

But Jesse wasn't done fighting, and when the state hounded him, confiscated lifesaving supplies such as fentanyl test kits, anti-overdose medications such as naloxone, and clean syringes, he doubled down. In 2018, he started the Church of Safe Injection, a religious organization, with all the rights and protections given to other churches. Jesse believed his harm-reduction work was protected by the First Amendment, which guaranteed religious freedom; it also dignified the work, adding a layer of respectability that changed the way Portland police treated the group when they distributed supplies.

"Why did I start the Church of Safe Injection in Portland?" Harvey asked in his 2018 *Portland Press Herald* opinion piece. "Because, overwhelmingly, the churches I've reached out to aren't interested in helping people who use drugs. They'll give them lip service . . . and maybe a pair of socks, but they won't really embrace them as Jesus would have done. They won't provide them with what they often need most: sterile syringes, naloxone, and nonjudgmental support.

"If this sounds blasphemous to you, it isn't. Pharisees have distorted God's word. If syringes had been around in Jesus' day, He would have supported safe injection. . . . All too often today, people who use drugs are offered only two choices: Get sober or die. Jesus would have rejected this shameful and lethal binary."

Just because you have substance use issues doesn't make you less human, or less deserving. Jesse knew that, and his message empowered people who were historically demonized, marginalized, and punished by the state. Like Jesus, Jesse uplifted the people who were pushed to the edges of "polite" society. *The last shall be first.* That was his life's mission, and also like Jesus, it was also that belief that killed him. Police departments in Maine coordinated their efforts to bully Jesse, subjecting him to unwarranted field sobriety tests, seizure of supplies, and harassment. The Lewiston Police Department, led by Lewiston police chief Brian O'Malley and his boss, Mayor Kristen Cloutier, issued a bulletin in June 2020 stating, "Jesse Harvey has been distributing hypodermic needles throughout Lewiston's downtown." The bulletin said Jesse was "NOT affiliated with a needle exchange organization, and therefore, it is not legal for Harvey to be handing needles out."

This bulletin was distributed to police departments across the state by the Maine Information and Analysis Center (MIAC), part of a nationwide terrorist-hunting network of "fusion centers," established after 9/11 by the Department of Homeland Security. It was a mandate to hunt Jesse down, threaten him, detain him, and interrogate him. Police were encouraged to use COVID-19 travel restrictions to force Jesse to stay home or face legal action. They had permission to search him for any reason, turn his life upside down, and bully him until he quit. And that's exactly what those cops did.

Like so many other activists hounded by the state, Jesse didn't survive this coordinated assault. Depressed, scared, isolated, and

overwhelmed, he spiraled into a deep despair that led to an overdose on September 7, 2020. It was fatal. I heard about Jesse's death as
I got off a plane with Sean. I was devastated. My phone was flooded
with messages. *Did you hear about Jesse?* Even in his last, difficult
months, Jesse and I talked frequently about what was happening to
him. He said the state was threatening him with criminal charges,
offering only inpatient treatment that was basically jail time with
a couple of detox supports. I tugged my mask down as I walked
through the terminal, feeling tears in my eyes as I took in the news.
It was too clear to me what had happened: one of our own had been
killed, not by his addiction but by the systems that felt threatened
by his very existence.

After his death, politicians praised his efforts—but only *after*.
Senator Angus King called him a "tireless advocate" whose loss is
"a tragic and painful reminder of the work we must do to confront
this awful epidemic, especially during the pandemic." Democratic
governor Janet Mills, a former prosecutor, adopted some of Jesse's
messages for her pro-recovery platform during her campaign. She
spoke about people in the recovery community in humane ways—
all while refusing to decriminalize safe injection and overdose-
prevention sites. She, like many other politicians, used warm and
fuzzy rhetoric to hide that nothing changes. The Church of Safe Injection is still a borderline-illegal organization—because something
that is good, moral, and just can also be illegal. Within weeks of
Jesse's wrongful death, with a fresh infusion of cash for a statewide
"opioid epidemic response," Maine added twelve syringe exchanges
and said they were considering adding more. In addition, they distributed thirty-five thousand doses of Narcan and claimed to have
increased access to medication-assisted treatment.

To me, it was clear which side the states were on: their own.

To them, the only good "addict" was a compliant one, and their narrow, hypercontrolled "recovery services" were so difficult to access that they might as well not exist for 95 percent of the people who needed them. People such as Jesse, who were willing to give direct aid to folks in need, were hounded into an early grave so that politicians could pat themselves on the back when they used his messaging but refused to adopt or support his methods. People who struggled with addiction were truly fucked in this system. The way harm-reduction organizations were treated by policymakers, police, and "respectable" state-funded groups proved it. The states had a stranglehold on recovery: they doled out a few scraps for our community and then blamed *us* for the mass deaths, disease, and despair. Our community was kept in a vise, and recovery organizations felt the squeeze acutely.

Although severely underfunded and overrun, community-based organizations are amazingly effective but dependent on grants, shoestring state budgets, and private donations. They weren't just up against addiction. They also had to contend with Purdue and the many systems that supported and enabled them, such as the FDA, pharmacies, and even the states themselves. Victims were caught between these two giants: one that wanted to stuff OxyContin down our throats, and one that wanted us to just disappear when we needed help. *How does David beat Goliath?* I wondered. To win such an unfair fight, David needed more than luck and good intentions. He needed a weapon that could bring down both giants—because they certainly weren't interested in fighting each other.

Throughout the case, I feared that we would be tokenized again, our words stolen for feel-good campaign slogans while our loved ones were left to die. The bankruptcy wasn't personal to the lawyers on any side of the case. It was business as usual for the states: one more deal with Purdue to line their pockets and keep money *out* of the hands of people like Jesse Harvey.

The victims on the UCC all knew that recovery community organizations, peer recovery, and harm-reduction supports, such as the Church of Safe Injection, worked. We'd relied on those services ourselves, and we had the data to support them. *Facing Addiction in America: The Surgeon General's Report on Alcohol, Drugs, and Health* said in 2016 that mutual aid groups and newly emerging recovery support programs and organizations are a key part of the system of continuing care for substance use disorders in the United States and that sustained wellness must integrate a range of recovery support services, including in schools, health-care systems, housing, and community settings. The report commented on the effectiveness of mutual aid groups and 12-step facilitation interventions; it described the evidence for the effectiveness of other recovery supports (educational settings, drug-focused mutual aid groups, and recovery housing) as promising. The report described recovery-oriented systems of care (ROSC), which embrace the idea that severe substance use disorders are most effectively addressed through a chronic-care management model that includes longer-term outpatient care; recovery housing; and recovery coaching and management checkups. Also, several studies back the idea that post-treatment monitoring (recovery checkups and "assertive approaches to continuing care") and support can elevate recovery outcomes for adults; recovery services provided by peers, community members, or other people who had lived experience with addiction were more effective. Harm reduction makes it possible to completely avoid or reduce injection-related health risks by providing a sterile syringe and proper equipment for every injection. Syringe service programs (SSPs) reduce HIV and hepatitis C virus

(HCV) infection rates by about 50 percent by distributing sterile syringes, safer drug use supplies, and education to people who use drugs.

It wasn't complicated. Yet, decision makers and state budget committees constantly bypassed commonsense recovery and harm-reduction principles when spending money. They'd earmark the cash for "opioid response," sit on it, waste it on billboards and slogans, do everything *except* fund grassroots support organizations, and then point the finger at the person who struggled as an example that those same organizations don't work. If they wanted to know what wasn't working, they should have taken a look in the mirror instead.

For example, in the midst of COVID-19, state funds in Sandusky, Ohio, paid for a billboard that said SOCIAL DISTANCING PREVENTS THE SPREAD OF ADDICTION. The billboard showed three "bad" stick figures using drugs, while a "good" figure stayed clear, six feet away—reinforcing the stigma that people with addiction should be ostracized and avoided, because whatever moral affliction they had was highly contagious. Seriously? I felt as if I were living in 1988 all over again. A $10,000 eyesore wasn't going to help anyone.

I knew from experience that the drug epidemic was not only stigmatized but widely misunderstood—even on my own team. For example, while Arik and the rest of our lawyers were incredibly smart and good at legal things, they knew next to nothing about recovery and addiction. When they heard the word *recovery,* they imagined 12-step groups and Malibu rehabs. When I mentioned funds for recovery organizations, they thought I wanted the debtor's estate to write a check to Alcoholics Anonymous. (Seriously!) Just as they had to teach me about bankruptcy law, I had to teach them about my side of the tracks.

Cheryl Juaire and Kara Trainor also served on the UCC, and they sat through every meeting, negotiation, and deposition. Cheryl lost her twenty-three-year-old son, Corey, to an opioid overdose and now runs an organization that supports families of loss; Kara was in long-term recovery and the mother of a profoundly disabled child born with neonatal abstinence syndrome (NAS). They knew what was at stake and who suffered most from Purdue's greed. Kara's recovery story was similar to mine, with long waiting lists, overcrowded recovery facilities, and few or no services. She also used medication to manage her opioid addiction, which eliminated many treatment options for her; this was before the "many pathways to recovery" model became popular.

I remembered a story Kara told me about her recovery: When she lived in Illinois and was struggling to stay healthy, she frantically looked for an available bed at a treatment center. Her addiction was ruthless, so bad that she opted for adoption after her second pregnancy because she knew she couldn't take care of the baby as well as her oldest son and the rest of her family. She experienced multiple relapses during the pregnancy, in part because the waiting list for maternal addiction-treatment centers was so long. Finding a place that was safe to go *as a woman* was hard enough. With her pregnancy or with a child, it was nearly impossible. Add to that her prescription for methadone, which kept her away from heroin, and she was excluded from virtually every recovery resource.

Postpartum, Kara was on a waiting list for more than a month before finding a place she could go with her older son while she was on methadone. Comparatively, Chicago had more recovery supports for women than Kara's hometown of Kalamazoo, Michigan. Still, she saw little change between 2005 and 2019, when the bankruptcy case began. She said, "In the time I got clean, I thought there would have been more resources, more funding. We have nothing. In Michigan, there's truly nothing, especially for women. When I started looking around to see what was available, it was nuts. I joined the UCC because I wanted to be part of something that would actually benefit people who were struggling. Who were in the streets and had nothing."

Kara, like me, lived in the gaps of the system. Her son was a daily reminder of the high cost of corporate greed and the total disregard Purdue showed for the people whose lives they ruined. She and I were both the kind of person that Purdue, the states, and the media held up as "degenerates," people who made themselves sick and then went crying to the government. We were determined to prove to these lawyers that those stereotypes were not only incorrect, but fatal: our lived experience exposed the many ways that states let our communities down.

The disconnect between the law that was being practiced and the real-world stakes of the case's outcome showed state complacency. In our power struggle, I was reminded that overdose rates continue to spike not only because of Big Pharma but because the infrastructures that supposedly help people don't even look at the evidence. The data, the white papers, the hours of evidence and testimonials that I could recite from memory—none of it mattered to the others. More than once, I sat in meetings tongue-tied because some of the most powerful state attorneys general didn't value victims' participation. They gave us a seat at the table, but until we got into negotiations, I didn't fully realize that it was purely symbolic. Our participation, our inclusion, was nominal: a concession to the fuss we'd made in the media and with our protests. But did they actually listen to what we had to say? I doubt it—or they would have acted differently.

Realizing our contributions were seemingly meaningless to most parties in the case was a hard pill to swallow. In some cases, Cheryl and I previously worked with these same attorneys general. We consistently showed up for Maura Healey, the Massachusetts attorney general, when her office was suing the Sackler family before they entered Chapter 11. While it was contentious with most state players, she was one of the few who kept our voices front and center. She boldly took on the Sacklers in her state; much of what she exposed made the case against the family possible. But she was only one of fifty.

This wasn't about rhetoric. It was about actions, not words. When the doors were closed and cameras were off, the same people who spoke with such compassion and understanding about overdoses didn't necessarily want to hear from us. They had the tools to fix the crisis: law firms, public health teams, and funding. But they didn't use them, or didn't use them correctly. Whatever they were doing was disconnected from what the community needed. If the states' way of dealing with the epidemic worked, we wouldn't have empirical proof of an increasing treatment gap and more deaths.

States also demonstrated their ignorance about basic ideas that are common, proven to work, and well supported by research and evidence. When I talked about harm reduction, the states thought I meant just a ton more funding for medication-assisted treatment (MAT). It seemed as if MAT was all they knew and was their only buzzword to throw into the conversation. *MAT, MAT, MAT*. To be clear, medication-assisted treatment works: it saved my own life. We need more access to it! It works best when we *also* have housing, employment, mental health support, basic health care, and other peer services. But try convincing the states to listen. Their programming for recovery was single focus: MAT only, opioids only, government-controlled only—and everyone else could take a hike. Substance issues vary by community; one specific treatment for one drug can exclude huge numbers of people. We are diverse, and so is our use. In my community, the gay community, it's mostly meth. Yet, the vast majority of state/federal funding only goes to treatment for opioid use disorder in areas where *they* decide it's needed. And sadly, under the current infrastructure, government-controlled programs are failing miserably at reaching those most in need. For example, back in sunny Florida, a 2018 study found that Black and African Americans experienced a four-to-five-year delay in accessing qualified treatment compared with whites. The inequities are distressing: the government's application of public health strategies remains unevenly distributed, favoring white communities over other races and ethnicities. It strikes me as so *American* and so *white* to be like, "We'll put all the money down one tube to help only areas where mostly white people are dying."

When my lawyer, Anne Andrews, was trying to convince me to apply to become a committee member, one of the things she said was, "If you get on this superpowerful committee, you will have the power to help dictate where money goes. And you can envision anything."

That got my attention. "Anything?"

Billions of dollars would be in play, she said. Think of the possibilities. We could designate an initial chunk of money from Purdue's estate and get it on the ground to help fill these gaps right away, before all the legal wrangling played out. This type of emergency fund was rare in bankruptcies, but not entirely unprecedented. In 2019, during the Pacific Gas and Electric Company bankruptcy, the court approved the creation of a $105 million housing assistance fund to help those who'd lost their homes in various wildfires, for which the California-based power provider had been held responsible.

The moment an emergency relief fund (ERF) became a possibility, it became my singular focus for the next seven months. I called Carol McDaid, a friend who advocates for public policy around recovery and treatment, and Daniel Raymond, who worked at Harm Reduction Coalition in New York City, and basically anyone else I could think of, and I asked them all what we could do with $200 million, which was the biggest number we thought we could get. As I wrote it, the ERF would be the largest investment in recovery community organizations, community-based harm-reduction services, and family support services *ever*. I imagined a world where people struggling with addiction had zero barriers to supportive services. I imagined robust funding that worked harder *and* smarter: money for recovery housing, peer recovery services, recovery community centers, harm reduction—all these things that had been proven to save lives but that always got the short end of the stick in budget meetings because policy makers don't prioritize people first. I imagined shifting the balance and spending Purdue's blood money on saving lives *immediately*. At the time, $200 million didn't sound like a lot of money, but it could begin to pay for the infrastructure we needed to finally do things differently.

A true "emergency fund" would treat America's overdose crisis like the burning building it was and send money to organizations on the front lines helping people. I hoped that victims would get individual claims payments in the final bankruptcy plan. But that could take months, or even years. We were losing 360 people a day to addiction; every four minutes, someone else was gone. An emergency relief fund could save lives *now*. Even that wasn't soon enough for me. I wanted this, like, *yesterday*.

We needed to go faster and think bigger. I wanted sustained recovery at the fingertips of anyone in America. I wanted to fund all these little organizations that literally picked people off the streets and helped them navigate a confusing and bureaucratic health-care system, help them find treatment, apply for Medicaid, find housing, apply for food stamps, and help them find jobs or job training. These interventions had been shown by studies to be highly effective, but they never got the kind of government grants that other services got—because, like my well-intentioned lawyers, the officials probably thought *recovery* meant "rehab."

The ERF was supposed to diversify the states' services and pay for direct aid that ultra-narrow government grant programs simply didn't see. Our ERF had the potential to create a template for other court settlements and state funding programs, should it prove successful. We did not need bailouts for the groups already turning a profit or the well-established organizations with deep pockets and good relationships with state and federal budget officials. But that meant cutting those powerful, recognized players out of the deal— and they wouldn't go down without a fight.

The first draft of the ERF called for $200 million to be taken out of Purdue's cash reserves and placed into a new not-for-profit 501(c)(3) organization, which would be in charge of distributing the money. It would have a seven-seat governing board, with two representatives appointed by the committee of unsecured creditors, two by the states, and two by Purdue, effectively sharing power between all groups, with the seventh member selected by the others to serve as board chair. Established nonprofit organizations and community groups that met certain criteria (for example, they couldn't be recipients of significant government funding, and they couldn't be claimants against Purdue) could apply for grants of up to half a million dollars. The governing board would decide who got what. Money had to be spread out evenly among the different states, and some would be earmarked for Native American tribes and NAS babies, or other special groups.

We first took our proposal to Purdue. It was their money; they would have to file the motion to create the ERF. We had a conference call with some of their lawyers toward the end of 2019. And it was . . . *weird.* They didn't seem to understand what we were doing. They kept saying they wanted the money to go out faster.

"Can you explain why you proposed a 501(c)(3)," one lawyer asked, "as opposed to other structures, where the funds might be quicker to use?"

We wanted the fund to be completely transparent. We wanted to make it a matter of public record where the money went, and we wanted to keep track of how many people it helped. That way, people would know if it was working. But Purdue didn't seem to care about any of that. The idea that they wanted it faster—even faster than I did—made me suspicious. Since when did Purdue care about helping people? After all, the overdose crisis had been going on for decades, and they'd never made a single move to mitigate the harm they caused, much less take responsibility.

Our proposal would have distributed funding in around six months. That didn't sound slow to me. I wanted to set things up, move quickly, and be transparent. Doing things right always took a little time. I mean, every week we took to hammer out a revised draft of the ERF was also a delay, and the Purdue lawyers didn't seem to have any problem with *that.*

Purdue lawyers suggested there were other, existing infrastructures that could be used to disburse the money. That could only mean one thing: the states would get all the money we wanted for the ERF and dole it out as they saw fit. This wasn't groundbreaking. It was what states had been doing with federal grants for years. This was what we all knew the states really wanted—and we knew it wouldn't do anything to slow the deaths. It was just more of the same. That made my spidey senses tingle, too. Why would Purdue propose giving more money to the states, who were suing Purdue's pants off? It didn't make sense.

So I explained why we wanted an independent fund. State agencies had already been a conduit for federal money. And, for the most part, they were *terrible* at spending it. Between 2016 and 2019, the US Department of Health and Human Services doled out more than $5 billion through various grants to ameliorate the opioid epidemic. (Which only got worse.) Nearly half that money had gone directly to state agencies; cities and counties received roughly $120 million. Rather than figure out a solution that actually worked, the federal government also created the State Opioid Response (SOR) grant in September 2018, which would over two years provide $2 billion for states to expand recovery services.

Yet, by the time that two-year cycle came to a close, half of all SOR funds dedicated to growing the treatment infrastructure remained unused. According to a December 14, 2020, report by the Government Accountability Office (GAO), $1.4 billion of SOR funds had not even been withdrawn from the grant account. According to *Filter* (filtermag.org), the GAO reported that "Alabama had utilized the highest proportion of its grant at 76 percent, while Michigan had squandered the most, using only around 33 percent." Also in 2020, the Department of Health and Human Services inspector general published a report, looking at State Targeted Response to the Opioid Crisis (or STR) grants. Of the money given out to states and territories to combat the overdose crisis, 61 percent of it remained unspent after the first year, and nearly a third of it remained unspent after two years. Nine states spent less than half of their grant money. Other grants were similarly left unspent, gathering dust.

The money the states were receiving, they weren't even spending.

"Maybe they should spend what they have first," I suggested. "If we start putting the money into their existing infrastructure, we're throwing two hundred million dollars away. The states are going to get billions in this settlement, and they probably won't spend *that* on recovery, either."

I also knew that treatment, which was synonymous with recovery for many of these lawyers, was already heavily subsidized by the government. Medications for substance use disorder were reimbursable through Medicaid. I knew we had to bridge the gap, but every time I thought we were making progress in explaining why this was so important, the bottom dropped out. I started to feel as if I were going crazy. Was I the only one this proposal made sense to? What wasn't getting through to the other side's lawyers?

A few weeks later, Purdue sent us their version of what the ERF could be. It was even worse than I feared: it was as if they were trying to repair the space station with a broken Popsicle stick. They wanted to spend some of the proposed funds on "education and prevention," that old-school "don't do drugs" curriculum that had already been debunked as useless. Some straight talk from ol' McGruff hardly qualified as tackling an emergency. When you read between the lines, Purdue didn't want to clean up the mess; they just wanted to send a message that you could prevent an epidemic that was already in full swing.

We had made it clear that we needed to spend the funding on services that would make it to the front lines right away. A

Yale University study, published in the journal *Academic Emergency Medicine*, found that people treated for opioid overdoses in ERs were not given what they needed to recover: providers pushed treatment but overlooked basic needs such as housing, employment, harm-reduction measures such as naloxone, and community-based care. Those unmet needs, big surprise, were always overlooked and undervalued as a solution. We wanted to change that by interrupting the cycle of overdose, ER, to back on the street, but it seemed as if we were the only ones who believed in the evidence that it would work.

I was discouraged by Purdue's version of the ERF, to say the least, but I could live with throwing a few million dollars toward "education campaigns." I can compromise with the best of them. Maybe they were naive, or uninformed, but that wasn't new to me. What was awful, though, was how they structured the governing board. They gave two seats to the consenting states and two seats to the dissenting ones, leaving the UCC with two seats and Purdue with one. That was totally disruptive and made the entire setup unbalanced. *And, boy, was it a setup from the very beginning.* Although the two sets of states disagreed on some things, they were essentially in lockstep on the ERF. This arrangement gave them a clear majority over victims and put states, not people, in the cockpit. Purdue clearly wanted the states firmly in control of the $200 million. To add insult to injury, their plan had few guidelines for how to spend the money, little transparency, and minimal accountability. Purdue wasn't interested in justice; they were making a deal with the states and ganging up on victims to keep us silenced and stuck.

I thought I was going to pop a vein. After the call ended, I immediately got on the phone with Arik.

"What the *fuck*," I yelled. My voice was so loud that Sean poked his head into my makeshift office to make sure I was okay. Our dog, Dollar, rolled off the bed and headed for the living room.

"We'll handle it," Arik said. "Our proposal is strong and it's fair. We aren't done yet."

The next time we met with the Purdue lawyers, I was tense, but I stayed quiet. I didn't want to jeopardize negotiations by blowing up on the call. I sucked on my vape pen and kept my arms crossed, trying to control my temper.

Arik told the Purdue side, "What you came back with was something that—unfortunately, there's no other way to read it—gave control of the ERF to the states."

The Purdue lawyers said, over and over, that wasn't their intention. But they never said they would change it. And they started to defend the states' ability to manage spending. They wanted control, and they didn't want victims to have equal power on the proposed board. They wanted a handshake deal saying that states would be entrusted to spend money in a way that benefited everyone—but I'd been around long enough to know that their assurance was meaningless. States had been complicit in the drug epidemic, with budgets that only made recovery harder to access, while reinforcing criminal justice systems that punished and incarcerated people that needed help. If the states were in control of the ERF, we'd only have more of the same.

"We think that the states have a lot to offer," a Purdue lawyer said. "Because not only are they dealing with this problem day in and day out, I think that they have a lot of very informed views."

Informed by what? I wanted to scream, but I held it in. The Purdue lawyers were infuriatingly polite. They did that thing where they made it seem as if they agree with you, but the actual substance of what they said was noncommittal. Finally, the lawyers said that they wanted to send both ERF proposals to the states, to get their input.

Arik was aghast. "You want to send *both* proposals?!" The states fund a lot of programs, but the intention of our ERF was to get funds on the front lines, to organizations that couldn't access state funding because it was tied up in relationships that states were already familiar with. Our ERF was supposed to bypass inequitable funding. This is why I was so adamant about the structure of the fund: because the states had demonstrated that when they were in control, very little changed. The states and Purdue, if they had the voting majority, wouldn't give anything away to groups that weren't already under government control.

"Yes," said Purdue's lawyers.

After a long pause, Arik said, "And your proposal is going to keep the states having control? This ERF is one of the things that the committee has staked a very, very large importance on. I really strongly urge you not to send something to the states that is like a menu of two proposals, one of which gives them control, and one of which doesn't. It just doesn't—it doesn't make any sense! And it's not something we're ever going to agree to."

"So, Erik—"

"It's *Arik.* My name is Arik."

"Sorry. We will get back to you on adjustments."

The Purdue lawyers seemed to think they could just make a few tweaks and be done with the whole thing. But we weren't going to accept that. Once again, the discussion ended without much resolution. I got the feeling that the resolution, whatever it was, wouldn't involve us. As Arik said, the states would be given two options: control over the $200 million fund, or no control. It was easy to guess which one they'd choose. Knowing this, we were willing to compromise on a few points to get our ERF proposal implemented. Without walking back much, we could add things to the proposal. Purdue could have its education and prevention. The state agencies could have some level of involvement. I went to the bargaining table with an open mind, trying to see a way where everyone could win. But the states rejected every single offer. They were determined to have it all their way.

Negotiations got worse as I lost faith in the entire process. I could feel our chance at justice slipping away. It didn't help that I was up against some ghastly people. If I was the most passionate and informed spokesman for the creditors' ERF, my counterpart on the other side was John Guard, the deputy attorney general of Florida— Florida, good old Florida, the state I was born in and nearly died in, the state that became synonymous with pill mills and horrible sober-living homes. Guard looked like Darth Vader with his helmet off. I'd be negotiating with him, and I was pretty sure he held me in as much contempt as I did him.

In one of our final ERF negotiation calls, I told the bevy of lawyers what I thought of the states' proposal: "Two hundred million dollars under your structure will not go very far and it won't do very much, because it's two hundred million dollars layered onto billions upon billions upon billions of dollars on things that are already funded."

John Guard, in a creepy, inauthentic tone that made my skin crawl, gave what sounded like a well-rehearsed speech: "One hundred and thirty people are going to die today from opioids. Our focus was to try to see if we could move the needle on the number of people that are going to die every day, and to do so in a coordinated fashion, so we're not working on cross-purposes."

Translation: give us the money.

I asked Guard how he could be so confident that the states and municipalities had the ability to get the money out quickly, given their history and our already-significant delays in this extended negotiation. We pointed out that what their side proposed wasn't an ERF: it was just a prepayment on the public side's claims. They were never going to agree to this money being controlled by nongovernmental entities.

"Not a single dollar is going to a state or a city or a county, and you know it!" said Guard. "This is not a payment on claims."

"Then why do you think the states and municipalities should have a monopoly on where the money should go?" Arik asked.

He was right, because there was little evidence that the states would do this better than an independent structure. In fact, the evidence said that it would take longer to get money on the ground if funding went through the high barriers set up by the states. My committee did plenty of talking on that point, but the highfalutin lawyers simply refused to hear it.

"The fact is that in most states the death curve is bending because money is getting out," said Guard. "In Florida last year, we dropped from seventeen people dying a day to fifteen people dying a day. So, I don't know, maybe two people dying a day is unimportant to the members of the UCC, but to the government officials in Florida it is extremely important."

At that point, I completely fucking lost it. "How dare you say that two people who die is not something that's a concern to the UCC? I'd like an apology for that. Because that's a disgusting cheap shot. I've lived in Florida. I failed through *your* treatment system multiple times. I almost died because of *your* system. In *your* state. On *your* watch. I've lost a good number of my friends in *your* jurisdiction. How fucking *dare* you."

The desperate-sounding Purdue moderator tried to jump in, but it was too late. This meeting was a train wreck that had caught on fire the instant it pulled out of the station. Arik told Guard to apologize to the committee for what he said about us not caring about two deaths a day. The suggestion was absolutely disgusting. As a state, Florida was extra-cozy with Purdue. In 2018, Florida's new attorney general, Ashley Moody, announced that her inaugural committee included Michael Corcoran, a Purdue lobbyist; at the time, Purdue was being sued by Florida's outgoing attorney general, Pam Bondi, for OxyContin's role in the state's overdose crisis. Ashley Moody was a former federal prosecutor and called herself a supporter of Bondi's opioid lawsuit. She was "passionately outspoken about the opioid epidemic, its effects, solving this crisis, and holding those responsible accountable," her spokesperson told the *Tampa Bay Times*. The paper also pointed out that Moody is married to a Drug Enforcement Administration agent. And she wanted Purdue's lobbyist, a longtime friend, on her team. It was too obvious to me that they were all in bed with one another—the government, the state, and Purdue—but *we* were the ones getting fucked. It just went to show that states loved patting themselves on the back for doing the bare fucking minimum while my friends lost their lives. Our ERF committee—the *survivors* of this epidemic—weren't to blame. Good intentions weren't going to save anyone.

The other side's lawyers jumped in to defend Guard's comment, and things only devolved from there. After explaining for a half hour why the states can't do their job, we resorted to biting our tongues. One of the state's reps muttered that a couple of people on the committee owed apologies, too. (They meant me, and they could go fuck themselves.) No one backed down, and no one compromised. Things only got worse. On my turf, I would have mopped the floor with these lawyers and attorneys general. But I was in their territory in the bankruptcy court, out of my element and at a serious disadvantage. *They held the power.* They showed up with their law degrees; Cheryl, Kara, and I showed up with years under our belt in this fight. Our ERF committee, not the lawyers, were experts. We knew what needed to happen. We didn't expect the states to be working against us—against the very people they were supposed to represent.

I couldn't believe that we'd created this thing, proposed it, pitched it, and now it was being squashed right under our noses. I would be surprised if there even *was* an ERF at the end of these miserable negotiations. Purdue and the states were obviously working together to keep that money under their control—and, more important, *away* from the people who needed it most.

By the time Purdue finally did share our joint proposal with the states, the states had written up their own version of an ERF, which is exactly what we were afraid of. When I saw the states' proposal, I felt my heart deflate. They had known all along what we wanted to do and made no attempt to compromise or even placate us.

Big surprise: the states wanted every single penny of the ERF. They wanted funds put into the same state agencies that already received federal cash, much of which had gone unspent for years—while the epidemic raged, on their watch, in their cities and towns and neighborhoods. Our ERF proposal was supposed to fill in their gaps and fund worthy efforts, but the states were only looking out for themselves. The 2020 election was right around the corner. They were looking for a political win. Their proposal gave more money to the same agencies and services that the final bankruptcy settlement would fund later in the process. Arik called their idea a "prepayment" on their claim. Some money now, lots more later. It was like a game of monkey in the middle, with victims leaping to catch a football that the states and Purdue tossed just out of reach.

The final kick in the teeth? The governing board in the states' proposal was to be controlled by state attorneys general's appointees. For the states, by the states. Not one penny for community-based services that weren't already in the states' favored cliques. The rest of us would be left carrying the physical, emotional, and financial debts of the overdose crisis while states got an advance on their billions and Purdue washed their hands of the whole thing. Once again, the two giants teamed up to trample victims, with complete, unchecked power.

"This can't be happening. It's a nightmare," I told Arik after we reviewed the states' proposal. "What about everyone else? What about the families?"

"Don't get so upset," he said calmly, trying to reassure me. "This is how negotiations work. They're going to start all the way on their end. We're going to start on our end. We'll come out somewhere in the middle."

But what's the middle ground between life and death? I was aware of how little the lawyers on both sides knew about recovery, addiction, and the community I represented. I could easily imagine them shrugging off their responsibility and signing away our lives.

Money for a guaranteed, realistic, road-tested solution was on the table and in danger of being stolen from the people who needed it most—people who weren't served by the same-old, same-old systems that were still sitting on hundreds of millions in funding. Kara, Cheryl, and I all had firsthand, lived experience with how thinly spread lifesaving resources were. We knew what was at stake. Yet, our passionate calls for a victim-centered ERF were ignored. Millions of people in my community, I knew, hung by a thread from hour to hour. How many of those people would these lawyers sacrifice just to make a deal?

My fear: every one of us.

7

LAST MONTH'S TUNA ROLL

At the beginning of February 2020, I hit a wall. I woke up one gray morning and stood in our yard, watching my dog nose the dead cactus plants. The sun was coming up over the distant red mountains, tinting the sky pale pink. A thin layer of frost was on the ground. I felt as though Christmas had never happened; Sean and I rang in the New Year mere weeks ago, but even that memory seemed far away, as though it had happened in another lifetime. The year 2020 was barely two months old and I was already exhausted. The Trump administration's frequent assaults on LGBTQ rights and its stunning failure to do anything about the ongoing drug epidemic were disheartening, to say the least. I was burned out.

On my iPhone, I scrolled through my Facebook notifications and clicked the links my friends had sent me. Overdoses had rebounded from 2018, and we were once again facing the worst year in history for substance-related deaths. Policy makers were pouring money into policing instead of compassionate interventions and mental health care. Another bad batch of fentanyl-laced heroin was making its way through rural communities on the West Coast.

The Sacklers popped up every once in a while. I saw reports that Mortimer Jr. and Jacqueline Sackler had retreated to a luxury ski resort in Gstaad for the winter after selling their Manhattan town house for a reported $38 million. Two hedge funds, DeepCurrents Investment Group LLC and Sunriver Management LLC, had cut ties to the family by redeeming investments by Kokino LLC, a private Sackler investment firm. Nothing about the bankruptcy. I scrolled and clicked until I realized I was shivering. I could see my breath out here. I called Dollar and headed into the house, still sifting through my texts.

"Did you see this?" said one message. I saw the news, all right. I just couldn't *do* anything about it. The long days and nonstop calls were starting to wear me down. I made coffee with my free hand while I skimmed an article about a new flu in Wuhan, some kind of SARS virus they said was spread in open-air markets.

"Is that for me?" Sean asked, slipping his arms around me and giving me a sweet hug. He snuck the coffee cup from under the machine.

"It is now." I smiled. He was the bright spot in my gray season. I watched him hunt for the cream in the fridge.

"I don't see enough of you," Sean added.

"When are you heading back to New York?"

"Too soon." I sighed. I started a second cup of coffee. My phone vibrated, and I looked down at it, out of habit.

"I am gonna take that thing out of your hand," Sean teased.

"I hate it. I'm so burned out. I feel like I'm in hell. It's the same thing, over and over. I don't want to hear their voices anymore. And I hate not being able to talk about it. This is front-page stuff, and it's just going to be sealed up and buried as soon as the case is over, like it never even happened."

He nodded and gently slipped my phone out of my hand, putting it facedown on the kitchen counter. "I know, babe. When this is over, things will go back to normal. It can't go on forever."

When he kissed me, I felt as if I could believe that. I missed him, although we lived together and spent every free moment planning our wedding, going on adventures, and enjoying our new hometown of Las Vegas. After two years of dating, I still couldn't get enough of Sean. Every time I got on a plane, went to yet another distant meeting, or left town, I missed him like crazy. He was the person who was closest to me, and between feeling cut off from my community and separated from my fiancé, I felt more lonely than ever. At the beginning of the case, I had been so confident that I could handle keeping quiet—even though my voice was my most powerful weapon, I could button my lip for a little while in service of the greater good. What I couldn't handle was missing my partner and my friends. Five months in, my sense of isolation was like a physical illness. It settled on me, making me feel dried out and aching for the people I loved.

Knowing that Sean was in my corner kept me going, most days. I kissed him again as I grabbed my coffee and my phone and headed back upstairs. "I've got a phone call with Anne. I'll be free in an hour!"

"It's a date."

Once again, I had to tear myself away from his beautiful smile to go back to the never-ending labor of committee work.

I got to my desk, and my sense of happiness faded like that early-morning frost. *Back to the grind.* I gritted my teeth and dialed into yet another call, trying to make sense of what was keeping victims from getting their fair share of the Purdue settlement. From what I could tell, the emergency relief fund was a threat to the states' pre-negotiated deal. I had the radical idea that victims deserved *everything*, and they saw that as infringing on *their* settlement, *their* plunder from the company they'd enabled throughout the drug epidemic. They wouldn't part with a single penny if they could avoid it. In each meeting and every email, every suggested rewrite, I could see the fund I worked my ass off for slipping away into a swamp of red tape, slowly being lawyered to death. But I wasn't going to give up without a fight. I stuck to my ideals. I knew it was the right thing to do—even if nobody was advocating for it except our ERF committee.

The thing was, the ERF *would* benefit states because it would let them off the hook for creating new programs, while also plugging the holes in their existing structure. The ERF, as we'd written it, could create visionary change for frontline community organizations—the forgotten heroes, the ones who always missed out in funding cycles. It would pay for the kind of change politicians loved to talk about but never managed to implement. (Finally, those campaign promises would come true!) Most important, it would save lives in an increasingly deadly overdose crisis that was only compounded by COVID-19. The ERF meant so much and cost *so little*. It was pennies on the dollar and checked all the boxes. Everyone won—which may have been why *everyone* didn't support it.

As the bankruptcy wore on, the ERF felt more and more like a dream and less like a reality. The lawyers were more interested in negotiations than reconciliation or meaningful restitution. A frustrating dynamic emerged: instead of working with victims or centering the people who suffered most, Purdue was doing everything it could to avoid pissing off the states. It was in Purdue's interest to play nice, since the states were the ones with real police powers and the ability to prosecute criminally. That gave them enormous power, much more power than the victims, who had no leverage and weren't petitioning outside the process. I started to feel as if the $200 million fund was being stolen right out from under us. At night, I couldn't sleep, thinking about what was happening. Our community could do so much with the ERF, but I sensed in my bones that it would end up being used as a nice bribe from Purdue to the states. Maybe I was being paranoid, but my instincts said otherwise. Any drug dealer would buy off the cop that busted them—I knew that from experience, from seeing the hired sheriff outside Dr. Brown's office in Broward County. The states were for sale, and a wad of cash and some contraband was enough to get them off Purdue's back. Like any other dealer, Purdue wanted to keep things friendly between the two parties. The states were enabling Purdue before the bankruptcy, and a payoff in the settlement was par for the course. The dealer pays the cop, and the cop looks the other way instead of breaking out the cuffs. The states already had all the power. Now they wanted all the money, too.

Although they kept up negotiations for appearances' sake, I was sure from the states' behavior that they never wanted an emergency relief fund. The consenting states (including Florida) wanted the deal they had agreed to prior to Purdue declaring Chapter 11. Any money siphoned out of Purdue for the ERF was money "off the balance sheet," money that they already considered to be theirs. As for the nonconsenting states, despite all their bluster about holding Purdue accountable, they, too, appeared to be holding out for a deal—maybe just a slightly *better* deal, with a little bit more money. In their eyes, the ERF might put that deal in danger. The only ERF these states would accept was a direct deposit into their treasury.

As for Purdue, they just wanted to nod their heads and appear agreeable. Maybe they didn't even see the difference between our two plans. Maybe they were equally afraid of both the committee and the states. To me, it seemed as if they simply didn't give a shit about any of it. They wanted it to be over. They'd leveraged the bankruptcy to avoid the massive civil litigation, and now they just wanted to hand over some cash and call it good. I felt as if some on our committee and a few of the lawyers representing us were the only people who cared; everyone else had an attitude of "So what?" To them, it seemed to be a done deal—one that completely cut victims out.

By this time, the one hope I still clung to was the judge. (It ended up being a false hope, but hope nonetheless.) Drain had said a number of times that he wanted to see an ERF and wanted to see it soon. In December 2019, after hearing about the stalled negotiations, he had told us all, "I hope everyone here does not let the perfect become the enemy of the good. Sometimes a lot of hot air can be spent on these issues when, really, compromise is warranted. I'm talking about the emergency fund and ultimately a distribution mechanism under a plan. So I don't mind raising questions about big thought issues, but narrow it down—quickly."

Everyone lived in fear of Judge Drain. People spoke to him obsequiously, as if he were God. When updating the judge on the ERF progress (or lack thereof), Purdue's lawyer was at pains to stress just how hard everyone was working, how much progress had been made, and, no, there wasn't an agreement just yet, but we were hopeful, everyone was hopeful, and so on. And the judge kept saying that we needed to compromise. So the question was, how angry would the judge get if we couldn't reach a compromise? And whom would he get angry at?

That February, our last shot at striking a deal came. Cheryl,

Anne, and I flew to New York for an in-person ERF summit (Arik met us in NYC). I was trying to stay optimistic, but I think I was the only one keeping the flame burning. None of our lawyers, even Arik, were terribly hopeful that we would be able to reach a deal. I knew that it was Drain's call—but whatever made it to his desk might smell worse than last month's tuna roll.

On that freezing-cold morning in February, we trudged up to the office of Purdue's law firm, Davis Polk & Wardwell. My glasses fogged up as I went in, and I shivered, unused to New York City's winters. I knew that, on the other side of the country, Sean and Dollar were probably snuggling up on the sofa without me. I sighed. This law office couldn't be further from home; it was like another planet. As my group walked out of the elevator, we were led past the reception desk through a hallway with fifty-foot-tall ceilings. A stunning collection of modern artwork decorated the office, making it feel more like a gallery than a lawyer's suite. Slanted ceilings opened into a beautiful view of Manhattan. We arrived at a conference room with an enormous square table and a kitchenette with a buffet fit for an upscale wedding, with gourmet omelets, bran muffins, and fancy jellies. This was all perfectly normal to the dozens of lawyers circling the room. They picked at the food, complaining that there weren't enough options, or that the hollandaise didn't look great. I couldn't help but compare the spread with the slushy orange juice concentrate and stale bagels that pharmaceutical companies left in the pill mill waiting rooms, those crappy breakfasts I'd grabbed on my way into a doctor's office to pick up another Oxy prescription. These lawyers looked as if they lived on artisanal croissants and organic egg-white scrambles. They were the people that were begrudging us our $200 million.

The Purdue team was there, including Sheila Birnbaum, who ran up to me and grabbed my arm when she said hello. (FYI, she was wearing a suit, not a kimono.) The two sets of states were present, including John Guard, who purposely avoided my gaze, and their lawyers. And—surprise!—the federal government was there, too, with representatives from both the Department of Justice and the Department of Health and Human Services.

"Great," I muttered to myself. I didn't know what side the Feds were on, but it was safe to say that it wouldn't be ours. The Feds claimed they were at the meeting just to watch and monitor what was happening, because they had an interest in this case. I'd heard a rumor that the DOJ was going to file a claim against Purdue and thus become one of its many creditors. Their presence in the conference room seemed to confirm that rumor. If the federal government wanted to become a creditor, it also implied that they would expect a check from Purdue, too. That was another party who wouldn't support the ERF, and another cop for Purdue to pay off.

Before the meeting, Arik had said to me, "Whatever you do, don't lose your cool. I'm going to do the talking in the beginning, and I'll talk as much as you want."

Ken Eckstein, the lawyer for the consenting states, began the meeting with a long soliloquy about how important what we were doing was. He said we should come to some agreement. He portrayed the states as the ones who were *really* carrying the burden of the overdose crisis; he described them as super-informed and competent. I gritted my teeth and stared down at my lap, trying to keep my temper from flaring. I couldn't *believe* this horseshit.

Then Arik began laying out our vision. Or at least, he started to. He got about eight minutes in, and I couldn't help myself. I tugged on his arm and said, "I'll do this."

I went into my pitch about why we set up the structure the way we did, why recovery organizations need money, why they can do so much with it, why the ERF needed oversight, and why the states had proved they couldn't be trusted to spend the money in a timely manner. As I cited statistics from the Department of Health and Human Services about how housing, recovery supports, peer counseling, and harm reduction have all been found to have positive outcomes on people's lives, one of their representatives interrupted to say, "I appreciate your references to HHS data and the United States surgeon general's report, but we don't share your opinion on any of this."

I was shocked. They were disagreeing . . . with themselves? That didn't make sense. Still, I kept pushing, unwilling to give it up.

"Everything that we've spelled out here is according to what your division in the federal government says is a best practice to give people a good recovery outcome," I said.

In the pause that followed, John Guard started his little shuck-and-jive routine again. He said, "The states are best equipped to spend the money. We have the infrastructure."

This fucking guy. I couldn't help myself. In spite of Arik's advice, I argued, raising my voice and shooting down every point he made. My cool? Nonexistent. I looked Guard straight in his eyes, but he avoided mine. He intentionally looked away, staring at his phone.

"I'd appreciate it if you'd look at me when I'm talking," I growled.

He wouldn't. Not even once. We went back and forth a few times. Finally, Guard turned to the Purdue team and whined, "Look, we're not getting anywhere. This is how we feel. We are the sovereign states. We've been harmed."

He picked up the three-ring binder in front of him and tossed it down the center of the massive square table, as if to say, *I give up.*

Before I could tell him to kick rocks, Sheila Birnbaum interjected, "We're going to take a break."

We were then split into groups, like kindergarten students. My group stayed in the conference room while the states and municipalities decamped to the hallway. The Department of Justice hung out in the kitchen by the buffet. Purdue played messenger, running little pieces of paper back and forth between us and the states with different proposals. We threw out some offers, and they were all rejected out of hand. I've been in a lot of rooms, and this was the craziest thing I'd ever seen in my life. Grown adults, passing notes— and not coming to an agreement.

Finally, I told one of the Purdue lawyers to convey this to the states: "Okay, we'll trust you. We'll go with your plan as it's written. But trust goes both ways, so we're going to ask for an equal makeup of your board, fifty-fifty. That means we're going to be able to call you on your shit if you don't spend the money the right way."

Again, the states came back with a no: no equal representation, no oversight, and no transparency. I was running out of things to concede. It's not a compromise if one side refuses to negotiate or even make an offer. They were sticking to their position, and I was getting desperate. I wondered, *Why do we even need the states to make a deal? They aren't supposed to be calling the shots.* All we needed to set up the ERF was Purdue and the committee, but it had somehow turned into a free-for-all, with the state and federal governments' lawyers sticking their hands in the pot.

I asked Sheila Birnbaum, "What the fuck are we doing running papers? This is insanity. Congress isn't even this nuts. Just make a decision here that we're going to propose this ERF as is to the court. Fuck the states."

"You can't do that," she said, horrified, as though I had proposed lighting John Guard on fire. (I admit, it crossed my mind.)

"What do you mean, I can't do that?"

"That would be a nightmare."

A nightmare for *them*—because Purdue would lose their buddy-buddy buy-off deal with the states along with control over the money. They were afraid. And when it came down to it, the states didn't need an ERF. The government didn't need it either. *We* did—victims did. It was life-and-death for us. I was fighting for a lifeline against these groups that were supposedly representing the *people's* interests. I was asking them to choose us, but these powerful lawyers had already decided that inaction would be just fine.

I flew back to Las Vegas with a lump in my stomach. I couldn't believe that all that effort had come to such a disheartening stalemate. When I got home, Sean was at the gym. I dropped my duffel bag and flopped on the bed next to Dollar, who let me scratch his ears.

"It's not fair, buddy."

He rolled his eyes, as if to say, *I agree.*

The next day, I checked in with Anne and the other lawyers, to see what they thought of the conference. Did we still have hope? Was there any point in persisting? But I couldn't get ahold of Anne—she was sick, a sudden fever and vicious cough that came on overnight. She was laid up in bed, taking Tylenol and trying to get some sleep. I shot her a text wishing her a quick recovery and turned back to the news. The flu from Wuhan was worse than they'd expected, the anchor said. We had confirmed cases of it in Seattle and New York City, popping up in the major international travel hubs on both coasts. It was called COVID-19 and could be passed through the air or by contact. *Oh, fuck,* I thought, running through the many places I'd been through within the last forty-eight hours. The airport. The subway. The hotel. The law office, where I'd shaken Sheila Birnbaum's hand—her *dirty* hand, no doubt. If Anne was sick, maybe I was, too. I'd been sitting right next to her, with our heads together, breathing in each other's face while we talked through our next move. I remembered the table of food, with open containers of cream cheese, jam, and fruit, which the lawyers had pawed through without a second thought.

The restaurant. The bathroom. The cab. I watched as the news anchor described the flu and showed a chart with a red line climbing higher and higher. It reminded me of the overdose curve chart, steep and deadly.

"This can't be good," I muttered.

It wasn't. Within weeks, most of America was under stay-at-home orders, and everything was being done over the phone and over video conference. Our bedroom became a command center, with a webcam, my computer setup, and a chair I could sit in for twelve hours straight. At the beginning, I assumed it was going to be temporary. Like everyone else, I assumed that we'd have six weeks of lockdown, it would be kind of a drag, and then everything would go back to normal. At least I was home, spending more time with Sean—though I was worried about my mom's health, since she was a cancer survivor and more fragile than most. As one state after another mandated masks and shut down nonessential businesses, my near-constant meetings for the bankruptcy migrated online. Everything we'd done in person was now conducted via Zoom.

The ERF's final step was a chambers conference on March 30, 2020: a private meeting between the judge and the lawyers. Normally, these occur in the judge's chambers, with his robe off, in normal clothes. But by now, those in-person conferences were via telephone. (I'm still not sure if Drain knows how to use Zoom.) Purdue asked the judge for an off-the-record phone conference to lay everything out. All thirty-six of the lawyers called in—no doubt with their little meters running, tallying up billable hours.

This was one of those rare moments where no one knew what was going to happen. We half expected the judge to lose his shit, completely irate at all of us. Judges hate it when parties can't compromise. He could have ordered us into mediation—that is, *more* mediation, since we were already in mediation with regard to the final settlement. He had the power to tell us who he thought should get the money. Technically, he could have made a final decision about the ERF at this meeting. This wasn't likely—but then again, judges can basically do whatever they want. What were we going to do, appeal his decision?

We knew that Purdue was under serious pressure from the states and the Department of Justice. Purdue planned on just telling Judge Drain that the committee and the states were at an impasse, then ask him what they should do. Those three parties had obviously agreed not to argue the substances of the ERF, with the assumption that the judge didn't want to hear the nitty-gritty of our ongoing fight. The important thing was to let him know that we were at a standstill and take his temperature on how to proceed.

"We're very sorry to be on the line today," said Purdue's attorney, Marshall Huebner. He droned on for close to ten minutes about all the hard work everyone had been doing, all the progress that had been made, how much every single person on the call (all thirty-six of them!) passionately shared the view that it was high time to launch a humanitarian initiative, blah blah blah. Lawyers never say in twenty words what they could say in three thousand; that's how they make their money. Finally, Huebner said that the negotiations were a failure—but not because of Purdue. He admitted that the ERF discussions had broken down and that the parties couldn't get to an agreed resolution on the issues that still remained. The delays themselves defeated the entire purpose of the ERF, which was supposed to get money out quickly. Huebner suggested that maybe it was best to add the ERF to the already-imposing dirt pile of issues being dealt with in mediation.

I felt my stomach sink as I heard the judge agree to sweep the ERF in with the other problems of the bankruptcy. Onto the trash heap, where it could be forgotten, gathering dust. This was it: the ERF was dead. They killed it. I listened, in shock, as the individual lawyers murmured their approval. I could almost sense their relief. The money was going exactly where they wanted it to—away from the people who needed it most. We wanted the ERF to focus on services that had materially been underfunded. They wanted those millions to line the states' pockets—or their own.

I struggled to breathe and keep my composure. David had lost because Goliath had better lawyers, more money, and sovereign powers behind him. The lawyers weren't going to reach an agreement that was favorable to the victims because they despised us and despised this project. No matter what was said in front of the judge, I knew the truth: they killed the ERF because they didn't want to share what they considered *their* cut of Purdue with "addicts" like me. All those months spent researching, planning, talking, arguing, compromising, cajoling—all those months working on the ERF—were meaningless to these people. We never had a shot at changing their minds, but they had drawn it out anyway, wasting time and driving up their invoices.

As the realization of what we'd lost dawned on me, Huebner was still talking. He droned, "This was really designed to be, in an ideal world, frankly, easy. It was a way to get a lot of money out as soon as we could to save lives, money that was not otherwise needed at any time in the near future."

Instead, he said, the fund was now more "grist for the mill." I felt as if I were at a funeral. The fund was cold. We'd lost it, lost our chance to do something meaningful. Now, the lawyers' words rang hollow. I leaned back in my chair, trying to stay composed as my heart squeezed in my chest. I understood that I could no longer trust anyone else at the bargaining table.

One after another, the attorneys spoke, congratulating themselves for their "work" on the ERF negotiations. They claimed the "extraordinary" amount of effort and time spent on the idea was a major accomplishment—for *them*. They made it seem as if the ERF had been the states' idea all along. I was numb. This time, instead of speaking up, I just let it happen. I felt a wave of grief pass over me as I watched my hopes for the ERF sink, finally vanishing completely.

Let it go, I willed myself. *Just accept that this was never going to be what you hoped.*

When it was his turn to respond to Huebner, Arik pointed out that many states had told us that a $200 million ERF spread over fifty states would not be meaningful. He reminded the group that the states had hundreds of millions of dollars of unspent federal grants for opioid response. He said that the creditors committee would rather have no ERF than the half-baked, ineffective fund the states were proposing. In truth, he said, we would rather let it die— even though we had proposed the fund and even though we had wanted it, fought for it, and made it a rallying cry. The ERF money must go to community-based services and stay out of government coffers, or else states were just using it as a prepayment on their eventual claim distribution. And since none of the other parties seemed to be interested in doing the right thing, we saw no point in belaboring the issue.

Drain muttered his assent. With my line muted, I sighed. I was glad no one could hear me. I was certainly glad we'd done this without cameras.

"I think it goes without saying that there is in fact a crisis that needs dealing with promptly," the judge said. "And my great hope was that that could be achieved. I'm not so sure at this point. There is more disagreement than I had hoped before this call started."

He urged all sides to compromise, to work it out, but not to spend too much money—in other words, not to spend any more expensive lawyer time. But he basically said we could figure out the ERF sometime *later*. If we wanted to keep fighting, we could— but those discussions would go on indefinitely and couldn't be restarted until several months from now.

It was judicial procrastination. The ERF was taken off the immediate agenda. It ceased to be a topic in hearings and in creditor committee calls. Nor did it figure much into mediation. I knew this for a fact: the groups who already held the power weren't willing to give up a dime for victims. When we suggested plugging a hole in the weak, underdeveloped infrastructure states have to respond to the crisis, they dismissed our efforts and killed the ERF to retain their control. The ERF would have been one of the largest investments in recovery community organizations, peer family supports, and harm reduction in the history of the United States. We wanted to trim the fat and take a chain saw to the middleman, but the middleman wouldn't permit that to happen. It wasn't a win-win for states—attorneys general wouldn't even get a look-good, feel-good political win out of it—so they blocked it. I was beginning to wonder if this

whole bankruptcy wasn't going to end up the same way, reinforcing the same punitive cycles of state violence and neglect on sick
people and their families while leaders smiled for the camera
and pretended to care.

The real kicker was that, for the duration of the case, Purdue's
cash reserves were open to pretty much anyone *but* victims. That
money all went to Madison Avenue. The bankruptcy was good for
business: whether lawyers worked for the states, Purdue, or a private interest, *they* were all getting paid on time, in full, and immediately. The victims, harm reductionists, peer support services,
family counselors, recovery community organizations, recovery
housing—the list goes on and on—they weren't the priority. Lawyers were.

The death of the ERF was a real blow to the movement, people
in need, and me personally. The loss put a deep, painful crack in
the hope I'd used to protect myself during the case. In spite of
everything, I wanted to believe that justice would be done, that the
meek would inherit the earth, that the last would be first. I suited
up every day, ready to get bludgeoned by these oh-so-reasonable
lawyers. I was willing to do that because I cared and because I had
faith that goodness could still win the day. In the case of the ERF, I
was wrong—and it broke my heart. Throughout this legal chaos, the
personal injury victims—actual *people*—came in last. It seemed that
everybody else put themselves at the top of the list and kept those
most harmed at the bottom. The ERF showed me how deep the division is between what the government is supposed to do—advocate
for people—and what it actually does. Our voices were not heard. I
started out with such high hopes. I thought they'd listen to us. Kara,
Cheryl, and I all had thought we were going to go in there and make
a difference. Now, it felt that our chance to do that was gone.

Why am I doing this? I asked myself after the final ERF meeting. *Why am I putting myself through the pain of losing, over and over?*

An earlier version of myself would have run straight out of that chambers conference, gotten high, and spent a few months (or even years) licking my wounds. I knew that wasn't an option this time around. I had to stay present, or we risked losing even more ground. When I reached out to her, Kara told me that she felt the same. In a way, showing up—even if it was to lose—was enough.

She said, "That's my long-term self-care and that's how I'm gonna have peace, by trying to help save other people's lives. When this litigation is done, thousands and thousands of people will be working in the field, trying to do the work that the money couldn't. We will continue to do the best we can. My recovery from addiction, when so many people are dying, is a miracle. I'm still here and I'm alive, and I have to do something meaningful with that. The work is the work. With my son, I want to be the best mother I can and that means staying clean and sober."

She was right. No matter how this shook out, I would keep showing up. If my voice wasn't heard, it wasn't because I didn't scream loud enough. We gave it our all. We did all we could. Dr. Amos Wilson said, "If you want to understand any problem in America, you need to focus on who profits from that problem, not who suffers from the problem." This experience taught me that *profit* didn't just mean money—it meant power, too.

8

LAWYERS, MEDS, AND MONEY

The ERF negotiations had withered away and were starting to rot. I was feeling pretty bitter about the whole fucking thing. As a full-time organizer, running a nonprofit, I was already stretched thin. My days were packed; it felt as if my volunteer work on this committee was taking up more hours than the sixty-plus I already logged weekly in my day job. It was a thankless, unpaid position—to put it simply, it was *exhausting* at every level.

I couldn't help but also notice that the same lawyers who talked as if our $200 million relief fund were some absurd extravagance were raking in millions of dollars every week, and taking their payments straight out of Purdue's cash reserves. That's money that should have gone to victims and abatement! In the first nine months of the case, more money was taken out of the estate to pay attorneys than the entire ERF would have cost. These lawyer fees were automatically approved, as easily as you set your credit card bill to autopay. Lawyers clicked the Pay Me button and got a check. Even the good lawyers, the guys on our side who spent hours advocating for victims, were getting paid. (Like, *paid* paid.)

Some law firms discounted their bills 20 percent—presumably a nod in the direction of "doing the right thing." Still, the invoices were sky-high. It wasn't lost on me that a family whose only child was killed by an OxyContin overdose would get less in the settlement than a corporate lawyer could make in a week on the Purdue case—regardless of which side the lawyer was working for.

At the beginning, I knew next to nothing about bankruptcy law and had no idea what lawyers billed. Legalese wasn't my first, second, or third language. I stumbled, trying to catch up. In addition to all the terms and loopholes that were bandied around in each meeting, the sheer number of lawyers working on the case was staggering. Purdue had a minimum of seven law firms working for them. Each firm could easily have sixty lawyers or more working on the case, plus another thirty or so assistants, clerks, and support staff. In addition, Purdue had *another* five firms doing consultant work. Those twelve firms alone billed the estate for more than $215 million in the first eighteen months of the case.

The lawyers who convened to dismantle Purdue and hack its bleeding corpse into settlements were truly terrifying. You did not want to be on the business end of these people: they knew their craft and were the best of the best. Their résumés alone would make anyone break into a sweat. For example, Purdue's lead bankruptcy attorney was Marshall Huebner of Davis Polk. He was the firm's "global head of restructuring" and, according to their website, was twice named Dealmaker of the Year by *The American Lawyer* magazine. So you know what *he* was there for. He once called himself and his team the "oncologists of capitalism." He described them as cancer doctors, slicing up corporate America with a sterile scalpel. That's how Huebner sees his job: go into a company, carve out the cancer, and let the company go on with the rest of its life. To guys such as this, the law was sophisticated butchery, and they were experts at it. A little blood on the floor didn't bother them at all. Huebner had overseen such bankruptcies as Ford and Delta Air—solid American companies that did in fact need restructuring. Their survival meant that jobs were saved and customers were well served. This bankruptcy was entirely different. Purdue was unreformable and had killed hundreds of thousands of people. This time, the company *was* the cancer.

Huebner's expertise came with a price tag. He billed Purdue $1,645 an hour for his services, an astonishing number that added up quickly. In the first three full months of 2020, Huebner made $973,424.50 from a drug company that was about to go down the tubes. I'm sure Huebner believes he's worth every penny. But I knew from being on these interminable phone calls with him that he was also incapable of opening his mouth without delivering a fifteen-minute monologue. He was paid by the minute, practically a dollar a word. At these rates, it was hard not to think Huebner and the others could have used their time a little more efficiently. They never said yes or no. It was always a speech—and in the meantime, the meter was running.

Purdue's platoon of attorneys included that cute little grandmother Sheila Birnbaum, of Dechert. I'd met her in New York. Her sweet-as-pie demeanor belied her intimidating powers. Now in her seventies, she was a powerhouse lawyer once known as the Queen of Toxic Torts. Birnbaum got her legendary status by defending corporations in mass tort cases, "everything from salmonella contamination to toxic spills to alleged injuries from cell phones," according to a profile in *NYU Law Magazine*. Birnbaum had been practicing law for more than half a century. Back in 2001, she was named by *Forbes* as one of the highest-paid corporate attorneys in the country. Two decades and several pay raises later, she was billing Purdue a staggering $1,350 an hour.

One hour of her time was worth what the average person pays to rent an apartment for a month. In a regular forty-hour work week, Birnbaum made $54,000—the cost of a year at Harvard.

Another prominent lawyer was Joe Rice, who represented municipalities and counties. (He's the guy who joked about peeking under Sheila Birnbaum's kimono. Real fucking classy.) According to *The Island Packet* newspaper, Rice is "one of the most successful trial lawyers ever," who represented plaintiffs in such landmark lawsuits as tobacco, asbestos, and the 9/11 litigation against al-Qaeda financiers. When you google Joe Rice's name, one of the first things the search engine suggests is *Joe Rice yacht*. That's because Joe Rice owns the largest yacht in Harbour Town, South Carolina. The 130-foot-long vessel, called a superyacht because of its size, is named *Rice Quarters*. It sleeps ten in five staterooms and can accommodate a party of fifty. You don't get a boat like that by taking a vow of poverty and devoting your life to serving others. You get it by jacking up your price and absolutely killing your opponents in court. During the COVID-19 crisis, when the government released billions to save small businesses through low-interest PPP loans, Joe Rice's firm applied for $10.35 million. Seriously? I doubt they were hurting for cash. The same year that so many family businesses closed their doors permanently and millions of Americans were out of work, Motley Rice was attempting to line its own pockets even more. In October 2019, the firm announced a $260 million settlement against opioid manufacturers Teva, Cardinal Health, AmerisourceBergen, and McKesson. In November 2020, it helped negotiate a forthcoming settlement of $26 billion from Johnson & Johnson and other pharmaceutical companies. I guess those multimillion-dollar contingency fees just weren't enough for Joe Rice.

In addition to the Davis Polk and Dechert firms, Purdue also hired Jones Day, the law firm that had previously represented such stand-up characters as the R. J. Reynolds Tobacco Company and the bin Laden family. Jones Day had even worked for former president Donald J. Trump and the Republican Party in more than twenty lawsuits, including legal challenges in the 2020 election. (Some Jones Day lawyers worried those challenges would undermine the public's faith in fair elections, but, hey—a billable hour is a billable hour. Whatever their worries, they still said yes to the client.)

There were other law firms, each one more intimidating than the other, and just as expensive. Purdue hired King & Spalding, Skadden, Arnold & Porter, and WilmerHale. Combined, they were billing the estate millions of dollars a month. That's to say nothing of the financial advisers, investment bankers, and consultants the company kept on retainer. To me, their presence was redundant. What was the point? Every time I saw a lawyer's invoice, I remembered that the money being wasted on lawyers and consultants belonged to a company that had all but agreed it wasn't going to exist anymore, at least in its current form. Purdue had already agreed to give itself away. All that was left to figure out was who got which pieces of its carcass. Yet, for some reason, we needed literally *hundreds* of lawyers and consultants to figure that out. Call me cynical, but it seemed like a fucking free-for-all. Who decided we needed so many lawyers? The lawyers. And what are lawyers great at? Justifying unjustifiable reasoning.

Purdue wasn't the only party with a legal bill that would make even Jeff Bezos wince. We—the creditors committee—had our own army of lawyers and consultants on retainer. They billed the estate for a ridiculous amount of money. I wasn't happy about it, but it was out of my control. Lawyers were like ants. If you had one, you had a *ton*. The entire restructuring division of Akin Gump—Arik's firm, one of the largest in the country—was on the case. Much of their effort went into the discovery process, which involved delving into *millions* of pages of Purdue's documents. We were Akin Gump's biggest client. They were literally getting paid to read.

Now, I like Arik. He's a great lawyer, with a strong moral compass, an all-too-rare quality for an attorney. He's smart, intuitive, and creative. He has a heart. But make no mistake: Arik was making a fortune on this case, too. He billed Purdue $1,425 an hour, even more than Sheila Birnbaum. In the month of November, he worked 164.9 hours on the case, and made $234,982.50. And that wasn't all. Our team had three other law firms, an investment bank, a financial consultant, and another firm providing legal services. In total, they billed Purdue $112 million during the first eighteen months.

Then there were the twenty-three consenting states, who had wanted to cut a deal with Purdue and the Sackler family prior to bankruptcy. They asked, early on, for their attorneys' fees (and two consulting groups) to be paid for by the estate. Hardly anyone objected, which seemed weird to me. Even the dissenting states were fine with the other group of states getting paid by Purdue, arguing in a motion that it would "enhance public confidence in the fairness and propriety of any outcome." The states were saying that they didn't mind spending a huge chunk of Purdue's money on lawyers—but an emergency relief fund would be going too far. What family, trying to cope with the grief and extreme expense of a loss, would say, "Yeah, feel free to give our share to the lawyer who makes more in a week than we do in a year. I'm sure they need it more than we do." Although I understood that Purdue wanted to dot their i's and cross their t's, it didn't make sense to say this massive expenditure was for the public's benefit. It wasn't *fair* and it wasn't appropriate. However, when lawyers make the rules, lawyers come out ahead. And that's exactly what happened.

The only group to object to the motion was the personal injury ad hoc committee, led by their attorney, Ed Neiger, who was himself working on contingency. In the motion they filed in November 2019, Neiger argued that it was crazy to start doling out money to lawyers before victims of the overdose crisis had seen a dime. Neiger noted that "little progress" had been made on the $200 million emergency relief fund the parties wouldn't agree to but couldn't stop paying their lawyers to argue about.

Drain approved of Neiger's point, but conditioned the lawyers' pay-on-demand arrangement on all parties making a good-faith effort at an ERF. That was another thing added to the pile of things that were conditioned on the ERF, along with the supposedly temporary stay for Purdue and the Sackler family. When the ERF talks collapsed, none of these things were rescinded. We continued on as though nothing had happened. I guess, to the people for whom the ERF was just a paper trail that sidetracked from the main case, that's all it was. "Good faith" was debatable, but who was going to debate it?

So, with Drain's implied blessing, the lawyers kept on billing Purdue. Among them was Ken Eckstein of Kramer Levin, who billed $1,350 an hour, and David Molton of Brown Rudnick, who billed $1,340 an hour. The consenting states had four law firms and two consultancy groups, which would together bill the estate $34 million through March 2021.

The other lawyers in the case—and they were legion—weren't billing the estate. They were billing other parties. In personal injury cases or other types of civil cases, plaintiff's lawyers usually charge one-third of the settlement. In a case of this scope, that meant hundreds of millions in legal fees. The nonconsenting states had lawyers, the Sackler family had lawyers, and of course the victims had lawyers; a motley crew, each representing different parties. There was my lawyer, Anne Andrews. There was Ed Neiger, who represented personal injury victims. (A little-known fact about Ed is that he is a die-hard Donald Trump supporter. He gave the maximum $2,800 to Trump's reelection campaign and another $10,000 to a pro-Trump super PAC. Neiger was even at Trump's New Jersey golf course for that now-infamous fundraiser that took place hours before the former president announced he had tested positive for COVID-19. Neiger escaped the event uninfected.)

These guys all liked to talk about fighting for the little guy, and maybe they were. But plenty of times, I was reminded that they had their eyes on the prize, too. After the ERF was tanked, the likelihood that victims would get a meaningful settlement shrank as well. A year or more after the final ruling, victims might get a small check. Every little payout meant one-third of that already-tiny check would go right back to the lawyers. Some of these lawyers were do-gooders, but they were *all* making bank. They stood to collect tens of millions off this case, whether they were on the right side of history or not. In the first eighteen months of the case, from the start to the debtors' filing their plan of reorganization, lawyers and consultants billed the estate $418 million. This is not including the fees from state and plaintiff lawyers. It's safe to say that lawyers for all parties will be paid well over a billion dollars combined when it's done and dusted.

Since Purdue's on-paper assets weren't the only things we were fighting over, the two sides of the Sackler family each had their own lawyers, too. Gregory Joseph of Joseph Hage Aaronson was the forever-perturbed attorney for Side B of the family, and Maura Monaghan of Debevoise & Plimpton represented Side A. Monaghan's website obscured her connection to the Sacklers and stated that her experience included representing "certain former directors and shareholders of Purdue Pharma, Inc." (Embarrassed about your clients, Maura?) Monaghan and Joseph were perhaps the only two lawyers in the whole clusterfuck who *weren't* taking money from the Purdue kitty. Their bills went straight to the Sackler family. I wondered how they slept at night, then realized that a king-size mattress full of blood money was probably pretty comfy, for them. They were sleeping *just fine.*

For most of the parties and people involved, this thing was pure business. That was painfully obvious with the legal team "representing" the NAS babies' group. The mismatch between these lawyers and the cause they claimed to represent was especially bad (and blatantly obvious). Kara, who sat with me as a representative on the UCC, was absolutely getting screwed by her own legal team.

Here's the short version of Kara's story. (The CliffsNotes, if you will.)

Kara Trainor grew up in the 1980s, in the suburbs of Michigan. She was a middle-class child of divorced parents; her biological dad was a professional hockey player, and her stepfather was a lawyer. She grew up traveling all around the country as a competitive baton twirler. In high school, she was a cheerleader and on the debate team. All-American, high achieving, good grades, going places. And blond, too! She was twenty when she found out that she was pregnant. Shortly after the birth of her first son, she began having back pain that was so severe that she went to the emergency room. A doctor prescribed her Vicodin.

Yeah. You know where this is going.

When Kara went to see her personal physician, she was told the same bullshit as so many other pain patients at the time: "Did you know there's a new pain medication that you only have to take twice a day, as opposed to six or seven pills?" What kind of sales pitch this doctor had from Purdue is anybody's guess. I'm willing to bet that Kara signed her intake sheet with a pen that had a pharmaceutical brand name on it and sat in a waiting room with posters for opioids on the walls, happy people running through fields of flowers, not a side effect in sight. She may have taken the pills the doctor gave her, but like so many people, she took them without knowing anything about what she was getting into. She was lied to.

As a young mom, Kara didn't have a lot of downtime to rest. (If you've ever chased a toddler around while you tried to work on a college degree, you know what that's like.) She couldn't catch a break. Kara took OxyContin for over a year. Her prescription doubled from 20 mg to 40 mg. Like many other patients, two doses a day wasn't enough, so her doctor instructed her to take three. (For the record, that's enough to knock a full-grown adult out for eight hours. It's not exactly aspirin, but that didn't seem to slow the prescribers down.) Kara's tolerance kept climbing. A year later, she was switched to morphine, and when she was cut off, she switched to heroin, which she bought on the street. When she got pregnant for a second time, she was put on methadone, which she would stay on for the next fourteen years.

When someone uses opioids during a pregnancy, their blood also carries those drugs into the cells of the developing fetus. As a result, the baby can develop neonatal abstinence syndrome (NAS). That means that the baby is born physically dependent on drugs and will likely go through withdrawal, just like an adult. The symptoms are similar, last for about the same amount of time, and are *not* fun. NAS is not caused by the standard medical interventions that some women elect to use during birth for pain management, such as morphine or an epidural. It's caused by regular, repeated exposure to drugs—such as the ones Kara took.

As the mom of an NAS baby, Kara wasn't the exception, or even unusual. I think she had unfair consequences for a behavior that is quite common. Opioid use is a secret for many parents. Nobody wants to cop to it. But the numbers don't lie: according to the CDC, an estimated 14–22 percent of women filled an opioid prescription during pregnancy. The Healthcare Cost and Utilization Project (HCUP) estimated that in 2016, seven newborns were diagnosed with NAS for every thousand newborn hospital stays. That is approximately one baby diagnosed with NAS every nineteen minutes in the United States, or nearly eighty newborns diagnosed every day, adding up to about 29,200 NAS babies per year. Does that make it okay? No. But it means that we have a huge population of people who are afraid to ask for help because they fear losing their children. People who don't speak up, who can't self-advocate, are powerless to defend themselves.

Kara's experience is one that many moms share: one-third of women who are in their prime reproductive years are prescribed opioids. That doesn't mean that these women all have substance use disorder *or* that they all get pregnant, but it does mean that many babies are exposed before anyone is aware of it. Opioid misuse can harm babies and moms; misusing opioids during a pregnancy increases the likelihood of prenatal obstetric complications by 600 percent, according to the CDC. Those complications include miscarriage, low birth weight, and an increased risk of sudden infant death syndrome (SIDS). Also, some women who misuse opioids tend to have poor prenatal nutrition and decreased general health, which adds to the physical stress of a pregnancy. They're also more likely to use other substances and may be exposed to blood-borne diseases such as hepatitis and HIV, which can have an adverse effect on a developing fetus.

Honestly? I don't think mothers are to blame here. You can be a good mom and still struggle with addiction. You can be a good mom and have pregnancy complications because you weren't informed about the risks of a medication. A lot of moms *do* use opioids, prescribed and unprescribed, and often before they even know they're pregnant. But opioid use is so severely stigmatized that we don't talk about it. In fact, dozens of states have laws criminalizing the use of drugs by pregnant women. So if you use during your pregnancy, you are actually a criminal. With those consequences, who would want to admit to less than perfect behavior? In November 2019, a woman who gave birth to a stillborn baby and admitted to using methamphetamine while she was pregnant was charged with murder—murder!—in California, of all places. Laws such as this can also be used against women who are taking methadone or suboxone as prescribed by their doctor, thus having the perverse effect of punishing women who are trying to stop using.

As I said, let's be real: not all pregnancies are planned or even anticipated. The CDC notes that maternal opioid use disorder rates at delivery more than quadrupled from 1999 to 2014; according to 2019 self-reported data, about 7 percent of women reported using prescription opioid pain relievers during pregnancy. Of those, one in five reported misuse of prescription opioids, defined as getting them from a non-health-care source or using them for a reason other than to relieve pain. Many women don't realize they're pregnant until they miss a period and have a positive pregnancy test—which is usually six weeks after conception or later. Substance use is the secret nobody wants to admit to: *I drank during my pregnancy. I got high during my pregnancy. I shot up during my pregnancy. I smoked during my pregnancy.* How many babies are conceived on a romantic getaway in wine country or after a tequila-fueled party? How many mothers sneak a cigarette or a joint during their pregnancy? These moms don't face the same consequences as mothers who have issues with opioids, which are considered less risky than other substances. According to a white paper by the Jacobs Institute of Women's Health, "Compared to the relative effects of alcohol, cocaine, or benzodiazepine abuse during pregnancy, opioids do not disturb the development of the fetus or harm living cells."

Kara was lucky with her first two pregnancies. She chose to let another family adopt her second son at birth, knowing she couldn't handle two young children alone. After giving birth, Kara went to treatment, but it didn't cure her. She still struggled with her addiction. Who wouldn't after years of opioid use disorder?

Her second pregnancy was healthy and normal, symptom-free. Then, in 2008, she met the man she would later marry and got pregnant again. (She was still on methadone. Doctor's orders.)

With this third baby, Kara's ob-gyn told her that her baby might not experience any withdrawal symptoms at all, and if he did, they would be minor and temporary. Kara was hopeful, but this baby was different from his older brothers. Riley was born experiencing withdrawal symptoms; he was taken to the neonatal intensive care unit, where he stayed for six weeks. The pediatrician at the hospital overseeing Riley made an unusual decision and prescribed the newborn methadone. Riley would take the medication for nearly a year. (As I said: doctor's orders.)

Riley grew up with severe developmental disabilities, and at nine years old he was still wearing a diaper and drinking from a sippy cup. Kara was going to change him, feed him, and provide full care for the duration of his life. It was a lot to take on, and she blamed herself sometimes. Who was going to tell her that this wasn't her fault? She was a great mom, but that didn't make her feel less guilty for using opioids during her pregnancy.

By 2018, Kara had crossed the threshold into long-term recovery and was living a completely new life. Despite the difficulties of raising Riley, she was happy and fulfilled, had a good community and a solid relationship with her family. She was scrolling through Facebook and catching up with a few friends when she saw a sponsored ad that said, "Do you have a child who was born with neonatal abstinence syndrome?" (Or something to that effect). Kara clicked on it and filled out a questionnaire. She had no idea what it was for. But soon enough, she got a call from an attorney, Claris Smith, at Cooper Law. They talked for two hours. Months later, Smith called back and told Kara, "We're gonna take your case."

Kara was like, *What case?*

"We don't know yet what litigation you're going to be part of," the lawyer added, "but we're going to take you as a client."

Kara's stepfather tried to talk her out of it. It was, he said, a mass tort case. It might not get resolved for decades. But she thought it might do some good to get involved in a case against opioid manufacturers, to help publicize the damage they'd done to families such as hers. But she heard from Smith only sporadically. Then, in 2019, Smith told Kara about the Purdue bankruptcy; Smith's firm, Cooper Law, under the umbrella of the Opioid Justice Team (OJT), was planning on putting together a class of victims. The OJT planned to file a claim for a piece of Purdue, using the logic that substance use disorder is a disability, "a medical problem with legal consequences."

That sounded convincing, and it certainly squared with Kara's personal experience. Smith told Kara, "I'm thinking of you as a class representative." Weeks later, Kara was on a flight to New York along with five other women to meet with the US trustee. That's where I first met her.

Prior to the bankruptcy, the Opioid Justice Team filed thirteen suits in different states on behalf of NAS babies, hoping to get before the federal judge negotiating the MDL settlement for the various classes—babies, adults, states, hospitals—impacted by the overdose crisis. At first, NAS babies were sucked into other packaged claims, under the umbrella of other causes, using a formula-type settlement much like that used in the 1980s for the tobacco litigation. That wasn't good enough for these lawyers: they wanted to break children into a separate multidistrict litigation for personal injury assessment. They were hoping to start a fund specifically for babies (not their families) that would constantly be replenished and renewable. Their fund, which would be part of the national settlement worked out by Judge Polster, would pay for the children's education, medical care, life expenses, and other supports for the duration of their lives. It would also give them a leg up in a system that isn't easy to navigate and is slow to provide financial support for people with substance use disorder and other disabilities.

That sounds high-minded and altruistic, doesn't it? So did

Purdue's marketing campaigns. (Just a little colorful side note: According to its website, the Opioid Justice Team's chief strategist is Stuart H. Smith, an attorney who, in 2014, was charged with cyberstalking after sending a threatening email to a city councilwoman. Smith pled guilty. He received two years of probation.) The Opioid Justice Team was saying all the right things, but I would say that what they *actually* did was more than a little weird. Get this: The OJT tried to get standing during the multidistrict opioid litigation by pulling a bizarre stunt. They filed a motion asking the judge to require all "women of child-bearing age" to take a pregnancy test, and test negative, before being prescribed an opioid from a doctor. *Handmaid's Tale* much? Needless to say, the judge did not grant that motion and later declined to give the Opioid Justice Team's clients standing in the court. Children and babies would be part of their original groupings; there wouldn't be a separate babies-only fund.

That wasn't going to work for these hungry lawyers; they wanted a piece of Purdue, which meant they needed a seat at the table with everyone else. They were granted their request to form an ad hoc committee for NAS babies and got two seats on the UCC sympathetic to their cause: my friend Kara and Walter Lee Salmons, the grandparent of children affected by opioids.

The next thing she knew, Kara was given a new lawyer, Celeste Brustowicz—whom she had never met. Brustowicz had been a defense lawyer for thirty-three years. She had represented foster families or suits about how a child was being cared for; her firsthand experience with social services came from caring for her younger brother. She got involved in the OJT when a friend called her up and said, "Let's do something about the opioid crisis and how it is impacting families." Brustowicz started reading congressional hearings from 2000 to 2001 about the efforts people were making to address the epidemic in such places as Maine, Pennsylvania, Kentucky, and West Virginia. She noticed that the states all showed the same pattern: in her opinion, in each case, all of the state's resources were laser focused on *adult* addiction problems. Brustowicz said suing on behalf of NAS babies would create solutions for the *children* affected by opioid manufacturers as well as improve their outcomes. It was a huge opportunity: an unserved, voiceless population who were automatically sympathetic to the public.

In an interview from 2018, Brustowicz said, "A lot of foster children, it's hard enough to get them adopted. If you had a choice of two babies, one with NAS and one without, you'd probably choose the one without. We want to make caring for the NAS babies more sustainable for foster parents." The money would, therefore, be earmarked for children's caregivers, to make them more appealing to foster families. These families, some who already receive a financial incentive to care for a displaced child with medical needs, were so important to helping kids; they provided more than shelter. But for my money, the issue wasn't the foster care system or even the kids' needs: the problem was these lawyers who were exploiting them both.

Brustowicz's opinion on mothers who chose to give their children up for adoption seemed a little less rosy: "It was clear to me that we had to do something for the children affected by this epidemic. Nobody was speaking up for them, not the babies born to dependent moms and not the children abandoned by parents who are abusing substances."

Abandoned? Brustowicz seemed comfortable with the stereotype of the irresponsible "junkie" parents, leaving their child behind so they could chase a fix. (Who knew what she thought of Kara and her decision to let another family raise her second son?) Also, whenever someone outside the recovery community says "nobody" is speaking up for us, that's a huge red flag, because we *are* doing the work. It means that the person claiming to be a "voice for the voiceless" isn't connected with the people who are screaming at the top of their lungs.

So, let's discuss why I am not alone in believing that the OJT's fund was a bad idea. First, it assumed that babies were cared for by foster parents, not their biological families. The OJT wanted a database of babies that tracked their development, needs, and changes from birth to death. That is a huge barrier to parents who have children in need. Who wants to be required to put their name on a registry as a person who uses drugs, society's idea of a *bad parent*? You may as well roll up to day care with a tourniquet on your arm. Brustowicz seemed to see NAS babies as independent of their families—as if, if the state's care was inadequate, an NAS-related fund would provide the financial support that an absent, sick parent couldn't. However, plenty of NAS children were still with their families. I mean, would we have a database of parents who drank alcohol during their pregnancies and while they were raising their children? You'd never be able to list them all. Alcohol use is common and just as destructive, yet it's normalized to the point of being a nonissue. Singling out opioid users, pain patients, and other families affected by opioids only reinforces the stigma of substance use.

Another red flag: this fund seemed to be a cash cow for the self-assigned legal team. If the Opioid Justice Team had a list of every child born with NAS, they could claim *all* of them as victims (or clients) and potentially take one-third of each claim, in perpetuity. *Cha-ching.*

I told Arik that I couldn't understand why the Opioid Justice Team was so singularly focused on tracking. Databases, numbers—

they cared more about that than the human beings each figure represented.

"Well, you know why?" he said. "Because it makes a larger class for them." There would be other opioid lawsuits, other bankruptcies in the future. OJT could make that "class" as big as they wanted, since the number of victims was both unknown and difficult to quantify. Their fund's database could be a never-ending flow of little data entries, each one symbolizing a lifelong, one-third personal injury payment to the lawyers in charge. They were already trying to beef up their fund, making all sorts of wild claims. In one filing, the attorneys wrote, "Nationwide, it is reported that a baby is born diagnosed with NAS every 15 minutes, nearly 700 babies monthly." In a later filing, that became two thousand babies born every month with NAS. Where were these numbers coming from? They contradicted the CDC's findings. That was all I needed to know to be convinced that these people were haphazard, self-interested—and taking advantage of a silenced, marginalized group of moms and babies.

Kara began to get a sense that the Opioid Justice Team was disorganized and inexperienced and may have had an agenda of their own, and I was getting the same impression. They would do weird things. After months of noncommunication, they sent her a bouquet with a card that said, "Never give up! Remember that you beat Richard Sackler." What? The case wasn't even over, and victims hadn't won a thing. If anything, we'd been getting our asses whipped. Kara's lawyers seemed to think she was stupid. (She was anything but.) Those Safeway floral arrangements . . . ? *Yikes.* It was bizarre and unprofessional and creeped us both out.

I liked Kara. She worked her ass off and attended every conference call and hearing diligently. During the ERF negotiations, I was eager to hear from her. What did NAS mothers need? How could we make sure pregnant women got support? But her lawyers, and all the NAS lawyers, most of whom fell under the aegis of the Opioid Justice Team, didn't seem interested in that. They wanted one thing: a medical monitoring program, essentially a federal database that would track babies born with NAS. It grossed me out, to say the least. "Cleaning up" the wreckage of the crisis wasn't the same as implementing meaningful change that would help moms stay healthy and access recovery supports, which would lead to more healthy children. The fund they proposed didn't address systemic change, try to reform the foster care system, or support families who were coping with substance use disorder. I thought that was a horrible idea, and a dangerous one. A list such as that could be used to punish mothers or confiscate children from their families.

Kara agreed with me about the dangers of such a database, but the NAS lawyers wouldn't listen. She texted Brustowicz, who never responded.

"I am not okay with this," Kara said to another one of the lawyers.

He replied, "Well, it doesn't matter, because we're going ahead anyway."

Victims' voices didn't seem to matter to the Opioid Justice Team. To hear them tell it, even babies with no symptoms at birth might still be suffering from the long-term effects of their mothers' misuse. The team cited a paper by Dr. Kanwaljeet Anand, a professor of pediatrics at Stanford University. The professor wrote that these children's "brain development has been altered by repeated exposures to opioid drugs in the prenatal period."

Sounds bad, right? Except that the widely accepted medical opinion is that NAS is fleeting—not permanent. NAS is definitely not a *good* thing. However, it's not necessarily the life sentence that the OJT made it out to be—unlike a lifelong registry in a nationally available database. The facts Anand put forward are at best controversial. Most research has found NAS to last no more than a few weeks, and there's little evidence that it causes any long-term physical harm, even though there can be exceptions—such as Riley, who is also diagnosed with autism. Reading about NAS, I wondered why he was kept on methadone for so long or even given the medication in the first place. Most neonatologists say that the symptoms of NAS can be treated by the same things that mothers all over the country are instructed to do with any newborn, such as swaddling, breastfeeding, skin-to-skin contact, and placing the baby in a comfortable environment. You know, *mom stuff.*

Some OJT critics said what I was thinking. "This is a quintessential group of plaintiffs' attorneys looking for a big payday, seeing the potential deep pockets of pharmaceutical companies that will likely be forced by one or more courts to pay damages," said Daniel Abrahamson, consulting counsel for the National Advocates for Pregnant Women. "They use junk science to concoct a dramatic and seemingly plausible claim to get a toehold in the opioid litigation. Their goal was to have a seat at the table when settlement discussions happened, so they could be in the room when monies were being divvied up."

With such a huge settlement on the table, plenty of vultures showed up for dinner. Lawyers were supposed to represent people's best interests, but their massive paychecks made me cynical. If it was about justice, why weren't victims first? One look at the case's balance sheets told me all I needed to know. Who was getting paid out first and foremost? Lawyers. Financial consultants. They got the first slice of a rapidly shrinking pie and left the rest of us to fight over the scraps. I thought the whole point of this fucking disaster was to hold Purdue accountable for its role in the drug epidemic. But behind closed doors, it was a very different story from the "justice will be done" rhetoric that many seemed to eat up.

This was a far cry from justice. It was laissez-faire economics at its finest. The depressing thing is that the heart of this case was a true public health crisis. Yet, independent public health experts were hardly part of the process. At times, they were hired as consultants, but never to give any kind of independent analysis. They were called in only to argue for one side or another, like expert witnesses in a civil trial. Imagine attempting to solve a financial crisis with a bunch of doctors who knew nothing about stocks. Or a constitutional crisis with a team of economists, with their charts and algorithms. How did that make sense?

The lawyers thought they were the sole solution to Purdue's terrible crimes. In their minds, the overdose crisis was a problem that would be fixed only by lawyers, judges, and elitists. Yet, I knew reckless capitalism wasn't ever going to heal itself—or do right by the people it hurt. Justice was hardly on our side. When the law is already imperfect and errs in favor of the powerful, that means only one thing: we were really, truly fucked.

9

TOOTHLESS

For all its power and prestige, Purdue is rotten to its core. As soon as you scratch the surface, you can smell the bullshit right through the paper-thin layer of respectability. The closer I got to the company's inner workings, the worse it stank. In April 2020, the creditors committee and the nonconsenting states filed a motion to enter discovery. We requested millions of documents from Purdue and the Sackler family: internal emails, PowerPoint presentations, board minutes, financial statements, marketing materials—pretty much anything stored electronically. If they had it, we wanted to get our eyes on it. We ended up with a literal mountain of information to sift through. The entire restructuring division at Akin Gump spent almost eight months going through it all—I've been told it was forty people, just *reading*.

My committee suspected the Sackler family had fraudulently been taking money out of Purdue, funneling the company's profits into their own piggy banks. Hiding it in offshore accounts, maybe, or even stashing it with girlfriends? The family owned the company, so they were free to take money out of the cash register.

However, the rules change in a bankruptcy: fraudulent conveyance is when you transfer money out of a company to hide it, so you can avoid paying creditors. When the Sacklers said Purdue didn't have more money to pay victims, that set off alarm bells for me. Of course they had it: they're a massive global company, owned by billionaires. You're telling me they can't come up with a significant settlement? *Bullshit.* Fraudulent conveyance is generally treated as a civil matter, but in some cases the people who do it can be criminally charged. As the creditors committee wrote in a court filing, "It is unnecessary to prove that defrauding creditors was the sole motivation of the transferor; rather, a transfer is intentionally fraudulent if 'at least one of the [transferor's] motives was an impermissible one.'"

That meant the Sacklers were on the hook to prove they weren't hoarding Purdue's profits to avoid paying for the damage they caused. There could be no settlement with the Sackler family until we knew how much they had. But the nonconsenting states had an even more pressing secondary motive. It was bigger than the family's billions. Our discovery process and the criminal proof it might turn up was the closest we would ever come to putting the Sacklers on trial. This was the only time we could do a thorough investigation of what the family knew about their company's fraudulent and overzealous marketing of their opioid products. We would be creating a public record, so everyone would know what the family was so eager to hide, cover up, and keep behind closed doors. In discovery, we could shine a light on the Sacklers.

Truth and reconciliation weren't in the family's best interest at all, and although they opened up their files to discovery, they weren't happy about it. Why would they be? Telling the truth meant admitting how badly they'd acted and sharing incriminating documents, WhatsApp conversations, and other information. We expected them to withhold certain documents, but the sheer tonnage of evidence they tried to keep from us was staggering. They handed over plenty of information, sure. But they also claimed that 57,259 documents fell under attorney-client privilege and should be exempt from discovery.

Those documents included approximately three thousand communications with two key Purdue figures: Stuart Baker and Jonathan White. They were both trusted advisers who gave primarily business, rather than legal, advice.

Jonathan White was an important Purdue insider and onetime board member. Stuart Baker, on the other hand, was like the Tom Hagen of the Sackler family: their longtime attorney, adviser, and consigliere. Baker's counsel identified 257 different roles or positions Baker held at one time or another at Purdue or at entities owned by Purdue or the Sackler family, including general counsel and executive vice president of Purdue. Jonathan Sackler once called Baker the company's "de facto chairman." As the committee wrote in a court filing, "Based on the available record, it is at least possible that Mr. Baker was the single most important executive in the entire network of companies and trusts owned by or for the benefit of the Sacklers."

Bingo. I knew from experience that the closer I got to the truth, the harder the Sacklers would fight to suppress it. If they wanted to hide those communications with Baker and White, that meant it was ultrajuicy. Compromising. *Incriminating,* even. The Sacklers were money motivated, of course. What billionaire isn't? While they cared about their reputations, I don't believe they wanted to give a single penny to the victims of their greed. They would do anything to keep their ill-gotten cash out of the hands of people who deserved it—people such as Aileen Lovejoy.

On Sunday, May 12, 2013, Francis V. Baillargeon III called his mom to make plans for their Mother's Day dinner. Every year, he went out to eat with Aileen Lovejoy, his mom—a single mother, widowed after her husband's heart attack. Francis was Aileen's only son and only child. He and Aileen were devoted to each other. They chatted on the phone about where they'd meet up later and how Francis's two-year-old daughter, Faith, was doing. Aileen hung up looking forward to an evening with her boy.

Hours later, she got a crude message from the hospital morgue: come identify your son's body. Francis, they said, overdosed in a drug house in Worcester, Massachusetts; the doctor's disgust was apparent as he delivered the news. As though Francis were nothing. As if he were worthless.

"My son was not a statistic," Aileen said. "He was a good man with a substance problem."

The coroner's toxicology report showed that Francis was killed by opioids—a deadly addiction that started after he sought medical help following a violent attack. He'd been stabbed with such brutality that several ribs broke. He was lucky to be alive, but because the hospital staff suspected the attack was the result of a drug deal gone bad, they discharged Francis as quickly as possible.

His pain was excruciating. "Those ribs never did heal. He walked around feeling like he was so weak on that side, you could put a fist right through him," Aileen said. Still, he kept working. He worked in kitchens, started a landscaping business, and hauled scrap metal for recycling. He hurt. But he kept on going, knowing that he was responsible for his family. He thought of the future: sending Faith to college, setting her up to succeed.

At Francis's funeral, which his mother paid for from her own slender pockets, Aileen said Faith was confused. She didn't understand where Francis was. She tugged on Aileen's hand and asked, "Nana, why are you laughing?" Faith thought Aileen's heartbroken sobs were laughter.

Francis's family was devastated by opioids. The dreams they had for Faith's future evaporated the instant Francis took his last breath. What is the life of that little girl's daddy worth? How do you replace a father, a future, a family?

Francis and Aileen both had a claim against Purdue Pharma. They are two of millions of victims of the drug epidemic. One living, one passed away. One family member who gets to see Faith grow up, and one who will miss every school dance, every driving-permit practice, every after-school event, every field trip.

Getting the money her family was owed was beyond challenging. Six years after Francis's unexpected death, Aileen was contacted out of nowhere by a fast-talking lawyer who said they were representing claimants in the case against Purdue. This lawyer said there was money for victims and survivors and said Aileen needed to fill out some paperwork to get a payout. Although Aileen wasn't hopeful for a significant settlement, she did hope there might be a little money—for Faith.

As a retired HR specialist, Aileen was no stranger to complicated paperwork, but what the law office finally sent over was a headache and a half. Even with the help of a paralegal or lawyer-in-training over the phone, Aileen struggled with the claim forms, especially the section where she was asked to "prove" that Purdue was at fault. Prove it? Where was she going to find that kind of information? Francis was forty-one when he passed, an adult, and his medical records were protected by the Health Insurance Portability and Accountability Act. Aileen requested them, waited, then waited some more. The person she talked to on the phone at the law office told her, "If you don't have proof, you can't be part of it," and without those documents Aileen wasn't sure she could make a legitimate claim.

What she found in Francis's file was devastating. The hospital sent over his whole folder: ten years of wellness checks, doctors' appointments, flu shots, and mental health visits. Her son fit into a manila folder, and as she carefully leafed through the printed pages inside, she saw that he *knew* he had a problem. For ten years, he'd been trying to get treatment. In every checkup, there was a note: he was seeking help. He asked everyone. Those requests were well-documented, but never went anywhere. After a decade of pleading, Francis, all alone, lost his life to the illness he was fighting. The records proved it. He wanted something better. He wanted out. The helping hand he reached for refused to save his life. After his tragic death, he was also being denied what he was owed.

To be addicted in America is to be invisible. Nobody wants to see you or acknowledge your existence. We step over someone sleeping on the sidewalk, look past a coworker's shaky hands, and choose not to ask questions when a loved one fills yet another prescription. Doctors who write those scripts don't want to think about addiction. Even those of us who *do* have issues with substances don't want to think of ourselves as sick. Addiction is taboo, and the less it's mentioned, the more comfortable people are. That is, the more comfortable *some* people are: namely, the ones who benefit from not being challenged. That's a huge problem, compounded because, living in that system, in a culture that *doesn't* want to talk about addiction, the people who need help stop advocating for themselves. They stop saying, "I have a problem and I need help." Not everyone is as brave as Francis, who asked for treatment up to the end of his life. Nowhere was that more apparent in the bankruptcy than in the claims process.

Arguably, every person in America had a claim against Purdue. The far-reaching impact of their greed affected families, businesses, municipal and state spending, the economy, and almost every aspect of our nation. Their efforts poisoned everything, which meant that, in my opinion, everyone should file a claim. I expected a long list of names—not just individual people, but their family members, neighbors, friends, health-care providers— *everyone.* I envisioned a noticing campaign that turned out big numbers. Nobody liked Purdue, and I predicted that, once the word was out online, it would spread like wildfire.

Purdue allocated approximately $23.8 million to the noticing campaign and hired a company named Prime Clerk to handle it. Their job was to create marketing to find personal injury victims and get them to file claims against Purdue. This campaign would be the largest of its kind in history. Everywhere you looked, you were supposed to see an ad: "Harmed by OxyContin? You may be entitled to compensation." You know, the kind you hear all the time on the radio about tires, mattresses, medications, and other consumer products. I wanted those notices on every social media platform, radio station, billboard, bus bench, movie screen, and local newspaper. If we had an option to get a plane to skywrite it or throw handfuls of leaflets from the sky, I wanted that, too. I was determined to get people the money they deserved.

Based on what I saw in my committee meetings, I worried that bigger interests would devour Purdue's assets. Most bankruptcies aren't that complex. You add up all the creditors, give them all a piece of the pie, and call it a day. But Purdue was different because it had zero secured debt and an astronomical amount of unsecured debt. That is, its debt consisted of people, corporations, and governments who were suing Purdue or would have liked to sue Purdue. The people could easily be pushed out by larger, more organized interests—groups with lawyers on retainer, who were fully aware of the case and what was at stake financially, such as hospitals, insurance companies, cities, states, and tribal governments. *Their* claims amounted to gargantuan, absurd sums. The insurance companies filed claims for $62 billion. A thousand hospitals filed claims for $172 billion. Four hundred Native American tribes claimed they were collectively owed $191 billion. Cities and counties claimed $900 billion. The fifty states in the union said they were owed a total of $2 trillion. More than seven hundred school districts claimed they were owed $26 trillion (more than the gross domestic product of the United States in one year). No one was going to get anywhere near these surreal amounts. They'd be getting fractions of pennies on the dollar.

But what was left for people such as Aileen and Faith? The vast majority of people affected by the overdose crisis were not corporations or governments. They were people who'd gotten hooked on drugs like OxyContin, or people whose family members had died of overdoses.

"A lot of the victims don't know that they were victimized. They may think that they're addicts. They may think that they have a moral failing or a character failing," Ed Neiger told the Associated Press. "There were people in a boardroom that caused them to become addicted to opioids."

Those same people were on the verge of getting away with it *again*. The fight to get the withheld documents would drag on for months, well into 2021. In the meantime, our lawyers discovered damning evidence that the Sacklers *had* drained their company of any cash they could in anticipation of a tsunami of lawsuits. They knew they were guilty, they knew they'd get caught, and they were preparing to cover their asses.

In discovery, we learned that between 1997 and 2007, the Sacklers withdrew just over a billion dollars from Purdue. They never took out more than $219 million in a single year, and never more than 15 percent of Purdue's net sales. That all changed in 2007— the same year the company pleaded guilty to criminal charges and agreed to pay $634 million in fines. That year, the amount of cash transfers to Sackler family entities began to grow exponentially. In 2008, the Sacklers withdrew $1.3 billion from Purdue, roughly what had been taken out in the previous twelve years combined. In 2009, the Sacklers took out $1.7 billion. The next year, $1.6 billion. Between 2008 and 2012, the family took out a total of $7 billion. The Sacklers argued that the transfers could not have been motivated by the fear of lawsuits because, in the words of Side B attorney Gregory Joseph, no one would have believed Purdue could "face meaningful litigation until 2017."

But documents dredged up in discovery obliterated that argument. In November 2006, just as Purdue was finalizing its plea deal with the federal government, Jonathan Sackler wrote a memo to his brother Richard, worrying that the pharmaceutical industry had been "enshrined as a permanent whipping boy for politicians, regulators, and the bar." He noted that despite the settlement, "contingent liabilities continue to hover over the business." Days after the settlement was filed in 2007, Richard emailed a friend of his, complaining that people were equating the marketing of Oxy-Contin to "drug pushing."

"Frankly," he wrote, "I don't know what to do. I'm not confident that this is something that will blow over. My sense is that it may get a lot worse in the coming weeks."

A week later, David Sackler wrote, as part of an email exchange with Jonathan and Richard, that the family should borrow money to make investments and diversify its portfolio. He wrote, "What do you think is going on in these courtrooms right now? We're rich? For how long? Until which suits get through to the family?"

Jonathan wrote back, "We should talk when we're together, but you should rest assured that there is no basis to 'sue the family.'"

David responded, "Well I hope you're right, and under logical circumstances I'd agree with you, but we're living in America. This is the land of the free and the home of the blameless. We will be sued. Read the op-ed stuff in these local papers and ask yourself how long it will take these lawyers to figure out that we might settle with them if they can freeze our assets and threaten us."

The home of the blameless. Wow. At the end of the day, the Sacklers were concerned about only themselves and holding on to as much of their fortune as possible. And part of that was making it as difficult as possible for victims such as Aileen Lovejoy to access, claim, and collect what they were owed.

Before Prime Clerk was hired for the noticing campaign, Neiger and the other personal injury attorneys had been advertising to sign up victims since September 2019. Remember, plaintiff lawyers were entitled to a percentage (usually 30–40 percent) of every claim they got paid, so it was in each lawyer's interest to register as many individuals harmed as possible. Those firms rounded up more than sixty thousand claims through their own ads. Their individual media blitzes were expensive (around $7 million or $8 million, from what I heard), reflecting the lawyers' confidence in a bigger settlement that would make the campaigns cost-effective. I envisioned the Prime Clerk campaign as even better. The exposure you can buy for $23.8 million is incredible, on par with a major political campaign in an election year. The goal was for every American adult to receive the noticing message at least ten times. It seemed realistic with that budget.

Bigger was better for this noticing campaign. The judge wanted it big, my committee wanted it big, and Purdue wanted it big. It was in everyone's best interest to at least appear to make a good faith effort to reach people, and what better way to do that than to blow a few million on a company considered to be the gold standard for noticing campaigns? Prime Clerk was presented to us—shoved down our throats—as the *only* choice. "They do everyone," I was told, and how would I know any different?

"To me, the failure of the noticing campaign epitomized how every element of the case went against the victims' favor," said Sharon Murillo, who served on the ad hoc committee of personal injury victims. "When our ad hoc committee was walked through the analysis, I was struck by their advertising choices. All I could think was *something's not right*. Considering what the estate paid for the campaign, the results should have been better."

Sharon knew that, statistically, millions of victims were out there—but when Prime Clerk's campaign turned up only 127,000 names, she was suspicious. Prime Clerk promised a "robust" campaign, but what did that mean? Looking closer, Sharon felt that the agency's methodology of making a claim was too complicated for the average person, with a budget eaten up by actuaries and seemingly poor marketing decisions.

"They were advertising in *Field & Stream*," Sharon scoffed. "Who even reads that? Prime Clerk seemed to be working with an outdated, out-of-touch media list. They couldn't seem to find our target audience—opioid addicts, not fly fishermen."

Sharon's family member, a well-educated man in recovery, didn't understand the online claim; the ads were unclear about where to go, whom to talk to, and what the process was. Many of the people we did reach found the six-page claims form long and confusing, like a cross between a tax form and an SAT, with essay-type questions such as "Describe all alleged causes of action, sources of damages, legal theories of recovery, etc., that you are asserting against the Debtors." The first question on the form was "Who is the creditor?" Like, what? Eligibility wasn't well explained either: the ads were ambiguous about whether claimants needed to have been harmed by Purdue. The form seemed to suggest that you needed to prove you had a prescription for OxyContin or another Purdue product, and who was going to have that proof, much less a written record of how the pills affected them? As Aileen found in Francis's file, prescriptions were often not included in medical records; pharmacists and doctors didn't coordinate care, which meant that victims lacked a paper trail.

"We had no idea how the claims would be handled. The individuals we were trying to reach were likely intimidated because they weren't aware of the steps in the process or how exposed they might be," Sharon said.

We'd hoped to get a celebrity for the TV commercial. Prime Clerk asked *me* to recommend some names, rather than using relationships of their own. This was the whole campaign in a nutshell. As far as I was concerned, the agency had no concept of their target audience, didn't understand how to use social media or microtargeting, and did zero work building trust in the communities they were targeting. Also, it seemed they didn't know anything about the overdose crisis *at all.* They bombarded traditional media channels with vague messaging, then seemed unsurprised when they didn't get the anticipated engagement. It also concerned me that after COVID-19 hit and Prime Clerk claimed they were pivoting to digital, I still wasn't seeing any ads on my phone. Since I was the target audience for this campaign, that made zero sense. My network was packed with advocates who were great at sharing information; this should have been all over Facebook, but I hadn't seen a single ad. I called Prime Clerk and said, "What are you guys doing with all this money? How are you running your digital campaign?"

Their response was a major red flag to me. I almost blew my top when they sent me their fifty-page Excel document with a laundry list of social media influencers in the addiction-recovery space, including Dr. Drew, Dr. Oz, and—what the *fuck*—me. I felt my heart rate increase as I struggled to stay calm and professional. I asked, "What does this list mean? Are you running ads on all these pages?"

The Prime Clerk employee on the phone said, "Oh, no, that's just our target list."

What?! I felt the wool being pulled over my eyes as the agency responded defensively, trying to explain why I, a perfect example of their target demographic, who even had my name on their *list of targets,* hadn't seen a single Prime Clerk ad in my social media feeds. I saw tons of ads for private law practices, such as Anne Andrews's and Ed Neiger's firms, but not a single one from the actual estate to file a claim. Getting a celebrity to be the face of the campaign would have been a huge boost, but nobody would touch Purdue. The celebrities who'd been outspoken against Big Pharma or used their platforms to raise awareness about the drug epidemic were never going to want their names linked to the Sacklers. (I don't blame them.) In the end, we got no responses from any celebrity. Once again, there was a huge disconnect between the money, the people on the ground, and the case.

Furthermore, there was the risk of defamation: Purdue and the Sackler family, ever sensitive to their precious little reputations, wouldn't hire someone such as Courtney Love, who was happy to bash them for their role in the epidemic. Love is out there and hates Purdue; she got into it with Joss Sackler on Instagram and has gone after the family publicly. The lawyers on Purdue's side essentially said, "Whoever we hire can't say anything bad about the company or trash us." Nobody's going to agree to that, with the stipulation that you can't say anything bad about the company or the family even after the ad runs. I wouldn't, and plenty of other people wouldn't either. Purdue wanted a pro-recovery celebrity who had never said anything negative about them, and you know what? People in hell want ice water. Such a celebrity didn't exist, and as we went through the options (Jeff Bridges was their top target), it was clear that, once again, victims would lose out while Purdue wanted to stay looking squeaky-clean.

In the end, Prime Clerk hired Héctor Elizondo, one of those supporting actors who look vaguely familiar but you couldn't name him if he showed up on *Hollywood Squares*. (You might remember him as the hotel manager in *Pretty Woman*.) The spot featured Elizondo walking in front of a black backdrop, begging the audience not to change the channel: "Please listen. This is important."

Whomp whomp. It sucked. What a waste of effort, money, and time.

I wasn't the only one who hated the ad. Former Nevada governor Bob List, who was on the victims ad hoc committee, said Elizondo "did not symbolize the typical victim of Purdue Pharma. The profile of those addicted would [be] a younger person who turned to it for medical or perhaps recreational use. That ad looked like something for a home health-care geezer."

In the fourth quarter, after the TV ad dropped and things were looking dire, List volunteered to bring together a group of digital marketing specialists—well known experts who knew how to dominate digital media—to shift the campaign forward. Prime Clerk said no thanks. As far as I was concerned, they didn't want to be creative or even focus on the campaign's outcome. They checked the boxes and got paid, and as usual, *we* were the only ones complaining. Like me, List was dismayed that Prime Clerk would spend so much money on print ads or one-off spots.

"The people who are suffering were not sitting on the sidewalk reading a magazine," he said.

Sharon Murillo agreed: the population of people Prime Clerk should've been focusing on weren't going to be eager to raise their hands and identify themselves as people with drug issues. Filing meant you'd be on a list, and even if there was no trial or even sworn testimony, that was enough to scare people away. Her family member commented that he was worried he'd lose his job if anyone even suspected he struggled with substances; he even avoided treatment when he needed it because of the stigma of addiction, knowing that it would leave a mark on his record that would prevent him from getting health insurance, life insurance, and medical care in the future. Even with his comparative privilege, he had enough misgivings that Sharon had to nudge him to file a claim.

I would argue that every step of the campaign, Prime Clerk turned left when they should have run right. Their playbook was upside down, backward, and inside out. This wasn't complicated, but they hit every stumbling block on the field because they didn't seem to see what was right under their feet. Think about it: You're running a campaign attached to Purdue, so the trust is already not there. Instead of wasting a budget on *Field & Stream* and reaching the wrong audience, Prime Clerk should've spent the majority of their print and TV budget on digital, which is cheaper, has more sophisticated targeting options, and can reach ten times as many people. Instead, Prime Clerk ignored everything we told them about their audience and leaned on a traditional mainstream media campaign. They got their $23.8 million and bought a ton of television ads. I'm willing to bet they were making a commission on TV ads or traditional media, too; digital offers less commission, if any. Big surprise, another person turning a buck on our dead friends. (Purdue estimated it incurred another $700,000 for the notices with a July 30 deadline, which means the entire campaign brought in over $24 million. For what?) Prime Clerk made a ton of money on this.

But few seemed to care if Prime Clerk had dropped the ball. Everybody was so hyperfocused on getting to the claims filing deadline in July and moving forward. The prevailing attitude was "Whoever gets there, gets there, and fuck anyone who doesn't." That, too, was totally counter to the attitude and beliefs of our community. We don't shoot our wounded and we don't leave people behind.

I'm certainly not the only one convinced that this effort was poorly designed, poorly executed, and showed no interest in making changes or fixes. COVID-19 complicated things, too: the agency said they had plans to do in-person outreach at such places as sober-living homes and treatment centers, but they were forced to cancel that stuff. The pandemic didn't have much of an effect on court proceedings—like so many other businesses across the country, we just moved to Zoom or did things remotely. But the coronavirus destroyed our ability to reach out personally to people and eventually worked in Purdue's favor. I thought we had a little more of a chance when the bar date was extended thirty days (instead of the ninety days the ad hoc accountability committee asked for), but COVID messed that up, too. The extension fell during an emergency period, when people were getting their water and utilities shut off and becoming homeless due to the pandemic. It was the worst time to create shorter deadlines. (Hell, even the IRS extended their filing deadline by ninety days. We apparently couldn't do the same.) As with everything else, the municipalities, states, and hospitals were all getting *their* claims filed. Institutions were protected from the crisis and set themselves up to collect, but individuals didn't have that opportunity. Once again, the big guys helped themselves and the little guy got a stick in the ass.

Toward the end of the claim process, certain Democratic attorneys general, such as Maura Healey of Massachusetts, started doing Zoom calls and posting on social media, urging people to file claims. They would say things like "Anybody who thinks they've been harmed by an opioid should file a claim. You are entitled to money."

That was more straightforward than the Purdue and Prime Clerk ads, but it was also incomplete. What they didn't say was that personal injury claims would be adjudicated differently from the claims of governments. Remember that states and municipalities argued that they were entitled to recover damages from Purdue for the entire overdose crisis, based on the view (set forth in some of their lawsuits) that Purdue kicked off the crisis. But that same logic wasn't likely to hold true for individual victims in court. Individuals had to have been directly harmed by a Purdue product. Eventually, they would need to produce an old prescription, receipt, or some kind of documentation, assuming that they even *had* that information, could remember when and where they were when it was prescribed, still maintained the executive function to complete the process, and were privileged enough to have official records of their medical history. It was an impossible barrier for many people.

On top of that, there was the deadline, which was enough to scare even the most prepared person away. The bar date, or cutoff for submitting claims, was initially set for June 30, 2020. But some parties in the case started calling for a three-month extension of the deadline, because of COVID. The loudest advocate for the extension was the Ad Hoc Committee on Accountability, a crew of parents of loss and anti-Purdue activists, including Nan Goldin, Ed Bisch, and Cynthia Munger. God bless this committee, that's all I can say. They were outspoken, fearless, and tireless in dogging Purdue in and out of the judge's chambers. Many times, they were the ones taking actions I wanted to pursue. When my hands were tied by my position on the UCC, I lived vicariously through the accountability committee. They were all longtime activists. Nan Goldin was first aware of the epidemic when her friends in New York's art scene in the 1980s and 1990s started dying of heroin overdoses; in recovery herself, she founded P.A.I.N. (Prescription Addiction Intervention Now, an organization formed to hold the Sackler family accountable) and coordinated sensational protests in Sackler-funded galleries to get pharmaceutical dollars out of philanthropy. Cynthia Munger, whose son is in recovery from opioid addiction after being prescribed Oxy-Contin more than a decade ago as a high school baseball player with a shoulder injury, is also on the committee. Ed Bisch's son passed away in 2001 from an OxyContin overdose; Ed was one of the first activists to shout from the rooftops that the drug was dangerous. Bisch got involved as soon as he read about the bankruptcy, realizing that the case was an opportunity to make the public aware of how deep Purdue's roots were in every aspect of American life.

"The Sacklers were protected by a 2007 agreement that said they got immunity for any crimes prior to that," Bisch said. "They also got civil immunity in the bankruptcy, which is a scam, because it was always about buying immunity for the Sacklers. This isn't any semblance of justice. It lets the Sacklers buy immunity for a small fraction of the Oxy profits. People get nowhere near what they deserve, and there's a lot of angry people with something to say about that."

The focus wasn't just seeing the Sacklers in jail, which Ed describes as "the ultimate dream," but sharing the sealed documents that the family had worked hard to suppress.

Bisch said, "When those documents are released, they'll show that what the Sacklers say in private is the opposite of what they do and say in public. *Wall Street Journal* and *Boston Globe* have published redacted documents from Purdue, and we want those unredacted. We want all the documents released, and we'll fight for that. Judge Drain has sided with Purdue on every major decision in the case; after all, he was handpicked for this, and that's not illegal but it's a screwed-up law that gives Purdue an advantage. We want those documents released. In the past, it's been amazing, the tone the judge took with Purdue. The politicians gave them a tongue-lashing, but there's no teeth behind that tongue, so far. Listening to the hearings, if you didn't know the judge was talking, you would swear it was a Purdue lawyer."

The creditors committee and the nonconsenting states conducted fifteen depositions—six Sacklers and nine Purdue insiders. I sat through almost every single hour of those depositions, and all I learned was that the Sacklers felt absolutely no guilt over what their company had unleashed upon the world, and that they thought they were the ones who were being treated unfairly. *Boo fucking hoo.* I also noticed that the consenting states were strangely absent in all of this. Those attorneys general, such as John Guard, who were so worried about money going to the emergency relief fund—where were they when it came time to try to wring a few ounces of accountability from the Sackler family? They mostly sat out the discovery process and kept quiet during depositions, patiently waiting for the lion's share of the settlement that was coming to them. It was disgraceful.

Yet, some moments in the deposition process were strangely fascinating. One surreal occurrence came the night before we were scheduled to depose Richard Sackler. At seventy-five, he was the most important Sackler still alive: the one who used to run Purdue, the one who headed up the research division that invented OxyContin, and the one who played a key role in deciding how aggressively the drug should be marketed. Twelve hours before the interview was to start, Richard's lawyers emailed our lawyers with information raising questions about his mental status. Was he going to plead mental incompetence? We had no idea.

However, we deposed Richard as scheduled, and honestly? He seemed perfectly fine. Cogent. He answered questions matter-of-factly and without any guilt or anxiety. Zero fucks given. Our lawyer Mitch Hurley questioned him, and his responses were almost insultingly casual. It was as if he were talking about the weather or the latest golf tournament, not people's lives.

Hurley asked, "You admit that OxyContin kills people sometimes, right? You just don't know how many. Maybe it's 1,553 in 2006 or maybe it's a different number, but OxyContin kills people. You know that, right?"

Richard answered, "Sometimes. People who take OxyContin and abuse it are taking a risk, just as big as they take when they abuse illicit drugs. It was a stated risk on the label, yes."

Hurley pressed on, asking if Richard had any remorse about the fact that a product made by his company may have killed more than fifteen hundred people in 2006 alone.

Richard's answer had more than a touch of the famous Sackler sangfroid. He took no responsibility of any kind for the deaths related to OxyContin; "Setting aside the number, I would have sadness and remorse—well, *remorse* is not the right word, but I would view any death as a tragedy, but I don't think that as the maker of OxyContin, Purdue was responsible for those deaths. I have great sadness, but I don't think that the manufacturer was any more responsible than the manufacturer of a car that's involved in a fatal accident."

The other Sacklers fell in line behind Richard, "expressing" some "remorse," while never sounding the slightest bit sorrowful or regretful, or taking any responsibility for what they'd done. Their vapid little comments were meaningless when so many lives were lost. Not one of these people shed a single tear over the deaths their products caused. Gillian Feiner, a lawyer for the Massachusetts attorney general's office, questioned Richard's son, David, who responded much as his father did.

When Feiner asked David whether he was ready to apologize to parents whose children were killed by OxyContin, he responded that he was terribly sorry for their loss. The grandparents who are raising their grandchildren? His sentiments were the same, but he was quick to let himself off the hook, saying, "I feel awful for their pain and their suffering—that medications have done a huge amount of good in the world have also been associated with pain and suffering from people."

The Sacklers had been well coached in avoiding guilt, I noticed. Neil Kelly of the Rhode Island attorney general's office deposed Mortimer D. A. Sackler (son of Mortimer D.), asking whether he felt any responsibility for the people, their families, and friends of those whose lives have forever been changed or ended as a result of Purdue's opioid products. All Mortimer could say was that his heart went out to anyone who used a Purdue product or any other product and lost a family member or overdosed. He acknowledged that the epidemic was horrible. But if his heart went out to the victims, his wallet did not. At the end of the questioning, he backpedaled, saying, "I do feel bad that Purdue medicine that was intended to help treat people in pain caused harm to other people who were struggling with addiction. Yeah, I feel bad about that."

Those platitudes were more than we got from David's sister, Marianna Sackler, who stonewalled Hurley through her deposition. The conversation went something like this:

Hurley: Do you have any guilt from living off the proceeds of the sale of OxyContin?
Marianna Sackler: No.
Hurley: Do you believe that Purdue bears any responsibility for the opioid crisis in this country?
Marianna Sackler: No.
Hurley: Do you believe that your family has any responsi-

bility for the misery created by the opioid crisis in this country?

Marianna Sackler: No.

And on and on. The Sacklers were proficient in this dance: they claimed they didn't know about the epidemic, weren't involved in marketing decisions, and were out of the loop. They had been well coached by their lawyers in the art of evasion. On top of that, it felt like tons of lawyers did a lot of grandstanding. No matter what the process turned up, nobody was *doing* anything with what we learned. At times it felt meaningless, just like the big-bucks budget for Prime Clerk. The court needed depositions to *look* impressive, meaningful, and tough. But nothing changed. I am convinced that even a full confession from the Sacklers wouldn't have affected the case's outcome. The family was going to walk, one way or another.

Interestingly, John Stewart, who'd been Purdue's CEO from 2007 to 2013, took the Fifth. Every single time he was asked a question—at least three hundred of them—during his deposition, his response was exactly the same: "The Supreme Court has held that one of the Fifth Amendment's basic functions is to protect innocent men who otherwise might be ensnared by ambiguous circumstances. I decline to answer the question on Fifth Amendment grounds." Mark Timney, another former Purdue CEO, also took the Fifth throughout his questioning under oath.

These people knew exactly what they were doing. Still, the accountability committee kept holding Purdue's feet to the fire and pushing to get the documents released to the public—so that people would finally see how the Sacklers had bamboozled their victims and used their unethically amassed billions to cover their tracks. Committee member Cynthia Munger said that assigning blame where it was due was the only way the people's justice would be satisfied. She hoped Purdue owners and company officials would be charged with crimes. "Until we do that and we stop accusing brick and mortar and not individuals, nothing will change," she told the Associated Press.

Purdue's stranglehold on the media as well as their massive legal influence made it unlikely they'd ever see the inside of a jail cell, Bisch said, but that was no reason to give up. He said, "We're getting a shit deal, and the whole thing hinges on making Purdue a public benefit company, keep on manufacturing OxyContin, and using that money to pay for treatment. They made thirty-five billion dollars gross on Oxy and claim thirteen billion dollars in profits, and there's rumors they've got more. But we'll never hear that story because they buy everyone. You can see from these documents that they signed those court papers in 2007 and immediately tripled their sales force, and when the sales went up, the deaths went up, but that's not in the papers."

The accountability committee wasn't focused only on financial damages: they primarily cared about making sure the significance of the case wasn't lost in a shuffle of paperwork. However, right out of the gate, they seemed to be at a disadvantage. They weren't as plugged in to the who's who of the case as they could have been. For example, they had a pro bono attorney named Michael Quinn, who was doing the best he could under the circumstances without getting paid. When their committee was formed, I suggested that Arik have a phone call with Quinn to see if we could help in some way. Arik set up a call with Quinn and Purdue's lawyers. (I wasn't on it.) Apparently, that first call was a complete disaster. Quinn had no idea who Arik was, or what the UCC was, and was not initially well versed in bankruptcy law, and the call ended rather awkwardly. However, quickly following the accountability committee's formation, Quinn knew he was up against real giants; he would later hold his own in stinging court pleadings that I would silently cheer on and reference during UCC meetings.

The accountability committee was serious about prioritizing victims. They are the ones who asked for a ninety-day extension of the filing deadline, as did the nonconsenting states. The consenting states wanted no extension. (Big surprise: Why support any effort that might cut into their portion of the settlement? Much better to let the deadline drift by, collecting as few personal claims as possible.) Purdue offered a thirty-day extension instead, reasoning that each monthlong extension would cost the estate $700,000. It was a shitty compromise, but with time running short, the creditors committee felt compelled to agree.

The judge approved the one-month extension, although he sounded a bit frustrated: "We're in the ninth month of this case. In some ways, this motion is a microcosm of the case as a whole. It has elicited strong views from multiple parties, and the parties were not able to reach agreement on something as simple as an extension of the bar date."

Drain was getting impatient. I can't say that I blamed him. The longer we waited, the less there was to fight about. Anne Andrews likes to say, "Bankruptcy is a melting ice cube." Each month, the case was burning through tens of millions of dollars of Purdue's money. The ice cube that everyone was fighting over was shrinking, and the longer creditors dithered over the deal, the less we had to divvy up.

Those negotiations took place in private (over Zoom) mediation, a long series of discussions between dozens of lawyers, including attorneys general and representatives of all the ad hoc committees and private litigants. Between them all stood two mediators, Ken Feinberg and Layn Phillips, who were appointed by the court, and who charged a combined $1 million every month. Now, I wasn't in the mediation sessions, but it felt to me as if these two guys were basically paid to pass notes between parties. *Must be nice.* It's no shocker that Feinberg was previously on Purdue's payroll; he collected about $12 million in fees from the company between 2005 and 2015.

The first step of mediation was for the lawyers of each party— hospitals, insurance companies, states, personal injury claimants, and so on—to make a presentation to the other parties, essentially arguing how much their side deserved, and why.

Anne, acting as lead negotiator for the victims, gave her presentation in the summer of 2020. She made a compelling case for who the victims were and why they deserved compensation for their loss and injury. There were a lot of numbers, a lot of statistics, but also some personal stories. She talked about victims who'd lost jobs, spent hundreds of thousands of dollars on treatment, whose loved ones had died far too young. She talked about people like Francis Baillargeon and his mother, Aileen: people deprived of their loved ones and the stability those relationships represented.

When I talked to Aileen, she said, "I think of my granddaughter's future. I'm not loaded, but I wouldn't keep a dime of that money. I think we deserve anything that would help her: the cost-of-living arrangements and college, plus inflation. That's what I'd be looking at, all those things that impact Faith's future."

Aileen absolutely deserved that money, and much more, from Purdue. Every person who was brave enough to make a claim did: we deserved our time back, our families, our hopes. Although the personal injury claims added up to trillions of dollars, we all suspected that we would never see anywhere near that kind of settlement. Purdue was just too powerful, and the groups we had to fight were too big, well prepared, and heartless to even give us a chance. The settlement with Purdue, including a few billion from the Sackler family, was likely to be around $10 billion, give or take. Anne argued that the victims were entitled to a minimum of roughly 20 percent of that, or $2 billion. Personally, I thought that we deserved way more, but $2 billion was just about the lowest end of fair.

David Nachman, a deputy attorney general for New York, was the unofficial lead negotiator for the states, who were pretty much all on the same page for claims negotiations. They had all agreed that their money would go to abatement—that is, preventing future harm from opioid use, including medically assisted treatment. (Interestingly, Nachman is married to a former pharmaceutical executive who was now working for a venture capital firm, Polaris Partners, with at least two possible abatement companies in its portfolio.)

After the victims' lawyers gave their hour-long presentation, Nachman was the first to speak up. I wasn't on this call, but I heard about it from a number of people who were. They all told me Nachman said something like "We don't think your claims pool deserves anything. We believe that the victims' amount is zero."

"How is it zero?"

Apparently, Nachman launched into a tirade about how the victims were the ones who had taken drugs and brought this on themselves, while the states were the ones trying to save people, who bore the brunt of the crisis, monetarily, by paying for health care and law enforcement. The prejudice against victims was astounding. Because addiction is such a taboo subject, states could attempt to play the sole victim, although they never suffered the same way as an individual.

At that point, the mediators, Feinberg and Phillips, stepped in. It was clear to me right away that these guys were far from neutral.

It felt like they treated the public side's claim as the de facto claim, as though the states' argument was far more legitimate than the victims'. Some politicians and lawyers believe that if you give money to an "addict," the first thing they're going to do with it is spend it on drugs. I believe they felt entitled to deprive broken families and people harmed of their fair share of the settlement because of discrimination.

How do you find middle ground with institutions who seem to think you're a worthless piece of shit? Well, it's not easy. We wanted $2 billion, they wanted us to have nothing. Eventually, they upped their offer to $300 million.

When I heard that offer, I said, "Three hundred million dollars? No. No fucking way."

A number like that was a nonstarter. We'd proved harm, shown evidence—and the problem was, these people just didn't care. Nothing seemed to affect them. I was convinced that they were cold-blooded, with ice water running through their veins. The mediation wasn't going anywhere if they couldn't acknowledge the basic humanity of victims, and they made it obvious that was never going to happen. This power struggle was the ERF negotiation all over again, my hopes just getting ground down to a nub as we struggled to reach across the aisle and negotiate with people who believed this was all our fault.

What's half of zero? Zero. As Ed Bisch said, we were getting nothing for nothing. At first, I thought I wouldn't settle for anything less than $2 billion. Then it was $1.5 billion. Then $1 billion. Anything less than a billion dollars, I thought, wasn't worth it. I felt the same desperation I had as I watched the ERF slide into the swamp of mediation, sunk by the states' unwillingness to negotiate with victims. I thought anything less than a billion dollars for victims was an insult and shouldn't be considered. This would be divided up among fewer than 130,000 people. (Each claim cost around $200 to recruit with Prime Clerk's ass-backward ad campaign.) Once the lawyers took their cut, it would leave each victim with a few thousand dollars—*maybe*. A few thousand dollars for a dead son or a lost decade. What was even the point? I couldn't imagine Drain approving a deal where the victims got such a small piece of the estate. Surely that would not play well with the general public.

There was a nuclear option: litigation. If all or some of the parties couldn't come to an agreement on how Purdue's money was to be allocated, we would have a sort of court proceeding within the bankruptcy—in public, on the record, in front of Judge Drain— where parties would present a case as to what money they deserved. The victims had hired Chris Shore from White & Case (a firm Anne called the "mad dogs of restructuring"). He was working on a litigation strategy and building a case as to why the victims deserved more money than the states wanted to give us. Part of that case was to attack the states, which had frittered away past abatement money or simply let it go unspent. (Yes, we had receipts.) On top of that, they hadn't done their jobs monitoring Purdue's marketing after 2007, shut down pill mills, or asked the right questions when the data they had showed drugs being prescribed at insanely high rates. Instead, they'd done what they'd always done: criminalized addiction.

In the addiction crisis, addiction was kicking the states' asses— and the best they could come up with was to blame us. *Groundbreaking.*

Shore put together a white paper, a sort of break-glass-in-case-of-litigation opposition-research project against the states. Part of it focused on how the opioid industry was able to buy influence at every level of government. Between 2006 and 2015, opioid companies and their advocates spent more than $880 million on political contributions and lobbying both state and federal officials. Between 2014 and 2019, Purdue gave $235,000 to the Democratic Attorneys General Association and $680,000 to the Republican Attorneys General Association. The Democratic AGs, mind you, were busily excoriating Purdue and the Sackler family every chance they got. But they'd still take their money. Even *after* Purdue declared bankruptcy, they still managed to donate another $75,000 to the Democratic AGs and $110,000 to the Republican AGs (as first reported by The Intercept). This was *in the middle of* the case!

At the end of the day, Courtney Love had a stronger backbone and better moral fiber than the elected officials who were supposed to be acting in the people's best interest.

The creditors committee was shocked when we learned about this. We filed a motion to stop Purdue from making any more political contributions, which they agreed to. The attorneys general associations agreed to give back the most recent contributions. But the damage was done, and the episode did nothing to decrease the tension between us and the AGs. I wondered, *if they hadn't been caught, would the attorneys general have changed their ways?* Probably not. There are a lot of perks to being in Purdue's pocket.

Even in the extreme isolation of my work, updates from the real world leaked in. My whole desktop was Purdue, the family, and the bankruptcy. I got a Google Alert anytime one of the Sacklers made a chess move in the news. That was my life, all day, every day.

Then, on May 25, 2020, the world caught on fire. A white Minneapolis police officer named Derek Chauvin sadistically murdered George Floyd by kneeling on his neck for a horrifying eight minutes and forty-six seconds. A cell phone video of the killing, which showed Floyd repeatedly saying, "I can't breathe," circulated online. I'll never forget watching it. This wasn't the first time a Black person was the victim of police brutality, or the first time graphic images of a Black person's death ended up on social media. The cops' response was straight out of the white supremacist playbook: feign remorse, promise to improve training, and trot out the dead victim's convictions and drug report. George Floyd had a few minor convictions and had been arrested on nine separate occasions between 1997 and 2007, mostly on drug and theft charges. He'd been to jail a few times. His toxicology report showed traces of fentanyl and methamphetamine. This information was used to smear Floyd and make him look like a "thug" or a violent criminal—and try to make it look as if Chauvin had done society a favor.

I looked at the photos of Floyd, and I didn't see a criminal. I saw someone I related to. He was the son of a single mom. He'd been a promising young athlete, gotten a good start at college. He had issues with substances. He had people who loved him. He was hustling, trying to support his family, and just trying to make it, without giving up his dreams. But that wasn't enough for Floyd, because he was born into a culture that was designed to punish and exclude him. Because he was born Black, he was born at a a disadvantage—which ended up making him an easy mark for Derek Chauvin. Unlike me, Floyd was racially profiled, discriminated against, and shuffled through the criminal justice system. He died. Chauvin killed him. If not for that cell phone video, I doubt anything would have come of it.

However, something was different this time. Massive protests gathered in Minneapolis and other cities as millions marched, repeating Black Lives Matter slogans and calling for justice. Sean, who was from Minneapolis, dragged me to the TV so we could watch the familiar streets and neighborhoods fill with people. We were both emotional, burning with pent-up feelings that had nowhere to go and no way to be expressed. The footage showed that we weren't alone. Images flashed on every screen: the country was on fire. In a pandemic, during one of the worst economic depressions since 1929, while a hotly debated election determined whether we'd have four more years of Donald Trump—everyone had had enough. America was a powder keg, and Floyd's killing was the spark that set it off.

The names and faces of other Black people who'd lost their lives to so-called protectors of the peace became a mantra: Sandra Bland. Breonna Taylor. Tony McDade. Elijah McClain. Tamir Rice. More deaths made news. Ahmaud Arbery, killed by white supremacists while Arbery was on a run. There were so many. In each case, the victim's character was called into question by so-called experts while police shrugged and said it wasn't anybody's fault. I didn't believe that, and neither did most Americans. It was more clear to me than ever that the system needed serious reform.

Floyd's toxicology report showed that he had two substances in his bloodstream when he died, though it's unlikely he was under the influence at the time of his murder. A group of emergency room doctors and psychiatrists wrote in *Scientific American,* "When Black people are killed by police, their character and even their anatomy is turned into justification for their killer's exoneration. It's a well-honed tactic."

Another letter, titled "The 'Collective Black Physicians' Statement' on the death of Mr. George Floyd," written on behalf of thousands of Black doctors and health-care workers in America, stated:

> Any mention of potential intoxicants of which Mr. Floyd may have been under the influence is meritless at this stage of the physical autopsy examination. In a medicolegal autopsy, the results of a urinary toxicology screen are often inaccurate. All substances must be detected and confirmed in blood and/or particular organs before it can be said that an individual was intoxicated and that death is a complication of that toxicity.

Floyd's substance use was leveraged in an attempt to discredit and dehumanize him. His Blackness was used against him. He couldn't win. We were not treated equally in the eyes of the law: I'm a white guy, straight out of a Warby Parker ad. At an earlier time in my life, my pockets were stuffed with contraband, enough pills to put me behind bars for years. Floyd was arrested for allegedly passing a fake $20 bill, the kind of thing I did back in the day without a second thought. Derek Chauvin wouldn't have looked at *me* twice. But he looked at Floyd and knew he could do anything he wanted, because Black men are stereotyped and profiled as "threatening." It made me sick to my stomach to see how the system worked to kill, suppress, and terrorize people—ordinary people, regular citizens. Nobody deserved that. I was newly aware of the innate bigotry of the country I loved. How do you fix something like that? Was it even possible? Or was the only real choice to just burn the system to the ground?

As summer wore on, negotiations became more and more complex. The NAACP filed a motion to enter mediation as a party. The organization was rightly concerned that not enough money would go to communities of color. That was good news: a powerful, respected group such as the NAACP was advocating for victims who had historically been left behind.

However, so many other parties were eager to do a deal and go home. The victims' lawyers tried to form an alliance with the hospitals, which would have let us control the creditors committee, four seats of which already belonged to victims. But the hospitals shrugged us off and signed a deal, leaving us facing the possibility of getting steamrolled, of being the only party left out. Judge Drain had given every indication that he would sign off on any agreement the majority of the parties agreed on—a decision made by imbalanced democracy, not consensus.

On Labor Day weekend, Sean and I were on a much-needed getaway—masked, gloved, and distanced—in Florida. We were supposed to be focused on each other and finally spending some time alone, but when my phone rang and I saw *Anne Andrews* pop up, I couldn't *not* answer.

"Seriously?" Sean sputtered as I pushed the accept button.

"I'm sorry," I whispered. "I'll just be a minute."

He rolled his eyes and walked away with his arms crossed. Even with a mask on, I could see that he was pissed. I tried to focus on what Anne was saying and hoped it was good news.

She told me that the public side was showing signs of cracking: all that noise from the accountability committee, plus the proof that states had taken campaign contributions from Purdue, was working in our favor. The states didn't want litigation—it would expose them and erode their "morally superior" position. The last thing they wanted was the victims' lawyers going on and on, in public, about how the states were complicit in the overdose crisis and couldn't be trusted to run pricey abatement programs.

Anne told me that the states had upped their offer to $600 million, to be paid out over five years. Ken Feinberg delivered the news. Anne pushed back hard. She told me she was swearing and screaming at the lawyers and the mediators every chance she got. (Have I told you how much I love Anne?) She told Ken we were willing to go down to $875 million, but that was as low as we would go.

After some more back and forth, a deal was landed on amounting to between $700 million and $750 million, depending on how much insurance money was paid out. Ed Neiger laid it out for us over the phone.

"Do I think that this is a good deal?" he said, sounding funereal. "I do not think it's a good deal. Do I think that it's better than the alternative, which would be to go to war with the states?"

He did. The lawyers at White & Case thought it was too risky to take our case to the judge, given that most other creditors had already signed a deal. The judge seemed pretty sympathetic to the states' claims. We couldn't go in guns blazing—much as I wanted to. In my heart, I hoped for a fight. In any other situation, I would have jumped in, swinging both fists. But it would have been like punching a wasp's nest. It was that same old dilemma: What do you do with an unjust system, with a process that all but guarantees an inequitable outcome? Do you compromise and take what you can get? Or do you burn it down? As an activist, I might have burned it down. But as a committee member representing thousands of other people, I couldn't do that in good conscience. Many of the victims needed the money, especially during the pandemic, with so many people out of work.

Besides, as Neiger said, "Even if we got north of a billion, or north of a trillion, it's still not going to deliver a lot of people justice, especially those who have lost loved ones."

We had wrung a little bit of money out for the victims. It wasn't enough. But it's what we got. We would try to wring a little bit of justice out of this horrible process, too. I nodded, thanking Anne and Ed for the update, then powered off my phone.

"How was it?" Sean asked as I walked toward him. I could see the pale pink edges of his eyes, the last trace of his bout with the COVID-19 infection he'd battled earlier that summer. He had a clean bill of health (and I appeared to be immune), but the health scare had made me even more aware of what I already knew: that our time on earth was always going to be limited, and I needed to do everything I could to show him how much I cherished him.

Dodging the question, I shrugged. "Let's go get some M&M's."

It was a problem that even chocolate couldn't fix. The case was wearing me down. At every turn when I hoped victims would have a shred of dignity, we were denied even the satisfaction of closure. The depositions and discovery process uncovered information that was crucial for the public to know about—but it came at a high price.

It wasn't lost on me that someone such as Aileen Lovejoy would collect a small sum, if anything at all. She'd never recoup even enough to cover the expenses of her son's funeral. She would continue to pay taxes, support her community, and beautify her neighborhood in a state where her elected representatives fought tooth and nail to keep settlement money *away* from her. How is that justice? I had hoped to be an advocate for victims, and once again, all I got was another lungful of rancid air as Purdue released its secrets. The company was revolting, and the Sacklers no better. I tried to console myself with the knowledge we had proof—but without action, what was that worth? I wanted justice, but when the system had no teeth and no appetite for change, the only people feeling the bite were the ones who'd been chewed up a hundred times already.

10

"A LEGAL FICTION"

When your house is burning, you call the fire department. But when your partner is a casualty of the overdose crisis, what number do you dial? Tim Kramer tried every number he could think of to report the harm done to his fiancée, LeeRae Conn, and her child, Kyle.

"When we met, I thought she had narcolepsy," Tim said. "Turns out, she was addicted to opioids. She was nodding off. These drug-pusher doctors gave her anything they could think of."

LeeRae was legally blind, but fiercely independent. Tim said she was self-reliant in nearly every way. She had special support devices that helped her live as though she could see, such as a money-counting machine that told her the denomination of the bills she was holding, and a scanner that told her what color her clothes were so she could mix and match. They rode a tandem bike together for outings around their Detroit-area neighborhood, Waterford. Yet, when it came to the nightmare of LeeRae's addiction, Tim was in a caregiver role. He was always vigilant, aware that LeeRae's doctor visits inevitably led to overdoses.

He tried everything. He cussed out her doctors, confiscated LeeRae's phone, and tried to get her into an outpatient program. He told her friends to stay away when he found out they were trading pills. He found LeeRae's stashes in their home's flower beds and inside the mailbox. He saved LeeRae's life multiple times—one night, he found her unconscious in the bathtub and hauled her out of the water, put her in the car, and took her to the emergency room.

"If I'd waited even five more minutes, she would have died," he said. But he couldn't stand between LeeRae and her doctors. Unable to intervene, he was forced to watch his partner slowly poisoned by perfectly legal substances that showed up with doctor's instructions. It was maddening. Finally, on the night of June 29, 2018, LeeRae went to sleep. Tim went into the bedroom and found her in their bed—dead. This time, he could not revive her. He was plunged into a second nightmare. He took over guardianship of Kyle, but wasn't able to adopt LeeRae's child. He struggled to get access to LeeRae's medical records. As he battled to protect the child he'd raised since second grade, make sure LeeRae got a decent funeral, and keep his head above water, Tim's grief turned to righteous anger. He'd had a first-row seat to LeeRae's substance use and seen for himself where the pills came from. He read the autopsy report, which said she tested positive for methadone, Xanax, Tylenol 800, OxyContin, oxycodone, and other medications she'd been given by doctors. Tim knew this wasn't LeeRae's fault. The sexy, funny, pretty, sharp woman he'd fallen in love with wasn't trying to kill herself or even have a good time with her medication. She was killed by a system that didn't care if she lived or died.

Six months after LeeRae's death, Tim formed a Facebook group called the Opioid Watchdogs Letter Drops. He organized letter-writing campaigns with other members in thirty states and Puerto

Rico to flood mailboxes with stories of loved ones lost to opioids. Tim contacted everyone he could think of, telling LeeRae's story and demanding justice.

"The township and the county law courts don't care. I sent letters to newsmagazines, *The New York Times*, the State of Michigan, the FBI, DEA, and CIA," he said. "I sent letters to everyone. Nobody cares."

There is no 911 hotline for this crisis. If there were, parents, loved ones, and families across America would be lighting it up around the clock. Instead, people such as Tim Kramer reach out to the institutions that allegedly have the people's best interests in mind and get no response. Whom do you call when the love of your life is killed by opioids? Who picks up the pieces? The Purdue bankruptcy felt, to Tim, like an opportunity to set things right. He received a few letters from a lawyer's office informing him that the "hearing date was changed," though he had no idea what that meant. Finally, he got an update with a phone number on it. Fed up and frustrated, determined to make his voice heard, he called.

He didn't realize that he was calling Judge Drain.

The US Department of Justice had no interest in Tim Kramer and LeeRae Conn, but they definitely cared about the bankruptcy. From the beginning, they lurked around the hearings. Their lawyers attended the emergency relief fund discussions and almost every deposition, too. They said, "We're just here to monitor what's happening because we have an interest in this case." An *interest*. It didn't take a genius to guess that the DOJ would be filing a claim, and we knew they were working on a settlement with Purdue and the Sacklers. The question was how much money they would ask for. A huge settlement, with the federal government taking the lion's share of the money, could upend all the agreements that were already in place.

On October 21, 2020, not two weeks before Election Day, we learned that Purdue would plead guilty to three felony counts: one count of "conspiracy to defraud the United States," and two counts of "conspiracy to violate the Federal Anti-Kickback Statute." Purdue also agreed to a civil settlement with the federal government to resolve its liability under the False Claims Act. They'd reached a settlement, and it was a doozy. In total, the deal was for $8 billion, which headlines around the world repeated without much explanation. (That's the thing about journalists: they love numbers because sometimes they look like facts.) The real figure was more complicated. For Purdue, the civil settlement was $2.8 billion, and the criminal fine was $3.544 billion. These two figures were claims; like other claimants, the DOJ would be getting pennies (or fractions of pennies) on the dollar. On that day, Purdue became a repeat offender—and the law did nothing except collect a check.

As part of the criminal fine, the Feds were also entitled to a $2 billion asset forfeiture. Of that, the Feds wanted $225 million up front. They were willing to forgo the remaining $1.77 billion, under two conditions. First, they wanted that money to go to the states' abatement plan. Second, they wanted Purdue to emerge postbankruptcy as a public benefit corporation (PBC) "to function entirely in the public interest." Although this sounds simple, it was a tall order. The definition of "public interest" was like blood in the water for lawyers, and defining what it meant created a feeding frenzy of nitpicking, debating, and negotiation that also caused great confusion and consternation for the creditors.

The DOJ settlement was a softball pitch for Purdue. A PBC postbankruptcy was the future Purdue wanted. They saw it as a modest public relations win, which it was (for them). They could spin it as a magnanimous gesture and portray the transition as a choice, not a mandate. They would appear to voluntarily turn themselves into a company that serves only the "public interest." Also, this transition created another upside for most creditors: a PBC would likely net them the most money, since all revenue from drugs sold would go straight to them and would be exempt from the corporate income tax. Everybody wins, right? Well, everybody except the people directly impacted. As usual.

To my surprise, the dissenting states were dead set against the PBC plan, and you know what? I agreed with them. They wanted Purdue sold. They said owning an opioid company would create a conflict of interest. ("Owning" it was a little bit inaccurate, since the states would elect a board of trustees, who would appoint a board of directors, who would hire and oversee management. But still, it did feel like robbing Peter to deal drugs to Paul.) Some of the states didn't want to give Purdue the satisfaction of turning itself into an entity that sounded as if it were a charity. And some of them argued that it would be better to keep Purdue in the private sector, since it could then be subject to the same oversight as any other company—which meant the company could still be sued should it, say, fraudulently market OxyContin. Not that they would *ever* do that, with their fucking spotless track record. It was true: the states didn't have a stellar record regulating the sale of OxyContin, and turning a huge pharmaceutical company into a public utility would be a headache and a half. Some of the creditors were pissed that the Justice Department was weighing in on the future of the company. That didn't seem like the DOJ's lane.

Although the negotiations with the Sackler family were kept secret, we knew the federal government had also reached a settlement with them. An article in *The New Yorker* by Patrick Radden Keefe predicted that the arrangement would be finalized before the 2020 election; he was right. It seemed to me that the bankruptcy and public opinion about the Sacklers might be good leverage for the Trump campaign, and sure enough, as soon as the DOJ settlement was announced, Kellyanne Conway tweeted something like "Look what President Trump has done, securing the settlement from Purdue." He hadn't done anything; his hands were full, managing multiple QAnon conspiracies and trying to wreak havoc in the electoral process. But it was obvious that seeming "tough on the drug epidemic" had value for the election, and if the campaign hadn't gone nuclear, Conway and her nest of publicity vipers might have created some more hoopla around the event. I think the Sackler family wanted the preelection settlement, too. Think about it: Under Joe Biden, there might be worse terms, or even no deal at all. The family was probably terrified of what might happen to them if Elizabeth Warren or another new whip-cracking US attorney general was in charge of the case. They'd make terms with Trump, the devil they knew, instead. I noticed that the case did accelerate in the weeks leading up to the election. Suddenly, the Sacklers weren't dragging their feet on motions and responses. They participated and cooperated—likely because their team was working overtime to make sure they got a deal before leadership changed hands.

The Sacklers agreed to pay the Feds $225 million to resolve its "civil False Claims Act liability . . . arising from the alleged conduct of" Richard, David, Mortimer D. A., Kathe, and Jonathan, according to the DOJ's press release. The false claims were old news: they took place during 2013, when the Sacklers approved a program called

Evolve to Excellence. Purdue, in an effort to turbocharge the flagging sales of OxyContin, sent sales representatives to high-volume prescribers "who were already writing twenty-five times as many OxyContin scripts as their peers, causing health-care providers to prescribe opioids for uses that were unsafe, ineffective, and medically unnecessary, and that often led to abuse and diversion." Evolve to Excellence? More like search and destroy. It was just another scorched-earth marketing campaign that put a few more bucks in the Sacklers' pockets and left hundreds of thousands of bodies in its wake.

What did the DOJ deals add up to? Well, not much. It was another perfectly legal shell game. Purdue, the company, was admitting it broke the law for the second time. The Sackler family were technically admitting nothing, and the Justice Department was not granting them immunity from criminal prosecution. However, the Sackler deal was seen by many as a de facto release, since the DOJ had clearly taken a look at the family's role in the overdose crisis but declined to prosecute them. It was more of the same treatment the Sacklers had enjoyed for decades. They lied, people died, and the government looked the other way. This time, the only real difference was that the government was taking some money—which could be seen as an indulgence, or an expensive Get Out of Jail Free card. The Sacklers could afford it. So, most people thought that a criminal prosecution, which was never likely, had now become all but unimaginable. The fantasy many of us survivors had of seeing the Sacklers in orange and black pajamas was just that—a fantasy.

You wouldn't know that by reading the news. That $8 billion settlement was everywhere you looked, and the media was treating the agreement as some kind of victory lap for the government—and the people they represented. The Purdue bankruptcy had been covered only sporadically over the last year, mostly as a human interest story. The hard facts and impressive-sounding dollar amount of the settlement pushed Purdue back into the headlines. DOJ ANNOUNCES $8B-PLUS SETTLEMENT WITH OXYCONTIN MAKER, announced *Politico*. PURDUE PHARMA PLEADS GUILTY TO CRIMINAL CHARGES FOR OPIOID SALES, read *The New York Times*. And so on. They're guilty, they're paying, blah blah blah. You'd think this actually *meant* something. Every cable news channel covered it. I was getting emails and text messages from family and friends, saying things like "So it's over?" People thought that this was the end of Purdue.

It wasn't, and the case wasn't ended either. Just because the DOJ got their deal didn't mean the victims had settled—and there was no media around that. If I'd written those headlines, I would have said, DOJ SETTLES FOR PENNIES, LETS SACKLERS WALK FREE WITHOUT ACCOUNTABILITY, VICTIMS STILL TAKING IT IN THE ASS. That would be closer to the whole story. In reality, the DOJ was getting in line to hold their hand out with everyone else. They were just another claimant. If anything, we on the committee were surprised that the dollar amount of the settlement was so small. Eight billion dollars wasn't that much money compared with the damage Purdue had done and how much revenue they'd squirreled away before they were forced into bankruptcy. Many creditors saw that as a good thing since it wouldn't disrupt any agreements or siphon too much money from anyone else.

At the next hearing, the lawyers were at pains to say what a "monumental" step this settlement was. US Attorney Lawrence Fogelman called it a "milestone event" in the US "effort to address the opioid epidemic." Judge Drain said it was "an extremely important development in this case." I thought that was all a load of self-congratulatory crap. The DOJ settlement, despite all the media coverage it got, was just another box for everyone to tick. The DOJ got theirs. Now, what about everybody else? Nobody seemed to be able to tell me when victims would receive any compensation for all they'd lost. Tim Kramer and the child he was raising were owed money, along with the thousands of other people in their same situation.

Arik told me a few times that I could find solace in that Purdue on paper was now a serial felony offender. But to me, that only underlined the injustice of it all. "On paper" doesn't mean shit, especially if you've got enough money to walk away from any charge scot-free. I've known people who went to prison for decades because of three-strikes felony laws. A friend of mine will never drive a car because she got three DUIs before getting sober. The Sacklers have blood on their hands, and they live their lives totally unaffected by the harm they caused. Not even a slap on the wrist. Nothing. They'd do more time if they were caught with a controlled substance—ironic, since they manufacture the same substance that puts people in prison. The harshness of the justice system doesn't extend to corporations or billionaires. Not a single person connected with Purdue ever went to jail, despite the company pleading guilty to multiple felonies on two separate occasions. I took no solace in that at all.

The one positive thing to come out of the DOJ settlement was *information*. All of our worst suspicions were confirmed, and many of the word-of-mouth anecdotes shared in the community finally had hard proof to support them. Documentation meant we weren't crazy, and we weren't imagining the crisis. This was corporate genocide, sanctioned by the state and abetted by medical professionals, all steeped in the stigma of substance addiction. According to the government's filing, the company sent sales reps to one hundred thousand doctors and nurses from 2013 to 2018. Thousands of these providers "Purdue knew or should have known were prescribing opioids for uses many of which were not for a medically accepted indication," which is legalese for "going to be misused or sold on the black market." The company also sent sales reps to pharmacies of the highest-volume prescribers, "including those that Purdue knew were writing medically unnecessary prescriptions, to ensure that Purdue opioids would be dispensed." They deliberately put pressure on prescribers to ramp up the number of pills they were doling out. It was all about the money. It was never about medicine.

Furthermore, Purdue paid illegal kickbacks to high-volume prescribers through its Key Opinion Leader corporate adviser and speaker program. Purdue also made payments to an electronic-health-record company called Practice Fusion, basically as a means to buy ad space. The medical software was programmed to recommend that doctors prescribe opioids to their patients. Purdue also paid kickbacks to specialty pharmacies "to fill prescriptions that other traditional pharmacies had rejected." So if commonsense pharmacists wouldn't hand over the Oxy, another person in a white coat would. Greed finds a way, and Purdue used every tool at its disposal to keep the cash flowing into its coffers.

This was always about revenue. Remember, in 2010, Purdue released reformulated OxyContin, which was supposed to be harder to snort or inject. Following that, OxyContin sales declined sharply. (Gee, I wonder why.) The revenue loss spurred Purdue to ramp up marketing and get their sales back to what they'd been before regulation interfered with their opioid free-for-all. According to the government, "Purdue studied the drivers of the post-reformulation OxyContin sales decline, and it attributed most of the decline to a reduction in medically unnecessary prescriptions, many of which were written for abuse through insufflation or injection, and increases in safeguards intended to hinder medically unnecessary prescribing." In October of 2011, a presentation was made to Purdue's board about a decline in prescriptions for 80 mg OxyContin, especially from Do Not Call prescribers. The push was on. The Sacklers endorsed a marketing effort beginning in 2013 that focused on high-volume prescribers to make up the difference. Through its own investigations, Purdue knew of various doctors who were likely prescribing opioids for diversion (that is, to at-risk users such as me). The company doubled down with that information and continued to send sales reps to these doctors to encourage them to prescribe more opioids at even higher doses. They didn't care if people got sick or died. All they cared about was their bottom line.

The information attached to the DOJ's Sackler settlement added weight to allegations that the family knew about and approved of the strategy known as Evolve to Excellence, in which the highest-volume prescribers, who wrote twenty-five times as many OxyContin scripts as a normal prescriber, were singled out and targeted by marketers. The government maintained the Sacklers "knowingly caused the submission of false and fraudulent claims to federal health care benefit programs for Purdue's opioid drugs that were prescribed for uses that were unsafe, ineffective, and medically unnecessary, and that were often diverted for uses that lacked a legitimate medical purpose." The filing asserted that at least some of the money transferred out of Purdue was done "with the intent to hinder future creditors and/or were otherwise voidable as fraudulent transfers." So there it was, in black-and-white—what advocates had been saying for decades. The government knew what Purdue was up to. And they quickly figured out how deep the rabbit hole went.

The government's filings included an intriguing subplot: A "consulting company" had helped Purdue come up with Evolve to Excellence. Though the company wasn't named, it could only be McKinsey & Company, the management consulting firm credited with transforming corporate culture in the 1960s. McKinsey had been connected to numerous scandals over the years, including Enron and the 2008 financial crisis. (You know, the corporate scandals that basically melted down our whole economy. No biggie.) The firm's clients have included a number of authoritarian regimes, such as Saudi Arabia, Turkey, and Ukraine. McKinsey has about two thousand partners worldwide, who each make up to $1.3 million per year. In America, the firm makes big bucks working with state-run institutions for unemployment and COVID-19 relief. According to *The Wall Street Journal,* New York governor Andrew Cuomo "awarded McKinsey a $9.9 million contract in March to advise the state on issues related to COVID-19, the illness caused by the new coronavirus. That included eighteen weeks of 'leadership counseling' at $42,500 a week. . . . McKinsey also did work for Massachusetts, some of which appeared to involve little more than forwarding others' material along. Researchers at Harvard University prepared reports for the state's health department tracking population movements. Consultants at McKinsey used the reports verbatim in material for the governor, according to a person familiar with the work." That's a lot of money just to forward some emails. Even worse, McKinsey helped put babies in cages: a *New York Times* report revealed that the firm was working with the US Immigration and Customs Enforcement (ICE) agency during widespread outcries and protests over the Trump administration's immigration policies, including separation of migrant children from their parents.

McKinsey's link with state and federal governments was already problematic, but when they worked with Purdue to market opioids, the outcome was deadly as well.

The firm's involvement in the Evolve to Excellence program was confirmed in a November 2020 filing by the nonconsenting states. (This was in support of our motion to compel Purdue to produce the documents it was withholding.) That involvement alone would have been bad enough, but the chef's kiss, as it were, was another piece of advice McKinsey had given Purdue.

By November 2017, their staff prepared to brief the Sacklers on ways to salvage business with health insurance companies by paying a rebate to the insurers for each patient who overdosed or developed opioid use disorder. Their analysis showed that paying a rebate could be an "attractive option" for Purdue if the payment was in the range of $6,000 to $14,000 for each patient who was harmed. The money would not go to the patient, but it would encourage the insurance company to keep paying for Purdue drugs. This buyoff was to ensure that the pill-to-patient pipeline was uninterrupted. It was bald-faced blood money, cash for bodies. (It also made me wonder why the fuck insurance companies felt that they were owed any money in the bankruptcy.) The filing proved that McKinsey thought Purdue should pay money to insurers for every patient who overdosed from or became addicted to Oxy-Contin. You cannot make this shit up. Even Purdue had the good sense to pass on this advice. Eventually, McKinsey was hired to disassemble the sales force that had "turbocharged" Purdue's sales. By Purdue CEO Craig Landau's own admission, the move came five years too late.

In 2018, shortly after Massachusetts had filed its lawsuit against Purdue, in which numerous board members were named as co-defendants, McKinsey partner Martin Elling emailed his colleague Arnab Ghatak: "It probably makes sense to have a quick conversation with the risk committee to see if we should be doing anything other that [sic] eliminating all our documents and emails. Suspect not but as things get tougher someone might turn to us."

Ghatak replied, "Thanks for the heads-up. Will do."

Eliminating documents? That meant they were shredding the evidence. McKinsey had plenty to hide—much of which probably never even made it into the depositions. It was sickening. The revelations put McKinsey in the same category as opioid manufacturers. They were coconspirators. Senator Brian Schatz of Hawaii tweeted, "It is essential that the next Attorney General pursue all of these criminals." And New Jersey governor Phil Murphy said, "The notion of putting a price on somebody's life is so offensive. It's beyond the pale."

In December 2020, McKinsey issued what was called, by *The New York Times*, a "rare apology," saying in a statement, "As we look back at our client service during the opioid crisis, we recognize that we did not adequately acknowledge the epidemic unfolding in our communities or the terrible impact of opioid abuse and addiction on millions of families across the country." That's the understatement of the fucking century. It was worse than Nixon asserting, "I am not a crook." These people *were* crooks, they *were* caught, and they'd never get more than a pricey slap on the wrist. It made me sick.

Months later, McKinsey agreed to pay forty-seven states, the District of Columbia, and five US territories $573 million, with the money earmarked for opioid abatement—basically, damage control for the mess they'd made. Separate agreements were reached with Washington, West Virginia, and Nevada, worth $13 million, $10 million, and $45 million, respectively. According to the agreements, McKinsey admitted no wrongdoing. No money went to any actual victims. Shocker, right? On top of that, McKinsey could make its payouts with the assumption that it would get some of its money right back from the states. For example, Maine's state government received a settlement of $3.14 million from McKinsey. Yet, Maine's Department of Labor was already paying McKinsey $6.44 million for a no-bid contract for advice on how to fix their broken unemployment system. The firm started the work on June 15, 2020, and then extended the work another month, stretching the project to close to nine months while they charged something like $27,000 per week.

McKinsey's settlement was put together with astonishing speed. State attorneys general chalked that up to one thing: no plaintiff's attorneys, and no outside counsel. "I believe that as state AGs we are more than capable of doing the work on behalf of our offices and recovering and delivering for the people in our states," said Massachusetts AG Maura Healey at a press conference. Others thought the deal came together so quickly because the states settled for peanuts. They were eager to get what they could, and with no regard for actual individuals or accountability to the public, they could speed ahead and make a shit deal that helped put the whole issue in the past.

"Five hundred million is a joke to McKinsey for what they've done here, it truly is," a plaintiff attorney named Hunter J. Shkolnik told the legal-news site Law360. "They're doing high fives in their boardroom for five hundred million dollars and a walkaway."

As usual, there were no repercussions for McKinsey. The firm did make one symbolic sacrifice by declining to reelect their top executive, Kevin Sneader. According to *The New York Times*, "The decision to deny Mr. Sneader a second three-year term as global managing partner came in a vote by more than six hundred senior partners, according to a company executive. McKinsey did not admit wrongdoing in the settlement, but both senior partners—who would have been voting in the election of Mr. Sneader's successor—were fired." After making a round of pseudo-apologies to the groups they'd been caught harming—still no word on those migrant families they may have helped to destroy—there's no reason to think the company wouldn't quietly go back to doing what they did best: making money by doing the most reprehensible, cold-blooded jobs imaginable. They could collect on both ends of the equation, invoicing the victims and perpetrators alike. They could pretend to be neutral by consulting with the states and also the companies that preyed on us.

"We deeply regret that we did not adequately acknowledge the tragic consequences of the epidemic unfolding in our communities," Sneader had said. "With this agreement, we hope to be part of the solution to the opioid crisis in the US."

McKinsey lost a few reputation points but made millions from the crisis. Once again, the only people *not* getting ahead were the people who were lied to, manipulated, and ultimately fleeced by a system that didn't care if they lived or died.

A backlash against the DOJ deal had been building even before it was signed. The Fed Up! Coalition (which included many of the same people on the Ad Hoc Committee on Accountability) wrote a letter to then–US attorney general Bill Barr, asking that DOJ officials meet with them before finalizing any settlement with the feds. They wanted the Sacklers prosecuted, wanted them to pay more money, and wanted Purdue shuttered instead of remade into a public benefit corporation. Members of Congress also wrote letters to Barr, opposing the clause in the deal that would remake Purdue into a PBC.

The feeling was that the Sacklers were slipping away from the reaches of justice, that the opportunity to hold them accountable in some way was passing by. So in early December 2020, the US House Oversight Committee, chaired by Congresswoman Carolyn Maloney, told the Sackler family they wanted them to testify. The Sackler lawyers refused, arguing that to do so would disrupt negotiations with creditors. The House threatened to issue subpoenas. Eventually, David and Kathe Sackler agreed to testify via video conference, along with Purdue CEO Craig Landau.

This was the first time Sackler family members were ever publicly questioned. Anyone hoping for some kind of admission, or an *A Few Good Men* moment, would be disappointed. I'd become deeply cynical about the process and wasn't expecting anything. These people had proved time and again that they were barely human. Cold-blooded and selfish, they were never going to do a single thing to take responsibility. I knew better than to hope. Sure enough, David Sackler, in a white conference room, peddled his usual bullshit: "What you have heard about the Sacklers from the press is wrong and distorted," and so on. You got Kathe Sackler, sometimes referred to as Dr. Sackler, looking as if she were about to fall asleep. None of them wanted to be there. None of them would cop to their crimes. Kathe's complete lack of remorse or self-awareness came through during one exchange with Congresswoman Maloney:

Maloney: "To sum it up, the Sackler family made billions of dollars by fueling an opioid crisis, over thirty-five billion dollars, that has claimed the lives of thousands and thousands of Americans and has caused an enormous amount of pain for families across the country. In light of all of this . . . Dr. Sackler, will you apologize to the American people for the role you played in the opioid crisis?"

Kathe Sackler: "I would be happy to apologize to the American people for all of the pain they've suffered and for the tragedies that they've experienced in their families. And I thought I did that earlier in my opening comments, that was my intention. I also am very angry. I'm angry that some people working at Purdue broke the law. I'm angry about it from 2007, and I'm angry about it now, again in 2020. I think that—"

Maloney: "I know you're angry and I'm sorry, but that's not the apology we were looking for. You apologized for the pain people have suffered, but you've never apologized for the role that you played in the opioid crisis. So I'll ask you again, will you apologize for the role you played in the opioid crisis?"

Kathe Sackler: "I have struggled with that question. I have asked myself over many years. I have tried to figure out, is there anything that I could have done differently, knowing what I knew then, not what I know now? And I have to say, there is nothing that I can find that I would have done differently, based on what I believed and understood then and what I learned from management in the reports to the board, and what I learned from my colleagues on the board."

Got that? Nothing she would have done differently.

Craig Landau, meanwhile, was eager to apologize for everything he could think of: "On behalf of Purdue, I'm incredibly sorry. . . . The company accepts full responsibility for wrongdoing." And so on. Some of the committee members, such as Congresswoman Katie Porter (a former law professor who'd written a book about bankruptcy), absolutely grilled the Sacklers:

> Porter: "Mr. Sackler, let me ask you. Why should the family not transfer back the 10.4 billion dollars to be used to pay the creditors in this case, including victims of opioid abuse?"
>
> David Sackler: "Well, for a number of reasons, I think the most important—"
>
> Porter: "Do you not have the money?"
>
> David Sackler: "Ma'am, I'm trying my best to answer one at a time. Would you like me to answer the money question?"
>
> Porter: "Yes, please."
>
> David Sackler: "As I said, in your opening questioning. Of the ten billion dollars that you referenced, roughly half went to taxes. So that money we do not have, it was paid in taxes. Does that answer your question?"
>
> Porter: "Okay. But you still have over four billion dollars that was not paid in taxes? Do you still have that money?"
>
> David Sackler: "We do. We still have that money."

Watching the hearing, I was struck by how many members of Congress, both Democratic and Republican, used their time to highlight the human cost of OxyContin and the victims of the overdose crisis. They even played videos from and about victims.

Tearjerkers, for sure, but never with any mention of personal injury payments. I couldn't help but think, *I wish the members of this committee knew how screwed victims are getting in this bankruptcy.* It seemed like a symbolic victory to these elected officials. They'd vanquished Big Bad Pharma, and the little people were safe again. I wished they knew what had happened with the emergency relief fund. I wish they knew what had happened in mediation. I wished they knew that money was intentionally being kept as far away from victims as possible. I wished the hearing would have been about more than just the Sacklers. A few weeks later, I had a phone call with some of the committee's staff, where I told them, "The public-side creditors have been doing everything they can to keep the money as far away from the victims as possible." The staffers had no idea, and from what it sounded like, neither did Congress.

If they had known earlier, would they have done anything? I doubt it. Actions speak louder than words, and although plenty of folks were willing to extend their sympathy, that rarely translated to meaningful change. Everyone was sorry. I was tired of hearing about how sorry they were. What I wanted to know was, when were the Tim Kramers of America getting a check in the mail?

Two days before the congressional hearing, we had a hearing in the bankruptcy case. It was just a couple days before Christmas. The hearing, done by telephone, was routine, with only a few motions on the calendar. But something extraordinary happened, possibly the most surreal moment of the entire case.

Purdue lawyer Marshall Huebner began with one of his trademark meandering monologues. God, that man could talk. He asked the judge to approve a procedural motion that none of the parties had objected to. The judge asked if anyone had anything to say about it.

Suddenly, a strange voice blurted out, "I don't know what the motion means. I got a few things I'd like to say."

It was Tim Kramer. He'd finally found the phone number for the court and happened to dial in during the hearing. After months and months of calling anyone he could think of, from the police to his congressional representatives, Tim had gotten hold of the one person who had any power in the bankruptcy: Judge Robert Drain.

"Excuse me, Mr. Kramer," Drain asked, confused. "Are you representing someone? And if not, what is your role in the case?"

Tim said, "My role is that my fiancée died and I became the guardian of her child. I became the representative of her estate. I got this letter in the mail. . . . It was a big fiasco to try to get to this phone call today, that's number one. And number two, Purdue and the Sacklers owe my stepchild money because they made the drugs that killed my fiancée."

Tim had told this same story to so many unfeeling, uncaring institutions and representatives. He told the judge exactly what happened to LeeRae Conn and what he needed from Purdue. This was the judicial equivalent of a 911 call: Tim was calling to report the damage and get the help he needed and deserved.

But what did Judge Drain say? The same thing as everyone else: you've got the wrong number, pal. He told Tim that the first matter of the day was a motion to extend the debtors' time to file a Chapter 11 plan. That didn't pertain directly to any particular claim in the case—which meant Tim's effort was meaningless. The letter Tim got, with the (wrong) number for the hearing, was some form of claim notice. Drain said over and over that, whatever Tim was saying, "it wouldn't pertain to this specific motion that's before me today."

Wrong number.

"Oh," said Tim. "Should I hang up then? Or should I stay on the line?"

"You could. Either one. Whatever you want. Does anyone else have anything to say on this motion?"

More voices were on that call—people like Tim, claimants who wanted to know when they'd get their share, and what they should do next. Drain dismissed them one at a time or sent them to a website to check their "claim status." It was a clusterfuck.

"Your Honor, I'm Maria Ecke, and my son—" a woman interrupted.

"Okay," said Drain, sounding pained.

"—David Jonathan—"

"Ms. Ecke, I'm sorry," said Drain, finally losing patience with the town hall format. Unlike Tim and the other claimants, Maria had a motion on the agenda, so she was allowed to speak. Her son had died eight days before Christmas in 2015. She and her husband had filed a claim for $242 million. She'd filed a motion for Purdue to pay that amount immediately. She read from a letter she'd written to the creditors committee, saying, "My son was worth much, much more than 242 million dollars, which I put on the paperwork to you. He was the great-great-grandson of the treasurer to the czar of Ukraine, Konstantin Makarenko, one of two living relatives. He was my firstborn, who died needlessly. There is clear and convincing evidence of Purdue Pharma's gross negligence and reckless indifference to the patient's health, well-being, and suffering."

The judge thanked her and addressed the motion as he would any other, in a sympathetic, verbose way: "It is of course absolutely true that one really cannot put a price on a human life or even, frankly, on an injury to someone who survives but has been harmed. At the same time, that is what courts do often because claims are asserted against companies and people for such loss, and the courts knowing full well that they're engaging in *a legal fiction,* nevertheless, do put a price on that loss and also determine issues such as causation and the like. Now, with respect to that motion, there is a fundamental principle of bankruptcy law which is that claims like this—unsecured claims—do not get paid until a plan is confirmed that sets up a mechanism and a distribution scheme for paying all of the claims asserted against the debtor. The rationale for that is a simple one. No individual creditor should get a leg up on payment over all the rest. Under the bankruptcy law, it is premature to provide for payment now. And so the motion before me which specifically seeks for such an early payment must be denied without prejudice."

Denied. Wrong number.

But there were other voices—people who were desperate to know what would happen next. Their family members and loved ones were dead. They needed help. Drain sighed, choosing his words carefully. Finally, he shut it down. He told the court that he held hearings only on what was scheduled before him. Hundreds of thousands of people had lost family members because of opioids, and he couldn't possibly take the time to hear them all—not even one, apparently.

"I don't think that this is the proper forum to do this," he said. "We simply can't turn these hearings into something that the law really doesn't contemplate, which is focusing on things beyond what is actually scheduled to be heard, that the parties prepare on, brief, and analyze. I'm not going to let you speak further on this. As much as I know your words are important, this isn't the right setting for it."

And that was that. The real victims, the people who'd fought and clawed and prayed and protested and hoped and petitioned to be heard, were silenced. Bankruptcy court wasn't the place for their voices—and if it wasn't, where were they supposed to speak? If Judge Drain wouldn't listen to them, who would? Ironically, without those claims, none of the other parties in the case would've had a leg to stand on—yet, the actual victims weren't ever invited to speak for themselves or given any chance to plead their families' cases. Victims were the building blocks upon which everyone's claim rested. The states, the hospitals, the insurance companies—their claims were based on casualties, on suffering, on loss. Those big corporations and institutions said they acted on behalf of victims. Yet the victims, real people, were nowhere in the entire process. They were an afterthought in the allocation negotiations. Their voices were drowned out in discussions about the future of Purdue, and whether to grant immunity to the Sackler family. They were stuck at the kids' table while the grown-ups, the big-shot lawyers and politicians, decided what would happen to them.

Many of these people, victims and family members of loss, needed the money. I remember speaking with a South Carolina woman who had two children. One had died of an overdose, the other was hooked on prescription pills. She was living without running water. She wanted to know when her claim was going to pay out. The answer was—probably never. There was no hope and no help. It was as though these folks were all calling 911 and getting a busy signal or listening to the same loop of hold music, forever and ever.

The people who were willing to keep fighting and keep the faith alive, such as Tim Kramer, didn't get more than anyone else. They struggled along with everyone else. They knocked on doors until their knuckles bled, reasoning that eventually they'd find someone who wanted to do the right thing. The longer they waited, the slimmer those odds got. Now, with the judge himself shutting the door in their faces, it looked like the end of hope. Months after he found LeeRae's lifeless body in their bed, Tim was still knocking. By then, he'd made peace with his grief. His stepchild was nearly eighteen, ready for the college education Tim couldn't afford on his own. He'd donated the special tandem bike, the money-counting machine, and the clothes-color scanner to an organization for the blind, so other people could benefit from the tools that had helped LeeRae while she was still alive.

He kept her white cane in the kitchen, just where she always left it. It would be there, every day, while he waited for someone to see.

11

THE BREAKING POINT

After my last call wrapped up, I ripped the headphones out of my ears and tossed them on the bed. The sun was setting and I hadn't left my desk chair for hours, getting up only for more coffee, a protein bar, or a quick trip to the bathroom. I stood up and stretched, feeling the joints in my hips and shoulders pop. How long had I been sitting here? It felt like an eternity.

The days went by in a haze of stress, each one gobbled up. My sixth sobriety anniversary passed. Valentine's Day. The first day of spring. My calendar was still packed with lawyers, meetings, and check-ins. Even during a pandemic, this part of my world had not stood still for one instant. Although the rest of the United States was staggering back to its feet—with the first doses of the Moderna and Pfizer vaccines distributed to frontline providers—the case hadn't slowed down at all. The committee and court calls were relentless as ever; even after eighteen months, the case was somehow feeling even more demanding.

I poked my head into Sean's office down the hall, gave him a hug and a kiss, and told him I was going for a walk.

"Do it," he said, distracted by his spreadsheet. "We'll order dinner when you get back."

"You're the best." I hugged him one more time, then laced up
my sneakers and headed out the door.

The empty sidewalks of my Las Vegas neighborhood were a
balm for my overworked brain. I cranked up the music on my
phone, trying to find the beat that would relax me, distract me, and
finally get my mind off the case. It took a lot. Claiming even twenty
minutes for myself was difficult. Sometimes, I'd get halfway into a
song and my phone would ring with another update. I punched the
reject button with a fury I'd never before felt. *Fuck off. Give me some
space.* I'd been so hopeful at the beginning. Now, I cringed when I
saw a lawyer's name on my caller ID.

At the corner, I glanced in both directions and crossed toward
a line of palm trees. Their fronds caught the dying sunlight, turning a brilliant pink that rivaled the neon signs of the Strip. They
burned against the crisp, cloudless blue sky. I walked, hardly paying
attention to where I was headed. It didn't matter. I just needed to
get Purdue out of my system. At the next intersection, I turned
toward the massive red mountains that jutted from the horizon.
A thin sliver of crescent moon hovered over one of the peaks, and
I focused on that as I hummed along with "Ophelia," my favorite
Lumineers song. Outside, I finally felt connected to myself again,
to my sense of place. The world kept on growing, blooming, fading,
and dying. I needed to be here, I reminded myself. Once I was back
in my office, I knew that this beautiful place would feel far away. I
took a deep breath of desert air, tasting sunshine and sand. I would
need all these smells and sounds with me when I returned to the
house. When the doors were closed and my phone was ringing off

the hook, I would be right back where I started—alone, miserable, and nauseated with worry.

In a way, things were looking up. I tried to count the positives of the last few months. The pandemic was in a downturn. Joe Biden was president. My loved ones and I were scheduled for the COVID vaccine. The world was trying its best to get back to normal. However, these blessings were totally overshadowed by the bankruptcy. It bled over every aspect of my life, and even at my most optimistic, I knew in my heart that it was done. Over. I wasn't anticipating my committee's next move. I could sense the great, miserable slide ahead as the wheels of the bankruptcy system cranked, processing Purdue as it had ground up so many other corporations. In a matter of months, this would all be over, and I was painfully aware that I had nothing to show for it.

No matter what I did, I couldn't fight the world on its own terms. I used every tool at my disposal, but regardless of how hard I tried or how many people I mobilized or what information was leaked, none of it seemed to make any difference. Every week, new stories broke. *The Wall Street Journal* reported wild conflicts of interest: Skadden, Arps, Slate, Meagher & Flom LLP and Wilmer-Hale, the law firms defending Purdue, received court permission in November 2019 to continue working for the company after it sought Chapter 11 protection. However, the firms didn't disclose their relationship with the Sacklers, and their common interest with related parties in the bankruptcy—or their joint defense agreement. This failure to disclose that they were repping both sides skirted bankruptcy rules meant to reveal potential conflicts of interest. I wish I could say I was shocked, but honestly? It was par for the course. Nothing I learned about these people surprised me anymore. Billions of dollars were at stake, and 99 percent of what should have been public business was being done behind closed doors. I was shut out, and so were the millions of people I was supposed to be advocating for.

Even after the point of no return, I kept trying to salvage small wins. There were a few. Every point scored for victims was hard-won, and I celebrated them. However, I was starting to pull back, too. The deluge of legal filings and calls didn't let up, and it was wearing me down. I had to plan—find some way to save my mental health and figure out a way to survive the aftermath. Purdue's executives would be fine. The Sacklers would walk away essentially untouched. The judge and the lawyers, they'd go to the next case. Everyone would invoice everyone else, cash the checks, and move on. The victims on our committee, including me, were the ones who would struggle to go back to normal—if we even knew what *normal* was anymore. After close to two years of being battered by the system, I was in bad shape. I was an experienced campaigner and was familiar with the sense of listlessness that followed a big launch. This was going to be a thousand times worse. I knew that, once the case wrapped up, I could be in big trouble—because there was nothing to celebrate. No parade, no confetti, and no congratulations. I would be coming back to my community essentially empty-handed. And you know what they say about messengers. They end up getting shot.

Bringing out more bad news wasn't something I was ready for. In spite of my best efforts, the nightmare was coming to life. The Sacklers were essentially leaving the case with immunity. Purdue, which we'd hoped would be burned to the ground, would become a public benefit company. I participated in near-daily negotiations, but things were looking bleak. I'd reviewed the lawyers' drafted letter to the victims' pool, but just the thought of sending it out shot my anxiety skyrocketing. The moment that email went out, there would be massive backlash. My heart broke for all of them, all the people we fought for and all the people this system failed. We would have to tell families, "Your loved one's life is worth thirty-five hundred dollars to forty-eight thousand dollars, maximum." That was pennies. It wasn't enough. I knew that, and I could do nothing about it. The final figure wasn't Anne's fault. Or the victim representatives on the committee. It was the outcome of everybody *except* the victims' groups driving that number down.

That was what made me sickest. We'd asked for a fair deal from the beginning. We offered Purdue and the Sacklers every opportunity to make reparations for the damage they'd done. We wanted justice. We were the only ones. Almost everybody else at the table did their best to get what they could for themselves. It wasn't fair or equal. It was 100 percent legal.

It took nearly a year, but by March 2021, we finally figured out how much money the Sackler family was worth: between $10 billion and $11 billion. About a third of that was tied up in a mix of small companies. That included pieces of their international pharmaceutical empire, such as Mundipharma, which in bankruptcy court parlance were called the International Associated Companies, or IACs. Eleven billion dollars is a pile of money. But you don't get rich by just giving your money away, and the Sacklers had no intention of playing anything other than hardball in their negotiations with how much money to contribute toward the final settlement. The victims? We were just another problem they planned to solve with some loose pocket change.

In the beginning, I hoped we would have some leverage, in the form of criminal prosecution. Maybe the government could force the Sacklers to play fair by treating them like the small-time drug dealers the government incarcerated without a second thought. However, the Sacklers weren't treated like people: they were treated like corporations, which have all the rights of individuals, plus billionaire privilege. It's no coincidence that there is rarely a criminal charge with a civil settlement between a big corporation and a state attorney general. The Sacklers were all but guaranteed to walk away from the bankruptcy with a civil release—the diet version of immunity from criminal prosecution. Instead of *creating* precedent, the states gave up their biggest bargaining chip and chose to look the other way. Certain attorneys general actually told the Sacklers' lawyers that the civil release served as a criminal release—a wink-wink deal. Everybody won. The Sacklers would never see the inside of a jail cell, and the states could say they didn't let them off easily. Just about everyone agreed that civil releases from both the states and the Department of Justice amounted to a de facto criminal release. Prosecuting the Sacklers would be next to unthinkable. For we victims and our payout, it was one less reason for the Sacklers to significantly up their offer.

At the outset of negotiations, the Sackler family had offered to pay $3 billion to Purdue's creditors. It sounds like a lot, but it wasn't a gouge. Much of this money would be recovered in the Sacklers' subsequent sale of Mundipharma and other IACs. This was roughly the same offer on the table before they declared bankruptcy, way back in 2019. Half the states (mostly Republican controlled) agreed to it then, and half the states (mostly Democrat run) rejected it. The breakdown was very much along party lines. Read into that what you will.

These mostly blue nonconsenting states had a different number in mind: they'd settle for $7.3 billion. To the Sacklers, that number was a stunt designed to maximize the ground they would have to cover to meet halfway. The figure was also going to cover some attorneys general's asses. They'd painted themselves into a corner in an election year, going on and on about how the Sackler family deserved to be in jail. Any deal they signed on to had to be a good one.

In reality, the parties were so far apart that any agreement was purely symbolic. They moved toward each other in inches. That didn't erase the miles between them.

The Sacklers countered with $3.225 billion. The nonconsenting states countered with $6.95 billion. The Sacklers came back with $3.275 billion; the states answered with $6.85 billion. The two sides were edging closer, but each counteroffer was less and less movement toward a midpoint. Soon, negotiations stalled. The mediators, Ken Feinberg and Layn Phillips, had little effect. In January 2021, they played what appeared to be their last card, since their term as mediators was about to end. They made a "double blind" offer to both the Sacklers and the nonconsenting states of $4.275 billion, meaning that each party got the number separately and was to respond to the mediator. That way, if one of the parties said no, neither side would know what the other said.

Both sides said no.

I was furious. I felt that we'd been robbed—because we were. The UCC was kept informed of this mediation phase, but never invited to the table or put in a bargaining role. We had front-row seats to the stalemate. I was getting negotiation reports and keeping my lips sealed, to avoid getting in trouble. At every turn, I wanted to go *off* on the pencil-necked, mealymouthed lawyers, calling them out for their ineffectiveness. Every day they delayed, hundreds of people died. More funerals, more broken families—none of that meant anything to them. Even as it became obvious that things weren't going to work out, I kept my mouth shut. I wanted to go to the press, but I didn't trust them. However, it felt like I was the only one. Shortly after the last call, Bloomberg ran a story about the stalled negotiations, writing, "The Sacklers are willing to add more than $1 billion to their cash contribution, bringing their total to more than $4 billion. . . . But attorneys general for states involved in the court-ordered mediation are seeking more than $5 billion to beef up addiction treatment and police budgets, the people said." How the fuck would Bloomberg know that? Everyone assumed that the state groups had planted the story. All I knew was, people were squealing, but it wasn't *me*. The Sackler lawyers were pissed. In a conference call, one of the attorneys referred to the nonconsenting states' "desire to move the negotiations to a public arena, and we are simply not prepared to do that."

That was news to me. This whole time I'd been too scared to do anything except play along. I didn't want to get taken to the shed—but then shit such as this was getting published. It felt like a slap in the face, yet another reminder of the way my naivete was being taken advantage of. The people who had nothing at stake talked. The people who stood to lose everything complied. And look where that fucking got us.

The clock was ticking. Purdue was supposed to submit a plan for reorganization by February 15, 2021. They could ask for up to a one-month extension, but March 15 was considered the final deadline. Purdue had said they would file their plan by then, with or without the Sackler deal. Without the Sacklers' money, some of the private creditors would not be getting their money on the same timetable they'd already agreed to. And the states would go back to suing the Sacklers, and the race to the courthouse would recommence. If that were to happen, an idea was floated for the states to share among themselves the proceeds of any successful suit, but enmity between the Republican and Democratic states was at an all-time high and there would be no agreement on such a proposal. The two sets of states were at odds over everything.

With time running out, Arik came up with a cunning strategy: the creditors committee, the consenting states, the debtors, and a group calling itself the "multistate governmental entities group" (the MSGE group, comprising more than a thousand cities and counties, plus seven tribal nations and a smattering of other jurisdictions) decided to team up and tell the Sackler family that they would be willing to negotiate off the mediators' $4.275 billion proposal.

"No one likes the idea of the Sacklers only paying 4.275 billion dollars, or frankly any dollar less than every dollar they took away from Purdue," Arik told the creditors committee.

But, he said, we weren't acting just for ourselves. He reminded us, "We are fiduciaries. We have to be in some way guided by what the creditors in the case think."

So, keep following the high-minded, altruistic principles that got us into this mess. We didn't have any choice: the high ground was the only thing left to stand on. I absolutely hated this strategy. I despised the idea of cutting corners: we deserved full Sackler value, every penny, nothing less. However, I was in the minority of the minority. I was getting used to that.

Arik's hope was that the nonconsenting states, fearful of being cut out of the deal, would sign on to it. They had to participate or risk losing out on billions of dollars. The four groups made the offer to the Sacklers, and the family agreed—only, they wanted to pay the $4.275 billion out over eleven years. They had an elaborate justification for it, but it boiled down to their not wanting to pay any quicker, and they didn't think they had to.

Smelling cash, the nonconsenting states came back to the table. After eating some crow, this deal looked a little better. Now, they were willing to negotiate around a $4.275 billion settlement, under two conditions: that the money be paid out over *four* years, not eleven; and, more important, that instead of being converted into a public benefit corporation, Purdue be sold immediately. This sounded slightly more reasonable to me—until I learned who the prospective buyer was.

By then, the only potential buyer for Purdue was Mike Burke. If you haven't heard that name before, don't be surprised. But he was certainly known to some who follow pharmaceuticals, particularly when it comes to pricing.

He was right on time for Purdue. For more than a year, the general assumption was that Purdue would be converted into a public benefit corporation: a new, presumably more ethical Purdue. NewCo, short for "new company," would still sell OxyContin, but would not market it (at least not aggressively). NewCo would also sell products that would help mitigate the impact of the opioid crisis, such as buprenorphine and naloxone. Revenue would flow back to the states, which would handpick a board of directors, which would in turn hire new management. The states could sell any part of NewCo at any time. Sounds good, right? Well, you know what that means: conflict. Time-wasting, money-burning, victim-screwing conflict.

The nonconsenting states began to grow uncomfortable with the idea of, as they put it, "owning Purdue." I think, by this time, many of us were. For a while, I thought that was just the AGs playing politics. But as the case wore on, I started to think they had a point. Replacing a corporation's entire management team would be an enormous undertaking, one that could take years. And there was no plan—no business plan, no plan for choosing board members, no plan on how to equitably distribute the revenue. What would guarantee that some of the states wouldn't run the company so as to maximize profit? Elected officials could be bought and sold by special interests. The Sacklers' philanthropy had a long reach, and who knew how far that grasp might go. Who oversees the government? Furthermore, there wasn't a whole lot of precedence for this. Turning an evil super-corp into a public utility was unheard of. There was no blueprint. Predictably, the process faltered as lawyers failed to rise to the challenge of their imaginations.

After the DOJ settlement gave weight to the PBC proposal, opposition to the plan began to spread to victims groups, including the Ad Hoc Committee on Accountability. In December 2019, Professor David Herzberg of the University of Buffalo and author of the book *White Market Drugs,* coauthored a letter to Judge Drain, arguing that turning Purdue into a PBC wouldn't do any good and might actually do some harm. (Drain himself had referred to Herzberg's book in a hearing as "the most comprehensive and up-to-date history on this issue," although Herzberg suspects that Drain had read a review of the book in *The Wall Street Journal* rather than the book itself.) Herzberg saw the bankruptcy as an opportunity for states to punish Purdue harshly and publicly by liquidating and dissolving the company, thus sending a message to the entire industry.

"If you give Purdue a shot at redemption," Herzberg said, "you communicate to the rest of the industry, 'You don't have to change what you're doing.'"

Purdue's outlook, revenue-wise, was not great. The OxyContin name was well and truly tarnished. The company's market share had shrunk considerably, and the market itself had receded as well. Drugs such as buprenorphine and naloxone, meanwhile, had only small profit margins. Big surprise, lifesaving drugs turned less of a profit than the ones that could ruin your life. It's worth pointing out that pain patients and people who needed OxyContin to manage chronic conditions weren't the ones driving Purdue's big profits. That was addiction revenue. Take away the overprescribed, diverted pills that flooded the market, and what was Purdue? A busted pony, trying to run on two legs.

"The main barriers to greater availability of addiction treatment drugs has been skepticism, stigma, and fear on the part of policy makers," Herzberg wrote in his letter to Drain. "Having a company with Purdue's bad reputation associated with addiction treatment drugs would worsen, not improve, those barriers."

I was coming around to this view as well. The best thing to do with Purdue would be to sell off its assets and give any proceeds to the victims. Everybody wins, except the Sacklers—that was my goal from day one, with victims at the top of the food chain. The states wouldn't get their abatement money; but then again, states had billions in other revenue streams from the federal government, such as the money sitting unspent in their budgets for "opioid response." But none of the creditors, save for a handful of victims groups, wanted this plan. The creditors wouldn't even *discuss* the prospect of liquidating Purdue. It would have meant less money for the states and, crucially, less money for most of the attorneys working on the case, and they, after all, were the ones running the show. That meant liquidation was a no-go, and the garage sale had commenced. Enter pharmaceutical investor Mike Burke, cash in hand (sort of) and ready to buy.

In the paperwork, Burke was referred to as BTcP Pharma, the company he owned. The debtors and the consenting states were against the Burke bid from the start and tried to discredit him every chance they could, calling him all sorts of names and dredging up a couple of unseemly episodes from his past. It was *juicy.* What interested me wasn't the gossip. It was the lawyers' strong reaction to him. The debtors were threatened by Burke's presence and hauled out the heavy artillery to defend their claim from him.

Burke had a history with pharmaceutical companies making expensive "orphan drugs," which were designed to treat diseases that affect only a small number of people. In the early 2000s, he was an executive at Ovation Pharmaceuticals, which sold—among other things—Indocin, a drug used to treat a rare congenital heart defect found in severely underweight premature babies. In 2006, Ovation purchased NeoProfen, another drug the FDA was about to approve. The Federal Trade Commission filed a complaint against Ovation, accusing the company of trying to corner the market and force hospitals "to pay monopoly prices." While the complaint was dismissed when the court found that Indocin and NeoProfen were in different markets, the pricing information it provided was notable. According to the complaint:

Once it acquired NeoProfen, Ovation immediately raised the price it charged hospitals for Indocin nearly 1,300 percent, from $36 to approximately $500 per vial. When Ovation launched NeoProfen in July 2006, it set a price of approximately $483 per vial, essentially matching Indocin's price. Ovation has maintained prices for the two PDA drugs at or above this level for more than two years.

Burke's job was to set prices for the company's drugs. In a 2004 memo, he wrote that Indocin and NeoProfen were "a group of medically niche small volume products that don't have substitutes and that are significantly underpriced to the market. In the U.S. we can price these almost anywhere we want given the product profiles."

Burke's next stop was to cofound Marathon Pharmaceuticals, and he was the company's chief business officer in 2017 when Marathon was hit with a similar price-gouging scandal. Marathon was poised to release deflazacort, a drug used to treat a rare type of muscular dystrophy in the United States. Its planned price tag was $89,000 a year, despite that it had been available in Europe for years at 2–5 percent of that cost. US senators sent a letter to Marathon's CEO, calling the plan "unconscionable." Marathon backtracked; it delayed plans to release the drug, then sold it to a different pharmaceutical company. Burke left later that year and founded MMB Healthcare.

In 2019, Burke's BTcP (a subsidiary of MMB) bought Subsys, a fentanyl-based drug, from the bankrupt company Insys Therapeutics. Burke promised to sell Subsys only to doctors treating cancer patients, to refrain from aggressive marketing. Burke, it seemed, had moved on from orphan drugs and was now buying up toxic-asset opioids—also known as bankrupt opioid companies. This made me more than a little suspicious. How did we know this wasn't the next Richard Sackler? In terms of acquiring pharmaceuticals at fire-sale prices, Burke's move made lots of sense. Adding Purdue to his portfolio was a shrewd business decision and created opportunities for him to raise opioid prices as the market recovered. But looking at his history, I saw all-too-familiar examples of the free market exploiting people with unique medical needs—and wondered why we had never discussed putting Purdue out for a real bid. Why weren't we looking for larger parent companies to buy it? Why were we entertaining offers from this private buyer?

As I recall, Burke's initial offer was to purchase all of Purdue's assets, except for its cash, for around $700 million. He offered an extra bonus payment of $300 million if Purdue continued to have exclusive rights to sell OxyContin by the end of 2024—that is, if generics hadn't entered the market by then. The offer represented more cash up front than holding on to Purdue, and it was a better deal if you believed that OxyContin sales were going to tank. It was, in many ways, more appealing than converting Purdue to a public benefit company and going through the whole rigmarole of flipping the organization into something nontoxic. However, the lesser of two evils is still *evil*. Something about the bid felt wrong, and as we learned more, I wasn't the only one who felt worried. The main problem, from the states' point of view, was that Burke would be putting in only about $20 million of his own company's money. The lion's share of the rest he would be borrowing from hedge funds, who would get repaid with significant interest. Many AGs didn't like that.

If you tell an attorney general that there's money going to hedge funds instead of state coffers, it's anathema. Hedge funds were notorious for messing with pricing for their own gain. They were also terrible at balancing the so-called free market and had demonstrated no ability to put principles before their payday.

The more we looked at it, the worse Burke's bid looked. In exchange for his up-front investment of $20 million, Burke stood to gain at least ten times that. It looked as if we were getting played. With this in mind, Arik and the nonconsenting states tried to convince him to change the structure of his offer. He did, and his new offer was completely different. Instead of borrowing money from hedge funds, he now wanted, essentially, to *borrow* Purdue from the creditors. He wanted to give creditors $20 million and a stack of IOU notes for the assets of Purdue, then pay us back somewhere between $700 million and $1 billion over the next seven to eight years. If he defaulted, the company would revert back to state ownership. Because of the structure of the deal, for tax purposes, Burke wouldn't be the owner of Purdue for a good long while. So that was a good little bonus for him. He was getting Purdue on layaway and still at an outrageous deal.

To the consenting states, this was crazy. The whole point of selling to Burke was that it was a sale. But with his restructured offer, suddenly it wasn't a sale? The nonconsenting states replied, no, no, it was a sale. To me, it was a Schrödinger's sale: once you looked too closely, whatever defined the deal evaporated, turning into a handful of maybes. The debate had become oddly metaphysical. Not to mention ironic: Republican-run states were pushing for state control of Purdue, while Democratic-run states were pushing for privatization, a sale to an arch-capitalist businessman. Up was down, black was white, blue was red, and so on. But that's how intense the polarization between the two sets of states was. They couldn't agree on anything.

The Sacklers bettered their offer to $4.275 billion paid out over ten years. That might have been good enough for the nonconsenting states if the other parties could be convinced to take Burke's offer, which looked unlikely. (Did I mention that the Department of Justice had to be convinced, too? Nothing was cut-and-dried with this. Everyone had to approve, which meant that nobody agreed.) In theory, a Sackler deal could be pushed through over the objections of the nonconsenting states. The judge would likely approve that if only one party objected. But the trade was that nonconsenting states would also be able to appeal. (Some circuit courts have ruled that you can't have a "nonconsensual third-party release" approved over the objection of some creditors. You know, in the interest of fairness.) So, if the nonconsenting states wanted to, they could appeal the whole thing all the way up to the US Supreme Court.

It looked as if they might. I was ready to say, "Fuck it," and roll. My mind kept drifting to the letter the lawyers had already drafted to the tens of thousands of victims who'd claimed a piece of Purdue. They would all be let down. That letter wouldn't tell them *why* we failed or even detail all the things we had tried in order to make sure justice was served. None of what I saw or heard in the meetings that cluttered my calendar would ever see the light of day. Justice would die behind closed doors, and all these folks would know was that they might get a check for a few grand to atone for the harm the company had caused them. Maybe if I circled the block again, I could put this off a little longer. The crescent moon had moved higher in the sky and was a piercing white against the now-dark silhouette of the midnight-colored mountains. I cycled through my playlist again, trying to buy a little more time. Early March in Vegas is freezing and windy, and even though I tried to hold out, soon it was so cold that I was shivering. I didn't want to go home: home was work and work was home. My bedroom was the courtroom. I was sick of it all.

I walked and walked until the icy wind was unbearable and my kneecaps started to stiffen. When I got home, Dollar was waiting for me on the couch. I cooed to him as I got a glass of water. The Lumineers still sang in my earbuds, so I lifted my phone to swipe them off. I could barely tap the screen. My index finger was blue from the cold. The skin around my nail was the shade of lavender. Yet, if I could, I would have been out there another hour, trying to burn off my anger. I flexed my hands, squeezing them into fists. At the beginning of this, I was so sure I could batter Purdue to the ground—that, superhero-style, I'd come in swinging and win the day for everyone who'd ever been harmed by the Sacklers. Now, I was just trying to stay alive. Stay sober. And keep on going.

CONCLUSION

The Way Out

The end of the case began the same way it started. On Monday, March 15, 2021, I was up late, near the end of the night on my coast. My phone lit up as it fed me the endless scroll of news headlines—updates I didn't need. I knew what had happened. My time in this fight was over.

Purdue files plan of reorganization. Company getting ready to exit. I groaned and swiped across my screen, erasing each notification as soon as it arrived. I knew what the filing said. I was too tired to go on, or to find the motivation to feign interest. I was beyond the point of fatigue. I felt a strange weight in my chest, as though my heart had transformed from muscle to lead. The torturous journey of the past eighteen months was coming to an end, and what I had to show for it was a sense of profound grief.

The first news headline I saw was from *The New York Times:* PURDUE PHARMA OFFERS PLAN TO END SACKLER CONTROL AND MOUNTING LAWSUITS.

"With drug overdoses still at record levels, it is past time to put Purdue's assets to work addressing the crisis," Purdue chairman

Steve Miller told *The Times*. "We are confident this plan achieves that critical goal."

Other articles quoted the Sackler family: "Today marks an important step toward providing help to those who suffer from addiction, and we hope this proposed resolution will signal the beginning of a far-reaching effort to deliver assistance where it is needed."

It turned my stomach. This first-take coverage made Purdue and the Sacklers look as if they were leaning gracefully into the world of philanthropy, like a late-career Bill Gates or Jeff Bezos. This was the outcome Purdue had wanted all along. This wasn't a bankruptcy, it was a heist.

Victims' advocates railed against the plan on social media—both for the ease with which the Sacklers were getting off, and the paltry sums of money going to victims. In an eloquent thread on Twitter, former prosecutor (and author of *Bad Medicine*) Charlotte Bismuth wrote, "As a former prosecutor who understands the scope of the devastation wrought by the Sacklers, I am appalled that they are able to buy such an extraordinary release in exchange for a mere fraction of their ill-gotten gains. I've never seen suspected criminals treated with such deference—but that's precisely why they fled into bankruptcy court (and this court in particular), where they knew their extraordinary demands would be entertained."

Lawyers started emailing and calling me, frantically begging for help.

"We have to get control of this," one of them said.

"There's nothing to get control of," I responded. "What the fuck do you want me to do? People are pissed. I'm pissed."

The lawyers blamed the messaging, the rollout, and the way the plan was announced. They seemed to think that a better spin would win people over and convince them to accept what was totally unacceptable. This was just a bad deal. It didn't matter if the lawyers thought this was the best deal we could get under the circumstances. It was still shit. There were no heroes in this story. I wasn't going to pretend otherwise, and I refused to clap for the people who'd done nothing to help my community. They had every chance to advocate for the constituents they were sworn to represent. They put us last. This was the outcome.

Predictable, prewritten press releases shot from the desks of attorneys general. The consenting-state AGs took measured victory laps. "Attorney General Ashley Moody has secured additional funding for Florida communities plagued by the national opioid crisis," read one. *For* communities, not *to* communities—which meant the state would keep their check, giving no money directly to survivors. True to form, the AGs' press releases were almost identical: some politician telling everyone what *she* had done, how much money *she* had secured.

The nonconsenting states released a joint statement: "We are disappointed in this plan. While it contains improvements over the proposal that Purdue announced and we rejected in September 2019, it falls short of the accountability that families and survivors deserve."

These states said they wanted major changes to the plan: more money from the Sacklers, a sale or liquidation of Purdue, a full release of all documents, and, lastly, a blanket protection for all Sackler-associated nonprofits who wanted to sever their ties from the infamous family.

In a video posted on Facebook, Massachusetts attorney general Maura Healey called the plan "an insult" and said it "lets the

Sacklers off the hook. . . . They shouldn't be allowed to keep their OxyContin fortune." Her video was widely and approvingly shared by activists.

Although the news continued to break early into the next morning, I couldn't put down my phone. I sat on the edge of the bed, in the dark. Sean rested, relaxed and dreaming with his head on the pillow beside mine. Although we lived in the same house and worked in adjacent rooms, I missed him. I felt that we didn't see enough of each other when every waking—and sleeping—moment was consumed by the case. I wanted my life back. I wanted *Sean* back. I listened to his deep, soft breaths and tried to match their rhythm with my own. To slow my pulse, so I wouldn't type something I'd regret. The messages kept popping up, bombarding me with new pleas, new information. I shook my head, trying to clear it as I wrote an email to Arik:

I had a very hard time sleeping.

"After 450,000 opioid deaths a bankruptcy plan emerges that would end Purdue Pharma. The Sacklers would pay $4.2b but admit no wrongdoing and would remain one of the wealthiest families in America."

In black and white—there it is. America is a place where, if you are rich enough, you can practically buy your way out of anything, including murder.

I am disgusted by this entire process. I am resigning from the committee.

I paused, thumb hovering over the Send button. Walking away, now? When things were so close to being finished? I wasn't sure.

I told myself, *You're tired. This thing is almost over. May as well see it out.*

I deleted the resignation, but sent the rest. Arik responded the next morning. He reminded me that it wasn't just $4.2 billion; the Sacklers were also giving up Purdue, a company worth several billion. But he said I shouldn't be disgusted with the process alone. If I wanted to blame anyone, he said, blame the states, and their inability to agree on a way to equitably share the proceeds from lawsuits filed against the Sackler family.

"Because of that," he said, "our ability to get the most money out of the Sacklers was compromised. That will be the untold story of this saga."

Others agreed. Lindsey Simon, an assistant professor at the University of Georgia School of Law, wrote in a Twitter thread, "However appealing it may be, blaming the Sackler negotiations for this limitation is a red herring. Yes, the Sacklers could contribute more money to the bankruptcy, but there's no indication that any increase would benefit individual claimants. The treatment of individual claimants under the plan is a direct result of the dominant role played by governmental entities in the case."

The very entities who were supposed to protect, support, and care for individual Americans had pushed us out. The system defended itself, to the very end—no matter what the cost was to ordinary people.

I wish I could say I didn't care, but I did. Caring made it worse. I felt the ache in my chest dull as I cleared another message from my phone. A year and a half ago, I'd been on fire and so eager to go toe-to-toe with Purdue. I was confident, at the beginning, that with everything out in the open, with the courts involved and the enthusiastic support of state AGs, we had a fighting chance. I brought my passion, ability, and lived experience to the table. I threw myself into this and trusted the process. That was a mistake. I *trusted.* On the other side of the filing that would finally end Purdue as we knew it, I could practically feel the massive, mechanical wheels of our system grinding me into a pulp. Months of sticking my hands in the wringer had brutalized my heart, my mind, and my soul. This was not a battle—it was butchery. It had taken me a long time to see who really held the carving knife.

When the National Prescription Opiate Multidistrict Litigation began at the end of 2017, some of us hoped it would yield hundreds of billions of dollars. We envisioned much of it going to support the victims of the overdose crisis—people in recovery, their loved ones, the survivors, and those that still struggled. We hoped the courts could be a venue for the kinds of reparations lawmakers would never provide. Nearly four years later, the MDL was turning out to be a huge disappointment. To compound that, the Purdue filing on March 15, 2021, was the final confirmation that all our hopes were truly dead. In the final settlement, the money sent to victims in the Purdue bankruptcy would total around $750 million, with payments spread out over a number of years. The states would receive billions of dollars, spread out over almost a decade. These were small, drop-in-the-bucket payments that would significantly be eaten up by lawyer fees. The writing was on the wall: we lost. Brian Mann, in a story for NPR, said it best: the Sacklers would remain one of the wealthiest families in America, never admitting culpability or taking the fall.

There it is, again. *Remain one of the wealthiest families in America.* This was always and only about the money for them—and for many of the other parties involved.

The MDL and the Purdue bankruptcy should have been about public health and reparations. Instead, it turned into a financial power struggle as states, hospitals, insurance companies, and pharmacies all vied for a refund on *their* losses in the epidemic. They had no misgivings about trampling on the people who should have been first in line—such as Tiffinee Scott, Aileen Lovejoy, Tim Kramer, and the hundreds of thousands of others who had a claim to a piece of Purdue. Those people didn't have the luxury of million-dollar legal representation. They couldn't pay millions of dollars a month to plead their case, as the Sacklers had. Charlotte Bismuth pointed out that the first family of Big Pharma had deep pockets and could afford advocates whose sole purpose was "to minimize the Sacklers' role in causing harm and protect their wealth. No one else has this." Normal people were at a disadvantage in court, she pointed out, and once the case made its way into bankruptcy—this court in particular—the Sacklers were all but guaranteed to come out ahead. In court, "they knew their extraordinary demands would be met," she said, and I agreed. The fallout from the case told me everything I needed to know about whom the system valued. I didn't need my phone to remind me of how bleak it was.

OxyContin would continue to be sold in pharmacies all over the world. It won't be aggressively marketed as it was before—well, probably not. That was the smallest of possible wins. But there was nothing to stop another drug company from aggressively marketing the next generation of addictive painkillers, or to prevent the Mike Burkes of the world from acquiring the patent and jacking up the price, just to gouge pain patients who rely on it. There was no protection in place for the communities most harmed. It had taken an indescribable, monumental amount of advocacy, mobilization, and effort to get victims taken seriously. We were stymied at every turn, undercut and lowballed. I couldn't imagine going through this again in another ten years, but I knew it was a possibility. The government wasn't interested in protecting individuals or even putting reasonable safeguards in place. The government would show up when the shooting was over, do a little cleanup, offer some sympathetic platitudes, and ride off into the sunset.

The fallacy of every court case is that somebody is the bad guy and must take the blame. This bankruptcy showed me how foolish that belief is. You may as well believe in the tooth fairy. With Purdue, more than one party was at fault—not just for the overdose epidemic, but for the epic fumbling of justice in the bankruptcy proceedings. I think the Department of Justice was just as much part of the problem as the states, given what they *could* have done and what they *should* have done. The DOJ probably had the most leverage against the Sacklers. The DOJ could have used many of the tools at their disposal— any number of federal charges, seizing assets, freezing bank accounts, suspending passports. Yet, they didn't. They didn't put the squeeze on the Sacklers. The DOJ worked only on reaching a deal, as though they were dealing with any other corporate interest. There was an incentive to keep things cut-and-dried: the Sacklers paid nearly $5 billion in taxes, with the federal government receiving (and keeping) most of that. You could say that the government was one of the biggest beneficiaries, if not *the* biggest, of the overdose crisis. That doesn't consider the cost of increased Medicare, Medicaid, and the money the government earmarked for abatement—but still. I think of what recovery community organizations, mutual aid groups, and frontline workers could do with $5 billion, and I am positive it would be more effective, humane, and sustainable than what we're doing now. To the legal system, every problem can be solved with more laws, more legislation. I am convinced that absorbing more funding into a system that is designed to discipline, punish, and exclude marginalized people is the worst possible use of our resources. Until we have recovery-focused leadership, I doubt that we will make serious progress in this area. The damage of the overdose crisis is done and can never be reversed. The best we can hope for is healing. And that path, that process—I don't know what it looks like yet.

There was nothing surprising about the plan of reorganization that Purdue filed—not to anyone who'd been paying attention. Purdue would be converted into a new company, NewCo, which "will be required to operate in a responsible and sustainable manner, and will be subject to the same laws and regulations as any other pharmaceutical company." It would sell opioids and "opioid overdose reversal and addiction treatment medications," with the revenue going to abatement trusts.

Even our pie-in-the-sky dream that the Sacklers would be charged for their role in the crisis came to nothing. They would almost certainly never face criminal prosecution. The family would walk away with immunity from civil litigation for themselves and several hundred of their associates, associated companies, and trusts. The immunity would extend to law firms representing them, such as Joseph Hage Aaronson and Milbank, and even to their crisis management firm, Goldin Solutions. In exchange, the Sacklers would pay $4.275 billion over nine years, to be repaid in part by the sale of their various companies.

The Sacklers' final bill was a fraction of their total wealth. That fact alone stands among the greatest injustices of the Purdue bankruptcy. It's eclipsed only by the pittance that went to victims. Between $700 million and $750 million was put aside for the roughly 130,000 personal injury victims. Actual people. The filing included a chart that broke down what each person was owed in points. *Points.* An addiction to a Purdue product was worth twenty thousand points; a death from a Purdue product was worth forty thousand points; a death from a non-Purdue opioid, such as heroin, was worth twenty thousand points; use of a Purdue opioid for more than six months was worth six thousand points; use of a Purdue opioid for less than six months without a resulting death or addiction would pay out the minimum award of $3,500. It was hard to say how much money each point was worth, but payments would likely max out at $48,000, for a death by a Purdue product. Forty-eight thousand dollars for a human life. When I saw this chart for the first time in the filing, I broke down in tears. This was the thing that hit me hardest. It was a game board, with me and my friends each assigned a dollar value. That's all we were. They moved us around like checkers, with no regard for our personhood or our lives. It was all a fucking game.

Parents of babies born with neonatal abstinence syndrome would receive three thousand to twenty thousand points, depending on how long the baby spent in the intensive care unit. But the NAS babies as a class would also receive $60 million for medical monitoring, an idea I was staunchly opposed to. Still, the NAS group wasn't satisfied. Scott Bickford, the lead NAS attorney, objected to the vagaries around how different victims would be evaluated. *He could object until the cows came home,* I thought. It wouldn't change a damn thing. No matter how you looked at it, the amounts were piddling. Some lawyers had spent months (with their meters running, no doubt) arguing over how to divide us up, how to draw and quarter us and assign an arbitrary value to our suffering, while collecting nearly twice what was paid out to survivors. It was sickening, macabre. I felt it like a gut punch. The people I'd worked with, talked to, and raged with—my own community—would not receive enough to even make a dent in their grief and loss and wreckage. I

Tier	Base Award	LEVELS (one of the below)	
		A	B
Tier 1A: PI *Addiction from Purdue Opioids*	20,000 pts	10,000 pts OUD Diagnosis, OR MAT for >6 months	20,000 pts Death from an Opioid
Tier 1B: PI *Death on OxyContin*	40,000 pts	N/A	N/A
Tier 2: PI *Purdue Opioids Use ≥6 months*	6,000 pts	3,000 pts OUD Diagnosis, OR MAT for >6 months	20,000 pts Death from an Opioid
Tier 3: PI *No Addiction/ Death from Purdue Opioids, and Purdue Opioids Use <6 mo.*	$3,500	N/A	N/A
Tier 1A: NAS *Addiction from Purdue Opioids, or Purdue Opioids Use During Pregnancy*	20,000 pts	10,000 pts NICU of 2-30 days, OR minor NAS-related injuries	20,000 pts NICU >30 days, OR Other serious NAS-related injuries
Tier 2: NAS *Purdue Opioids Use ≥6 months*	6,000 pts	3,000 pts NICU of 2-30 days, OR minor NAS-related injuries	20,000 pts NICU >30 days, OR Other serious NAS-related injuries
Tier 3: NAS *No Addiction from Purdue Opioids, No Purdue Opioids Use During Pregnancy, and Purdue Opioids Use <6 months*	$3,500	N/A	N/A

saw the news that FEMA would cover part of the funeral expenses of COVID-19 victims. There was no such allowance for overdose victims. Once again, we were left to fend for ourselves—to take our pain, our lost hopes, and our suffering and wonder what on earth we were supposed to do next.

The proposed plan was long: 93 pages, plus another 320-page disclosure statement. There were dull details I won't bore you with, interspersed with a lot of Purdue patting itself on the back for generously solving a crisis that it helped ignite in the first place. But there were also all kinds of vagaries. For example, the Sacklers were committing to releasing documents to be held in a "public document repository" but weren't exactly committing to giving up all the documents—only some, saying, "the scope and terms of which are to be mutually agreed." In other words, *we'll figure that out later.*

To me, it sounded as if the filing were saying, *Stay tuned for more.* The plan was littered with pending business. The Sacklers and their associates were prohibited from "engaging in the manufacturing or sale of opioids, *subject to exceptions to be agreed*" (emphasis mine). Placeholders in a plan of reorganization are not unusual. Plans are filed like this all the time, with the understanding that parties will fill in the finer details later. But some of these finer details seemed pretty important. In what ways, exactly, would Sackler family members be allowed to sell opioids? And why would that even be a consideration?

Other issues were still to be resolved. The public schools got nothing under the plan, and they were none too pleased about that. The Sacklers still wanted a dozen or so names added to their magic list of VIPs with immunity. Probably the biggest and weirdest open dispute was between the public side (the states and municipalities) and the private-side contingency lawyers. The public side thought the attorneys were making too much money. Some of the states simply wanted more money to go to the clients. But some of the states were arguing that the private-side lawyers should forgo some of their fees and give them to the *public-side lawyers.* The justification for this demand was that the private-side lawyers were making way more than the public-side lawyers, and this wasn't fair, because there would never even have been a bankruptcy without the states' lawsuits and the multidistrict litigation. *Lawyers.* They only care about fairness when it's *their* fucking invoice.

So, the filing wasn't the end. But it was the beginning of the end—for Purdue, and for my role on the committee. When my involvement in the case ended, I would leave knowing that *this would happen again* unless the same ordinary people the government flagrantly abandoned in our time of need mobilized to influence, reform, and eventually change the courts. The massive systemic transformation needed would take years, even decades, to accomplish—but the tools we needed were there. In the right hands, we could one day realize a more just government than the one that let the Sacklers walk away from the wreckage they caused.

In the future, the government must get in line behind the people it claims to represent. Victims must come first. One thing I've learned about mass tort cases that enter into the bankruptcy court is that there are thousands or hundreds of thousands of victims. In bankruptcy, these people have to get in line behind corporations and governmental entities. They are treated like small numbers on a large ledger. This is a great injustice. A fair bankruptcy process would put victims at the top of the pyramid and place the burden of proof on governments and corporations as to why *they* deserve to cut to the front of the line. A government for the people and by the people puts *people* first. Until we do that, we can't call ourselves a justice-loving nation.

We must also ban venue shopping by corporations. A number of law professors—notably Lynn M. LoPucki of UCLA—have pointed out that the bankruptcy system is corrupted by venue shopping. In this practice, a corporation entering bankruptcy can choose its own jurisdiction and thus, in most cases, its own judge. This option is unavailable to private citizens. For the record, it's also unavailable to average businesses, but easily available to large corporations. It results in a sort of competition among judges over who is more friendly to debtors and corporations. There's an incentive to keep positive relationships at that level, way over the heads of ordinary people.

Now, I am not suggesting that Judge Robert Drain was bent on letting Purdue and the Sackler family off the hook. Drain had empathy. He played by the rule book given to him. His errors in the case were small. He was tough on the nonconsenting states, treating them as impediments to a process. He was, at times, deferential to Purdue's lawyers. Most of all, Drain impressed upon all parties, over and over, the need for a quick resolution. He wanted to push the process along as fast as possible. With good reason—every month, millions of dollars went off Purdue's balance sheet and into the pockets of lawyers. But the emphasis on speed had its downside, too. Among other things, it allowed the Sacklers to run out the clock on discovery. It made it harder to look for another buyer for Purdue, and harder to negotiate with the one potential buyer we did have, Mike Burke. And Drain declined to appoint an examiner, which would have added a layer of oversight and transparency to the proceedings.

Perhaps, given another six months, nothing would have changed except Purdue's cash reserves. But behind the scenes, everyone felt as if the bankruptcy were a moving train full of burning garbage. Our choice was to get on or let it pass by.

The respect Drain showed Purdue's lawyers made the others want to keep Purdue on board with any agreement because we knew that Drain would be reluctant to overrule the debtor. That had a moderating effect on proceedings—and not in a good way. All the lawyers were concerned with forming a consensus. That's what killed the emergency relief fund. Again, this is not to say that Drain is a terrible judge. He isn't. I think that a vital point of reform is acknowledging that it is absurd for corporations (or anyone else) to be able to pick their own judges. But, hey, this is America.

In the end, the Sackler family gave up less than half their fortune in exchange for civil immunity and de facto criminal immunity. They bought their way out. This was a deal negotiated with the majority of Purdue's creditors, but it was forced through over the objections of half the states in the union—the more populous half—as well as many victims. The legality of the release is somewhat disputed and may be decided by the Supreme Court. (That's a strong *maybe*. I wouldn't be surprised if this goes no further.) I believe that this sort of ransom should not be allowed over the objections of a major class of creditors. We must make third-party releases harder to obtain. At the least, those third-party releases should have a layer of judicial review and oversight. They should be treated as an exception to the norm. Instead, giving the Sackler family and their cohorts immunity was treated as a foregone conclusion. The attitude was, they would walk. White-collar criminals aren't held to the same standards as street dealers, and that is something that should definitely change.

Days after the filing, Congress unveiled a bill that might have been useful a year ago, but was purely symbolic now. Democratic representatives Carolyn Maloney of New York (chair of the House Oversight and Reform Committee) and Mark DeSaulnier of California put forth the Stop Shielding Assets from Corporate Known Liability by Eliminating Non-Debtor Releases Act, or the SACKLER Act. The bill proposed closing "a loophole to prevent those who have not filed for bankruptcy from being released from lawsuits brought by the federal government, as well as states and local governments in bankruptcy," according to *The Hill*.

However, this was a case of too little, too late. (Though it might do some good in the future.) The House bill came nineteen months after the Sacklers' first indication to get a nonconsensual third-party release through the bankruptcy, which predated Purdue's official Chapter 11 filing. If Congress was so concerned about this, why didn't they enact this bill at that time? Perhaps the initial deal of $3 billion over seven years, plus a $10 billion to $12 billion payout to creditors, seemed robust. It certainly made for exciting headlines. Yet, after the UCC did discovery on the Sacklers—finding evidence that Congress would later take credit for—some in the government suspected they needed to go harder on the Sackler family. Again, none of the money the DOJ extracted from the family would ever be given directly to victims. It was for the federal government. If they cared so much about protecting *people,* they would also have enacted an ERF-type law, creating some kind of trust that would support the families and individuals harmed by the Sacklers. The SACKLER Act *sounded* good—but it's tragically ironic that it likely won't apply to its namesake.

Some action around bankruptcy reform is beginning to shape up, but it's clear that much more must be done. Senator Elizabeth Warren has put forward a bankruptcy bill that would make key reforms to the bankruptcy system. (And it's a good one, too.) Most of Warren's ideas are focused on granting to average citizens the same bankruptcy protections long enjoyed by corporations. Among other things, it would streamline the bankruptcy process for individuals, end the prohibition on discharging student debt through bankruptcy, and allow people to protect their cars and homes in bankruptcy. It would also close the "millionaire's loop-hole," which currently allows wealthy debtors to shield their assets in "irrevocable trusts" based in one of a handful of states. Here's the part that might have made a difference in Purdue: Warren's plan would strengthen the law prohibiting fraudulent transfers, which the Department of Justice maintained the Sackler family had done.

It would also add criminal penalties to anyone who aids or abets that transfer.

Writing this, I wonder if these reforms are even possible. Can a broken system reform itself? I don't know. As the Purdue case wound down to its natural conclusion, I hoped that we would leave this dark chapter of history behind. The COVID pandemic was coming to an end, and America seemed to be coming back. But that didn't mean our problems were solved.

I had spent almost two years of my life being consumed by the case. I had hoped for justice, but all I got was a feeling of deep disgust and revulsion. The lawyers and power brokers who controlled the process said they wanted victims involved. But they never listened to us, never gave us any degree of agency. We were a bargaining chip for the attorneys and big groups and used to beef up corporate claims. In spite of our own lawyers, we couldn't fight the system. Every way we turned, we heard the same song: "We do things this way because this is the way things are always done." I was shocked, again and again, to find intelligent, educated, well-intentioned people fighting tooth and nail to defend and uphold a system that was just as toxic and destructive as Purdue itself. We owe it to ourselves, to our children, our country, and our future—all of us—to prevent the unspeakable tragedy of Purdue Pharma from ever happening again. Purdue had many accomplices in the release of the Sacklers. This would not have happened in a just system—yet, until we reform our system, it can never be just, equal, or fair. I believe that.

Reckless capitalism, the almighty dollar, and the status quo won the day. I should have seen it coming. I am glad that I didn't. If I had known what was ahead, I don't know if I could have made it this far. The lesson beaten into me, again and again, was brutal and simple: *bankruptcy laws don't work for average citizens, but they work really well for the one percent.*

I've spent years fighting to get those of us in recovery, people who use drugs, and family members impacted by addiction treated with a modicum of respect and humanity. I'll continue to do so. Now that my voice is no longer needed in this case, I can go back to what I love. I can speak openly again. I can return to my community. My heart is heavy and my soul is tired, but as disappointing as this has been, I know I did the right thing. Even though we were counted out from day one, we kept fighting. I listened. I learned. I was committed to telling the truth.

The story of Purdue unsettled my life. Its conclusion changed me forever.

Perhaps it will change you, too.

AFTERWORD

Alea iacta est. That's Latin for "the die is cast." It means that the outcome is set in stone, and everything leading up to it cannot be stopped or changed. Looking back over the final grueling months and weeks, my sense that the case's conclusion was predetermined was as strong as ever. Any meaningful role I had to change the trajectory of this tragedy had long since been over. The system protected the wealthy—at the expense of ordinary people. Nothing was really going to change, after all. At least, not on the inside.

Outside, the world was beginning to happen again. In April 2021, just a few short weeks after I received my covid vaccine, I got on a plane and flew to New Jersey. Even with my mask on, I could smell the early spring blooms of the east coast as I arrived at the recovery home just outside of Marlboro for my first overdose response training in twenty-two months.

The plan was to distribute several thousand naloxone kits and meet with family groups and recovery homes around the state—the people who'd been on the front lines during the pandemic. It should have felt like old times, but instead, I realized how profoundly disconnected I was. What had I been doing for the last two years? Compared to this, it felt like a whole lot of nothing.

After the training, I sat around in the living room of the recovery home with a few guys, eating pizza.

"So, what do you do?" one of them asked me.

I paused, my slice a few inches from my mouth. I couldn't tell them all I'd seen and heard over the last two years. But I couldn't lie, either.

"Have you been following the Purdue bankruptcy?" I finally asked.

Their blank stares told me they hadn't.

"What's that?"

"It's—well, it's a legal thing," I said. "You know about Purdue, right?"

"What's Purdue?"

In a flash, I realized that they didn't know or care about Purdue or the family that created it. They didn't connect their own struggles to the billion-dollar corporation that was splashed all over the news. They probably hadn't even seen the noticing campaign.

"Just some company," I said. "Whatever, it doesn't matter."

If my fellows at the recovery home didn't know about Purdue, the bankruptcy hardly seemed to know about real people, either. A couple weeks later, on May 24, 2021, the UCC voted to accept the settlement with Purdue. I felt total grief as our committee entered our vote. In the conference call afterward, everyone else was patting themselves on the back—but victims were a footnote by then. Even the hope that the money the states would get in abatement would all go to support treatment and recovery was up in the air. To me, it looked like we were in for more "business as usual."

A bill called the Stop Shielding Assets from Corporate Known

Liability by Eliminating Non-Debtor Releases (SACKLER) Act was supposed to ensure that individuals couldn't use bankruptcy courts to evade responsibility. As I write this, just a few weeks away from the plan confirmation hearing, it is still waiting for its first committee hearing in Congress. Looks like the SACKLER Act won't affect the Sacklers one bit, after all. The loophole, which the stalled legislation addressed (and that the Sacklers exploited), was not closed.

The Sacklers were walking away with their wealth intact. Although they'd eventually make an initial payout, their settlement will be spread out over years; in the long run, assuming a standard healthy interest rate, they could actually end up richer than before. On top of that, it's looking like executives and employees at Purdue would also collect an additional $34.7 million in bonuses as the bankruptcy wrapped up.

The die was cast—but everyone still had to play along. That was the only way this game would end. It was a train wreck, to the very last.

On the afternoon of June 25, I lay down for a power nap, sticking my phone under my pillow. Moments later, I jerked awake to the insistent buzzing next to my ear. *Cheryl*. From her first unsteady inhale, before she even spoke, I intuited that the worst had happened.

"My son is dead," she said. "We're at the sober living home. Peter found him."

Cheryl, whose first son Corey was killed by an accidental overdose, had lost her second son, too. I was speechless. Her son Sean had been in recovery for some time, with good support. He devoted himself to helping others find relief from addiction through a faith-based program in Massachusetts. He was a parent himself.

Once again, Cheryl had paid a price higher than any judge or billionaire could ever compensate her for.

"I'm so sorry," I told Cheryl. "Is there anything I can do?"

"Yes. Let the lawyers know I won't be available."

I told her that I loved her and then we hung up.

I rubbed the tears out of my tired eyes and tossed the phone aside. At that moment, I stopped caring about the case. Cheryl had lost her son—both her sons. Those of us who were still limping along had sacrificed years of our lives to a doomed cause. We'd never get our time back. No amount of money could make up for what we lost.

On July 7, the finality of the case managed to get even more bleak—any hope that a meaningful shred of justice would be achieved was eliminated. Fifteen of the twenty-four nonconsenting states officially folded—and their ringleader was none other than Maura Healey. The pugnacious Massachusetts attorney general was ready to make a deal, a deal she'd spent the entirety of the case fighting—and a deal she'd promised families and victims she wouldn't agree to unless substantial changes were included, including no release for the Sacklers (a sticking point on which Healey eventually caved). Joining her in agreement were some of the most vocal (former) nonconsenting states including: Colorado, Hawaii, Idaho, Illinois, Iowa, Maine, Minnesota, Nevada, New Jersey, New York, North Carolina, Pennsylvania, Virginia, and Wisconsin. Fifteen of twenty-four. A strong majority.

These states agreed to a deal that was almost identical to the one in place for months now (some would argue the broad strokes were almost identical since the beginning of the case). I was furious, but once again, couldn't say a word. Although I was made aware of the break in the nonconsenting states on July 3, the deal was kept confidential until it was announced in the mediator's report on July 7. It turned out that the reason for secrecy was because Healey wanted time to make political calls and attempt to flip the remaining holdout states.

The changes that the fifteen nonconsenting states folded for were moot, in my opinion. The Sacklers would regain the right to put their names on buildings once their payments were completed—though, with their damaged reputations, nobody was likely to name anything after them for a long time. Some of Purdue's privileged documents would be public, but many of the Sackler family's most guarded secrets will remain shielded—since the document repository only applied to information that Purdue (as a company) had access to. And the Sacklers only agreed to boost their settlement amount by roughly $50 million. The remaining $175 million will come from a charitable trust once belonging to the deceased Beverly Sackler, money the family had no use for anyway.

These were Cadmean victories, at the expense of every single victim of the American overdose crisis.

There is no happy ending to this story. I still can't reconcile what I had hoped for with what we got. Although I had accepted the resolution of the case, I didn't like it. It felt twisted to me— unhealthy and wrong. My only choice was to go back to the community I loved.

I had missed them. I'd be glad to be home again.

ACKNOWLEDGMENTS

This book and all of the real-world pains we went through took a team.

First and foremost, I want to thank my family: my mom, Barbara, and my sisters, Lorraine and Katy. I could not have done this without you. Sean, thank you for supporting me every step of the way. You have my heart, and your love made it possible for me to be brave as I took on this story.

Thank you to my fellow victims on the Unsecured Creditors Committee: Cheryl Juaire, for your tireless advocacy and friendship over the years; Kara Trainor and Walter Lee Salmons, for your passion and endless fighting spirit. You gave a voice to those who have been too often silenced in this process.

Every single day, the Ad Hoc Committee on Accountability did the difficult work of pursuing justice in impossible circumstances. Your courage gave me strength. Thank you for being true to the core and your mission to ensure that the real stakes of the Purdue case—the human cost of Big Pharma's greed—were never forgotten. Each one of you inspires me to stay passionate and stay loud.

Thank you to the committee members: Ed Bisch, Nan Goldin, Cynthia Munger, Barbara Van Rooyan, and Emily Walden.

I would also like to give special consideration to the contributions of Harrison Cullin and Megan Kapler, and all of the members of P.A.I.N. and OxyJustice. And of course, the committee's fearless pro bono attorney, Michael Quinn.

Thank you to the Ad Hoc Committee of Personal Injury Victims. Without hesitation, you stepped up and fought tooth and nail for victims in this case. Your efforts were not in vain. The Ad Hoc group was composed of individuals who suffered themselves, or whose loved ones, such as a child or a parent, suffered and died as a result of a Purdue opioid addiction. The Ad Hoc group members are: Kathleen Scarpone, Robert F. List, Esq., Jill Cichowicz, Diana ("Dede") Yoder, Will Allphin, Lindsey Arrington, Chad Sabora, Nicholas Boatman, Sharon Murillo, Julie Strickler, Claire Rudy Foster, and Tiffinee Scott.

Thank you to my dear friends Garrett Hade, Melissa Patruno, and Heidi Gustafson for putting up with me while completing this project, plus the entire team at the Recovery Advocacy Project for their work in bringing our efforts to scale. Thank you for making sure we have our place at every policymaking table in America. The work is just getting started, and America will continue to hear from us—especially Stuart P. Smith, Aaron Kucharski, Ana Maria Hernandez, Carol Cruz, Courtney Allen, and all of our organizers across the country doing the work that matters.

Thank you to Foster and Hillel Aron for helping to bring this chapter of my life into words. And a special thanks to Kevin Reilly, Laura Clark, Gabrielle Gantz, Martin Quinn, and the entire St. Martin's Press team. And to Elizabeth Shreve and Tim Sullivan for helping to share the message of *Unsettled*. I am blessed with an incredible team, and I know that your support makes all the difference.

A very big thank-you to those who have believed in our work since the beginning: especially Sharon Murillo, Kristen Williams, and Thomas Sandgaard. Thank you for giving the recovery movement the opportunity to continue amplifying our voices. We couldn't do this without you. Your action and vision help bring recovery to millions of people, welcoming them into the community and making change that saves lives.

I'd like to make special mention of my attorneys Arik Preis, Anne Andrews, Ed Neiger, and Joe Steinfeld for fighting every day in this case to make sure our voices were heard.

And to every American who feels unheard, left behind, or shut out—you're not imagining it. You deserve to live in a nation that values you, and you deserve to be represented by people who genuinely have your best interest at heart. The individual is the soul of our nation, and when we forget that, we leave ourselves behind. Thank you for being *you*. You are the future I will continue to fight for.

In memory of

SEAN P. MERRILL

March 15, 1979–June 25, 2021

Given all that I've recounted in these pages, and all that I've lived through in my own life, I feel an urgency to help others. I have lost too many friends and loved ones. There have been too many funerals and memorial services to attend.

Many among us face acute needs just to survive each day. As you read this book and reflect upon your own lives, I hope you will be inspired to find the causes close to your heart, and find ways that you can give back. To that end, Cheryl Juaire, who was a crucial figure in the bankruptcy fight, recently lost her second son to an overdose. The not-for-profit organization she founded, Team Sharing, is on the front lines—providing critical services to family members who've all experienced a loss greater than any one book or piece of policy can change. I encourage you to learn more about Team Sharing's work, and support them where you can.

Team Sharing is a leading national organization of parents who have lost a child to overdose. Through social networking, community advocacy, and grief support services, Team Sharing provides support and friendship to grieving family members—while working to raise awareness of substance use disorder and its impact on our communities.

Learn more about their work at
teamsharinginc.org

INDEX